BREATHING AS A TOOL FOR SELF-REGULATION AND SELF-REFLECTION

*Minna Martin, Maila Seppä,
Päivi Lehtinen, and Tiina Törö*

Translated by Hilkka Salmén

KARNAC

Originally published in Finnish under the title *Hengitys itsesäätelyn ja vuorovaikutuksen tukena*
© Minna Martin, Maila Seppä, Päivi Lehtinen, and Tiina Törö
Publisher: Mediapinta Oy 2014, Finland

First published in 2016 by
Karnac Books Ltd
118 Finchley Road
London NW3 5HT

British Library Cataloguing in Publication Data

A C.I.P. for this book is available from the British Library

ISBN-13: 978-1-78220-383-4

Typeset by V Publishing Solutions Pvt Ltd., Chennai, India

Printed in Great Britain

www.karnacbooks.com

BREATHING AS A TOOL FOR
SELF-REGULATION AND SELF-REFLECTION

CONTENTS

DISCLAIMER

In this book, every effort has been made to emphasise the importance of medical investigation of symptoms associated with imbalanced breathing to exclude or diagnose severe pathology. The authors and the publisher expressly disclaim any and all liability arising from use of the methods presented in the book. They also disclaim any and all liability for a person's failing to seek examination and treatment by a registered health care professional on the basis of the information provided in the book.

ACKNOWLEDGEMENTS

We would like to thank the Finnish Association of Non-fiction Writers for financial support for the revised edition of the Finnish original version of this book and the Kopiosto copyright society through the Finnish Association of Translators and Interpreters (SKTL) for their financial support for the translation. We also wish to thank our breathing community, and guest authors of the book, for their good cooperation. In addition, we would like to thank the colleagues, participants in our training groups, and patients who have given us permission to describe their experiences. We would like to take this opportunity to thank all those who provided valuable feedback on our manuscripts at various stages of writing the book. We would particularly like to thank Aira Laine, psychoanalyst, for encouraging us to have the book translated into English (see Laine, 2012). We wish to thank the people of various professions and medical specialties who made their contributions on understanding breathing and functional breathing disorders and developing comprehensive treatment for such problems. In addition, we would like to thank all the professionals from various fields who have participated in breathing school instructor training. Their input has served to forward our cause. Our warmest thanks go to our patients, who were our most important teachers. This book could not have been written without their cooperation. Finally, we would like to thank those who are personally most important to us: our spouses, children, parents, siblings, other relatives, and friends, who faithfully supported us during the writing process.

Of course, the process did not end with completion of the Finnish manuscript. We would therefore like to extend our warmest thanks to Hilkka Salmén for her competent translation into English and to Hilary Coleman for her review and linguistic revision of the translation.

ABOUT THE AUTHORS AND CONTRIBUTORS

Minna Martin is a psychologist and psychotherapist with advanced level special training in cognitive-analytic therapy (CAT) and training in psychophysical psychotherapy. In 2015 she was named Psychologist of the Year in Finland. Her first professions were physiotherapist and physical education instructor. Along with her work as a psychologist in student health care, Minna Martin works as a psychotherapist and trainer. She provides training for professionals in the use of the psychophysical breathing therapy method and leading of social anxiety groups. In addition, she has given lectures on these topics at international congresses. She has developed both individual therapeutic approaches and various types of group work based on psychophysical breathing therapy. Minna Martin has written articles for professional journals and books, as well as guide books for patients with various problems. In the team of contributors to this book on *Breathing as a Tool for Self-Regulation and Self-Reflection*, she is the author and editor with the primary responsibility for the work.

Maila Seppä originally trained as a movement therapist. She is one of the main forces behind the spread and establishment of psychophysical psychotherapy in Finland. Working with her patients she noticed the close connection between the regulation of breathing and emotions. She developed a short-term therapy method to teach first-aid techniques for controlling anxiety and to use breathing as a route to the mind. More than 700 university hospital patients have attended the breathing school run by Maila Seppä. But her work has not been restricted to patients alone. Personnel groups from numerous fields have seen Maila Seppä to learn to cope with their work and to get to know themselves, their patients, or their students better. Today, more than 300 people from various groups of health care professionals around Finland have participated in the training for breathing school instructors that was developed from Maila Seppä's work.

Päivi Lehtinen is a special psychologist, licentiate in psychology, psychodynamic psychotherapist, and family therapist, who has also studied physiology. She has worked for thirty years as a psychologist in a general psychiatric outpatient clinic at a university general hospital, and her cooperation with Maila Seppä dates back many years. Päivi Lehtinen has developed a treatment method for people suffering from symptoms of imbalanced breathing, with the breathing school method (a psychophysical breathing therapeutic short-term therapy group) as a central element. Another main area of her work is cooperation with patient groups from the department of gynaecology, such as women fearing delivery.

Tiina Törö is a graphic designer and relaxation therapist, with a Bachelor's degree in graphic design. She has experience of working with people recovering from mental health problems. In addition, she has acted as the executive manager of a patient association, as a leisure-time instructor for the elderly and as a leader in *Hengittävä hiljaisuus* (breathing silence) retreats. She is a trained breathing school instructor. As a person prone to developing breathing symptoms herself, Tiina Törö represents the book's largest target group in the working group.

Other experts contributing to the contents of the book

Nina Jaatinen, physiotherapist, sex therapist: functional pelvic floor disorders and pelvic floor physiotherapy, Chapter Four.

Outi Kallioinen, psychiatric nurse, psychotherapist: early interaction, Chapter Seven.

Sirkka Kaunisto, physiotherapist: insufficient ventilation and physiotherapy of respiratory diseases, Chapter Four.

Matti Keinänen, docent in psychiatry and clinical psychology, training psychotherapist: mental breathing, Chapter Six.

Benita Lillrank, specialist in occupational health care, problem-solving psychotherapist: as medical specialist for the book, she read, commented on, and revised the text.

Tarja Majasuo, midwife: childbirth and fear of delivery, Chapters Four and Seven.

Rauni Nissinen, clinical specialist nurse, family therapist, couples therapist: breathing in couples therapy, Chapter Seven.

Miina-Liisa Värelä, soprano: voice production and singing, Chapters Three and Eight.

In addition, the book contains numerous vignettes based on experiences that our colleagues, participants in training, and our patients have given us permission to use.

CHAPTER ONE

Introduction

*Somewhere deep, very deep,
a light, tiny breath is born,
involuntary, but the first
expression of the self.*

The approach taken by this book is a psychophysical one. This means an approach based on the mutual interaction between mind and body. There is some literature available in English on the psychosomatic aspects of breathing and psychophysical treatment methods in which breathing plays a central role. Nevertheless, it may be difficult to fully appreciate the wide significance of breathing from the available literature. Literature describing psychophysical aspects of breathing has not yet reached the mainstream of medically and theoretically grounded treatment. This book has started to fill the gap by taking a many-sided, comprehensive look at breathing, psychophysical breathing therapy developed by us, and the use of breathing as a tool in many professions and in many problem areas.

The book is intended for the training of professionals in health care and psychotherapy in particular. Its main target group is people helping patients with functional breathing problems, anxiety, and tension or stress symptoms. Practitioners working with patients with respiratory or other somatic diseases, as well as midwives and doctors helping women to give birth, may also learn new ways of thinking and acting from the book.

The book is suitable for school and kindergarten teachers, pastoral care workers, and others engaged in social or educational tasks or nursing. It will be useful for professionals in fields where breathing and the use of the voice are important, such as musicians and those working in the theatre, teachers, educators, and other people using their voice at work. It is also suitable for people offering physical training or guiding relaxation or mindfulness exercises. In addition to these groups, the book may provide tools for anyone interested in breathing and interaction.

The mindsets and treatment methods described in the book developed through many decades of cooperation between the movement therapist Maila Seppä and the special psychologist Päivi Lehtinen. This is how *breathing school*, a psychophysical short-term therapy group originally meant for patients with hyperventilation or somatic symptoms of anxiety, came about (Chapter Two). Development of the method and the theory behind it continues in cooperation between Maila Seppä, Minna Martin, and Matti Keinänen. The method has subsequently been applied in both individual and group therapy to help people suffering from many kinds of symptoms and problems (Chapter Seven). For this reason, the method is today more widely called *psychophysical breathing therapy*. We hope that psychophysical breathing therapy with its various applications will inspire health care professionals to further develop their interactive skills and methods of working with various patient groups.

Psychophysical breathing therapy involves numerous interwoven aspects. It is based on the knowledge on the psychophysical regulation of breathing described in the book (Chapter Three) and the significance of balanced breathing for physical and mental well-being (Chapter Four). We add to this the understanding of the significance of early interaction for learning ways of breathing and developing the stress regulation system (Chapter Five). The psychotherapeutic frame of reference is based on object relations theory and, particularly, the ideas of Donald W. Winnicott (1951, 1987). Studies of early interaction and the neurobiology of early childhood have also added to our understanding of how the regulation of breathing develops in interaction.

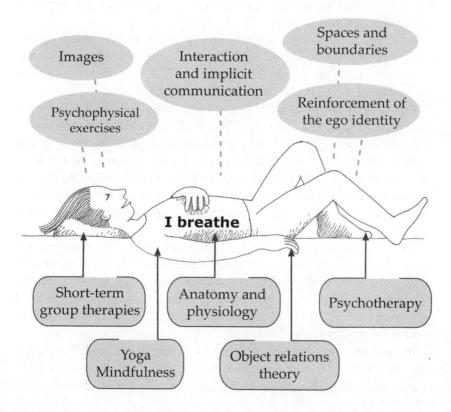

The influence of non-Western medical practices that have already to some extent become integrated in Western medicine, such as mindfulness and yoga, can be seen particularly in the psychophysical breathing therapy exercises described at the end of the book (Chapter Eight). Breathing is the thread or, in this connection, rather the breath connecting various types of theoretical views and practical experiences.

Breathing represents the interface between many fields of science and many professional groups. It is a no-man's-land and yet belongs to everybody. In this psychophysical terrain we offer breathing as a new, albeit thousands of years old, type of conscious therapeutic method. We do not offer a method or techniques that patients could be taught and that would immediately eliminate their problems. We offer a way of being, observing, and living. The teachings in this book can be applied as preventive and therapeutic measures for many types of work. In addition, we provide professionals with means of coping, avoiding burnout, and finding their own breathing space. You can start reading the book at any chapter. Certain basic views and concepts are therefore repeated in several chapters.

Breathing is the basis and the basic expression of life. Breathing can never be completely grasped or understood. It is as if there were at the bottom of breathing an opening to a world that is unknown, frightening, unfamiliar, and therefore impossible to picture.

Where does the first breath come from, usually accompanied by a loud cry: "Here I come, I am, and I'm alive"? Where does the last breath fade out and disappear? It is no coincidence that the Latin word *expirare* and its derivatives, the English *expire* and French *expirer*, have a double meaning: not just to breathe out but also to die. Breathing always involves, even if unconsciously, the presence of death. Any disturbance in breathing, laboured breathing, or becoming conscious of one's own breathing are therefore often difficult to face.

As we approach the unknown emptiness, sense its opening, we cannot see or feel anything because the spirit itself is not accessible to examination. Nevertheless, it has always been described. Art, rituals, religions, and myths have expressed it. A creative state is experienced as sacred, for it allows us to get in touch with the primary forces of life, with divinity (Rinpoche, 1992).

In Judaism, *ruah*, breathing, refers to the Spirit of God filling Creation. In Christianity, too, there is a deep connection between the Holy Spirit, without whom there is no life, and breathing. The creation story in the Bible says that the Spirit of God was hovering over the surface of the waters. And further: then God created man out of dust and blew into his nostrils the spirit of life, and so man became a living soul. An African bishop sought an equivalent for the word *spiritus* in his language. He finally translated it as "holy breath". Indian Veda scripts tell that the world was created from God's exhalation. In Buddha's teaching, the Sanskrit word *prana*, meaning "vehicle of mind", is used for breathing (Stinissen, 1988). The concept of *mental breathing* (Chapter Six) developed by psychiatrist Matti Keinänen (2006, 2015) is suitable for describing many of the basic aspects of our work in breathing therapy. It refers to mental mobility and good self-reflective and mentalisation abilities. The psychosemiotic concept of *khora* can be used as the basis for mental breathing:

A new person lives in his mother's womb in a state preceding images, words, and thoughts. This basic state is preserved in that person throughout life as the womb and cradle of creativity. The concept of khora was created for this original state creating images and words. The word comes from Greek and can be translated as "space" or "place of infinite dimensions". Even though the "memory of the womb" is personal, it has a living connection to what is common to us. In addition, it is the source of collective and cultural images. In orthodox Christian images, khora refers to the Virgin Mary as the mother of God and a temple (Kristeva, 1984; Siltala, 1993). Mental breathing created and formed in interaction receives its strength and energy from this source. As the child being born gives up the safety of the womb, he has a long journey ahead. He retains the memory of the womb, khora, his earliest image, as a resting place. The pulsation, variation between unity and separateness of that place provides space for creating other images of oneself and the environment. Khora has no shape; it is associated mainly with rhythm, going away and coming back, opening up and closing. It pulsates in the moment that is always present and thus escapes definition. Even as we try to explain it we have already hopelessly lost its authenticity. In our book, khora exerts its effect behind the text and the figures, and it is strongly present in the breathing exercises in Chapter Eight.

Before health care and psychotherapy assimilated breathing in their work, understanding of breathing was the province of religions, philosophies, and arts. This is why we wished to present the above views as background factors affecting our work, even though we will not come back to these themes later. Instead, we present in the book old and new information that is based on clinical experience and research and associated with the psychophysiology and psychology of breathing. Even though we draw on many sources, the various views fit together well, complementing each other.

CHAPTER TWO

Psychophysical breathing therapy

Maila Seppä, Päivi Lehtinen, Minna Martin

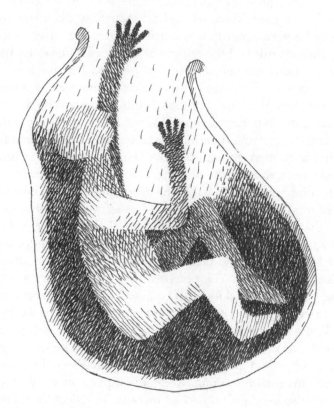

*Inside and out you feel
simultaneously
cool and warm;
you feel the movement.*

2.1. Development of psychophysical breathing therapy

In the early 1980s, patients presenting at psychiatric outpatient clinics with unexplained physical symptoms had often undergone somatic tests and examinations in various specialities which had revealed either no disease, or a disease explaining only part of the symptoms. Typically, the patients did not mention their anxiety or panic sensations, the attack-like nature of their symptoms, or a need to make changes to their lives. They mainly expressed worries concerning the bodily symptoms that were being investigated. Panic disorder was not introduced as a diagnosis in Finland until 1987, and the effects of imbalanced breathing associated with panic disorder and other anxiety disorders were not commonly known. According to current psychiatric diagnostics, most of these patients fulfilled the criteria of one or more anxiety disorders, often panic disorder. Some of them may have had depression.

Even before the diagnosis of anxiety disorders became more multi-faceted, psychologist Päivi Lehtinen studied the psychophysiological literature on the hyperventilation syndrome. It helped her understand her patients' symptoms (Lehtinen & Laine, 1988). Päivi Lehtinen had heard that movement therapist Maila Seppä specialised in breathing. Their reflections formed the starting point for a cooperation continuing for several decades that led to the development of a comprehensive treatment model and a new type of short-term psychophysical group therapy that was named *breathing school* (Lehtinen, 1995; Lehtinen, Tammivaara, Seppä, Luutonen, & Äärelä, 2000). The model was used for over twenty years and breathing school groups were attended by more than 700 patients. The presence of physical symptoms that the referring physician considered to be associated with hyperventilation proved to be a useful criterion for referring the patient for breathing school. When Päivi Lehtinen and Maila Seppä retired, this group therapy ended. Nevertheless, the method continues to be used for a very wide range of patient groups by people who have been through breathing school instructor training. Methods applied in breathing school groups are also used for individual therapy. To reflect the more varied therapeutic practice, the method is now called *psychophysical breathing therapy*.

It is rather interesting that at about the time the breathing school method was established, Jon Kabat-Zinn (1994, 2013) in the USA was contemplating how patients with psychosomatic symptoms could be helped. He says that these patients were considered incurably ill because no functional treatment methods existed at the time. Kabat-Zinn started developing a structured therapeutic method combining meditation and yoga (mindfulness based stress reduction, MBSR). Breathing school was based on the German breathing therapy (see Mehling, 2001) and psychotherapy tradition but, like Kabat-Zinn, Maila Seppä included in her treatment method influences from many other sources, such as yoga and traditional meditation. Many people recognise both similarities and differences between these methods. In her treatment method, Maila Seppä emphasised the significance of a person's own feelings and interpersonal interaction for the regulation of breathing.

Breathing school was developed virtually from scratch. Early during its evolution, little information was available on other equivalent breathing therapy methods. Today it is clearly easier to find such information (see Caldwella & Himmat, 2011; Heller, 2012). One form was that of Jan van Dixhoorn, a Dutch physician, who started developing his method at around the same time as Maila Seppä, that is, in the late 1970s (van Dixhoorn, 2007). He has stated and shown in many of his publications (see 2009) that breathing therapy is a useful method to combine with other treatment for patients with somatic diseases and symptoms, particularly when no clear reason can be found for the symptoms and accurate treatment methods can therefore not be assigned. His method was originally developed to help people with voice problems. However, van Dixhoorn has performed his best-known studies on the effect of breathing therapy on the rehabilitation of patients with myocardial infarction. The aim of van Dixhoorn's breathing therapy is to help patients improve their ability to observe their breathing and thus to regulate tension in the mind and body. He uses both direct and indirect breathing exercises for treatment. Indirect exercises and images can be used to avoid excessive control of breathing and thus to avoid disturbing breathing. The treatment is a process. Progress depends on how the patient responds to the exercises. Van Dixhoorn emphasises the significance of the relationship between therapist and patient and the often remarkable effect of treatment on psychophysical well-being. The aims and methods of treatment are largely the same as in the method we describe in this book. One of the differences is that in the breathing school method psychotherapeutic and physical elements are purposely intertwined.

The aim of psychophysical breathing therapy is to help patients learn ways of breathing that are better for their well-being, and to find first-aid measures for alleviating acute anxiety. Breathing becomes more balanced if patients learn to recognise, put into words, and work on tension and anxiety and to build up their self-compassion and -experience. In the method, the therapist has the crucial function of being a model for identification, who facilitates calming down. Many patients say that when symptoms appear they remember what was said in breathing school or individual breathing therapy: "You can always breathe."

Stepped care model for patients with symptoms associated with imbalanced breathing

- Examination and assessment by a physician
- Assessment by a psychologist or psychiatrist
- Assessment by a breathing therapist
- Short-term breathing school therapy group
- Final assessment by a breathing therapist
- Final assessment by a psychologist or psychiatrist and referral for further treatment, if considered necessary.

People attending breathing school were offered the possibility of additional individual or couple visits to the health care worker referring them for treatment. At these visits, patients had the chance to work on thoughts or feelings appearing during breathing school that could not be brought up in the short-term therapy group. The therapy model was comprehensive, that is, at every stage of the process it was possible to refer the patient for other treatment considered necessary in addition to breathing school, such as assessment of the need for pharmacotherapy or further somatic tests and examinations. The stepped care model gave the patient and health care worker time to process the situation and to find a suitable therapy method for each individual. Even today, it is recommended that working on breathing be combined with other forms of therapy according to the patient's needs. However, as health care has become increasingly hard-pressed, it is not necessarily possible any more to apply as thorough an assessment process as in the original model described below.

2.2. Patient assessment process

The necessary somatic tests and examinations are performed for each patient. In the best case, the very fact that no physical disorder is found may come as a relief for the patient. The physician performing the physical examination is in an important position. Explanation of the situation by an understanding physician will make the patient feel safer. The patient may be sufficiently helped by a physician telling him about the impact of imbalanced breathing and bringing up the effect of any mental stressors on breathing and the patient's symptoms. The physician should mention that despite the examinations a disease explaining some of the symptoms may later be found because the sensations associated with imbalanced breathing are similar to the symptoms of many somatic diseases. In addition, the physician should mention that diagnosing a somatic disease does not exclude a functional breathing disorder but that the patient may have both.

The interplay between mind and body should be explained in more detail. The patient should be told that symptoms may have been triggered by an affect or thought about to surface that provokes anxiety or that the patient cannot accept. The patient should be asked whether he has noticed any change in his breathing in stressful situations. Any means the patient has used to feel better should be observed. Many have found that calm breathing will calm them down. The patient's situation and history should be examined. Information on childhood experiences will help to understand the current situation even if such experiences are not more extensively discussed at this stage. Any current or more long-term stressors should be sought. The severity of symptoms, functional capacity, and any need for psychopharmaceuticals should be assessed, and a preliminary psychiatric diagnostic evaluation should be performed.

The interview should be conducted in a calm, informative atmosphere appreciating the patient's experiences and thoughts. The assessment process is considered a significant mini-intervention. The patient's interest in his own thoughts, feelings, and bodily sensations should be aroused by asking about these without expecting immediate answers. In addition, an attempt should be made to make the patient assume responsibility for himself and become interested in doing something about his well-being. These people present with bodily symptoms and usually expect the physician to have a solution that will make them well again. Imbalanced breathing often acts as a protective measure against mental anxiety. Therefore, one should be careful about bringing up mental problems or symptoms.

Patients with functional breathing disorders referred for specialised care have often had symptoms for a long time and should therefore be referred to a psychologist or psychiatrist if such resources are available. The examining physician can lay a good foundation for breathing therapy by encouraging the patient to have such therapy and talk to a psychologist or psychiatrist. If breathing school is considered to be a suitable form of therapy, the patient should be referred for assessment by a breathing therapist. Active encouragement is necessary in referring for therapeutic assessment (Lehtinen, Tammivaara, Seppä, Luutonen, & Äärelä, 2000).

2.3. Breathing school, short-term psychophysiological therapy group

Maila Seppä, developer of the breathing school method:

> Breathing school is based on my early childhood, my mother's cradle songs, and calm being in the midst of the war. When in my work as a movement therapist I encountered anxious patients, my early experiences were activated in me, producing an understanding of the significance of fears and the soothing other.
>
> I attended dance therapy groups for several years and continued in a psychophysical training group held by the German psychologist Bernd Walber-Baltz. There is a long tradition of breathing therapy in Germany, and this was reflected in the teaching. When working as the second group therapist in cooperation with a psychotherapist I learned to understand the significance of images as tools. In group therapy, we particularly studied the change of body image. This is where the body image drawing exercises I use in breathing school come from.

2.3.1. The framework of breathing school

Object relations theory and research on early interaction have significantly influenced the philosophy behind breathing school and the methods used there. The child development theory of psychoanalyst Donald W. Winnicott (1951, 1987), and his notion of the significance of the sense of being for the development of the true self provided the theoretical background for helping people suffering from anxiety or panic. The main breathing school exercises are based on the concepts of *being* and *doing* and their integration. The exercises are also associated with yoga and meditation exercises that have influenced many self-care methods.

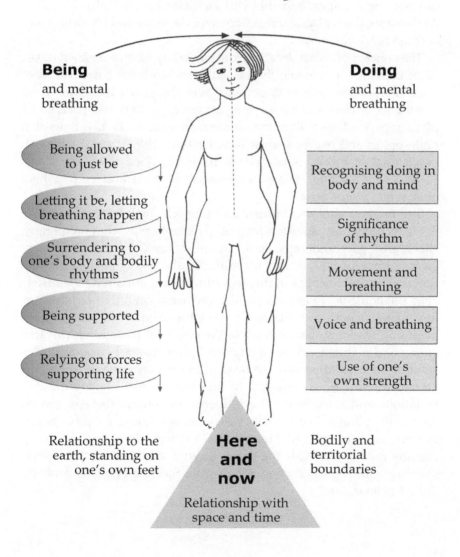

Being and doing
Consciousness and integration

Being
and mental
breathing

Doing
and mental
breathing

Being allowed
to just be

Letting it be, letting
breathing happen

Surrendering to
one's body and bodily
rhythms

Being supported

Relying on forces
supporting life

Recognising doing in
body and mind

Significance
of rhythm

Movement and
breathing

Voice and breathing

Use of one's
own strength

Relationship to the
earth, standing on
one's own feet

**Here
and
now**

Bodily and
territorial
boundaries

Relationship with
space and time

The method is based on a thorough knowledge of human physiology, body structure, and muscle work. At the assessment stage, the patient is told about the main features of breathing physiology, muscle structures participating in breathing, and the consequences of imbalanced breathing. When guiding the patient, the breathing therapist should keep in mind the multiple effects of breathing on human health. She should invite the patient to use introspection and images. Becoming conscious of changes in breathing enables the patient to connect with the affects and thoughts causing the changes, and this will facilitate his mental processing. At the same time, physical reactions will decrease and breathing will become more balanced.

The concept of *mental breathing* developed by Matti Keinänen (2006, 2015) provided a valuable theoretical framework for what had been learned from working with patients over the years. It provided the breathing exercises and the teaching of "being" with roots, space, and a place in psychological thinking. In the literature, the French-Bulgarian philosopher and psychoanalyst Julia Kristeva (1984) and the Finnish psychoanalyst Pirkko Siltala (1993) have described this early stage, *khora*, as the undifferentiated experience of mind and body, where images and words arise.

The method was also influenced by psychoanalytic theory, cognitive psychotherapy, solution-focused psychotherapy, trauma therapy, short-term psychotherapy, and group therapy. Concepts that are basically psychoanalytic are, for example, the role of anxiety and the function of the defences in dealing with it, and attention to transference phenomena. Two concepts derived from cognitive psychotherapy, vicious circle and automatic thoughts, have been used to help breathing school attendees analyse the effects of thought on the activation and maintenance of feelings and physical stress reactions. The solution-focused approach can be seen in the way patients' problems are faced: they are encouraged to find new ways of facing difficult situations and sensations. The influence of trauma therapy can be seen in the effort to keep patients' experiences during the process sufficiently safe and therefore tolerable. Short-term therapies and group therapy methods provide the therapist with valuable help for understanding group phenomena. (See Dewan, Steenberger, & Greenberg, 2012; Kajamaa, 2003.)

Healing elements of group therapy and short-term therapy in breathing school
• The group has defined common targets • The group consists of people with similar symptoms. Similarity is comforting, and differences help members to see problems in proportion • In a group, it is possible to study the significance of distance and closeness in human relations • Alternative ways of acting and more approving attitudes are created • The time limit steps up the tempo of the work and encourages participants to apply what they have learned to their own lives • At the end of the group work, significant feelings arise, which are examined and which encourage the separateness of the participants.

Psychophysical breathing therapy is constantly developing and is alive in today's world. On the one hand, much of the most recent research data confirms the knowledge gathered in breathing school groups. On the other hand, new data expand the scope of use of the method. Brain research and the associated neuropsychoanalytical knowledge, for example, have confirmed the notions of the significance of implicit, non-verbal knowledge and unconscious bodily expressions and the possibilities of influencing these. Other therapy methods also have interfaces with psychophysical breathing therapy and influence it in ways that may be useful for the therapist.

Theories and methods behind psychophysical breathing therapy
• Psychoanalytic theory • Object relations theory • Mental breathing • Research on early interaction • Brain research

- Neuropsychoanalysis
- Cognitive psychotherapy
- Group therapy
- Short-term psychotherapy
- Solution- and resource-focused psychotherapy
- Trauma therapy
- Yoga
- Mindfulness.

2.3.2. Therapeutic contents of the breathing school method

Individual assessment by breathing therapist before
group meetings

When a patient comes for an assessment visit, it is important for the breathing therapist to give her sufficient space. The therapist breathes calmly and is present. The patient is not interrupted or given instructions when she reports why she came to the assessment visit. This does not mean that the therapist does not react to the patient's account. It is natural to encourage the patient by asking further questions or by non-verbal messages. Receiving means listening with a keen ear while at the same time being conscious of what is happening in your own body, thoughts, and feelings. This provides information on the essence of the symptoms and allows an assessment of how the patient may benefit from psychophysical group therapy.

The patient is told that the aim is to simply look together at and wonder about how she breathes and thereby to learn to understand her problems related to breathing. The patient lies down, the therapist sits down close to her and touches her arm. A calming touch message, "Don't worry, everything is fine", often reaches the patient better than words. Then again, physical touching may arouse problems related to closeness that the patient has and provide an opportunity to discuss these. The therapist tells the patient about partner exercises used in breathing school and their significance. It is stressed that each group member will have the right to choose how she participates in the exercises.

The patient is asked to close her eyes and listen to her breathing. Then the therapist and patient examine together where the breathing movement is felt and where the patient believes the bottom of her breathing lies. Images are used to bypass the pressures of breathing "correctly".

The therapist helps the patient during inhalation by pulling gently on the patient's ankles or by lifting the patient with her hand placed under the patient's back at the waist. These measures are meant to encourage the downward movement of the diaphragm to deepen breathing. Many patients already find more space for breathing as a result of these manoeuvres used for examination. After the examination, a picture is drawn of the patient's way of breathing. The drawing can be used to tell the patient about the aims of breathing school, such as attempting to influence exhaling, letting go, and allowing a pause in breathing.

Hyperventilation

Chronic
hyperventilation

Flowing breathing

In the examination, it is important for the therapist to observe and describe rather than teach or provide explanations. The patient should, however, be given feedback if he is found to be using his auxiliary breathing muscles. The patient should be asked to breathe more consciously by blowing out softly, at low pressure. Other individual suggestions for influencing breathing should also be given.

> *A woman treated in hospital for exhaustion came for an assessment visit. She had been told to contact me but she had not been willing to do so until this was made a prerequisite for further treatment. She came to the meeting unwilling and prejudiced. When leaving, she turned at the door and said: "On my way here, I decided that if you told me with as much as one word how I should breathe, I would leave immediately." She later said that all her life she had tried to please others and this had exhausted her. She attended breathing school and during it obtained the energy and tools for listening to and expressing her own needs.*

The patient is told about the working methods in the group. He is asked to speak about his fears and fantasies related to breathing school. The discussion can be used to point out the importance of the patient taking an active role in bringing about changes and to talk about how individual this work is. The patient must not be promised anything or coaxed to join the group but rather held back and asked to consider attending breathing school.

Breathing school

The breathing school intervention consists of twelve weekly group sessions of ninety minutes each. There are six to ten participants per group. Age, sex, and severity of symptoms should be considered, as far as possible, when choosing members for a group. The first two group meetings are introductory meetings, after which the patients are required to commit themselves to attending all group meetings.

Themes and aims of breathing school
• Learning to be, giving yourself permission to be as you are • Having permission not to have to relax, concentrate, or master anything • Recognising one's own bodily sensations, sensing, wondering, and listening • Encouragement for approving presence and the experience of being supported • Finding and appreciation of one's current breathing rhythm • Exhalation exercises, and finding the pause after exhalation • Inhalation exercises • Breathing exercises with the help of images, playing, and use of voice • Attitude to gravity, and use of gravity in exercises • Attitude to verticality, and recognition of live movement of the spine • Exercises combining breathing and movement • Power of thought in the regulation of breathing and bodily functions • Boundary exercises: picturing body boundaries alone and together with someone else • Exercises related to space and territory

- Exercises related to own strength
- Observation of changes in breathing in pair exercises
- Further development of self-reflection throughout the existence of the group by giving space for verbalising experiences and feelings.

At first, preconceptions about having to concentrate or relax or the need for prior knowledge or skills are vented. The participants are given permission to feel as they feel, look and be of the age and size that they are. The excitement and anxiety felt by everyone at the beginning of the group work is noted and shared. An agreement is made on joint group rules and boundaries. The fact that exercises are not obligatory is discussed, noting that it is most important to become conscious of one's choices and of what is happening in oneself. Exercises are often done with eyes closed to avoid "performing" breathing, instead of letting it happen naturally and without comparison to others. This also makes it easier for participants to get in touch with their own internal experiences. The group leader should keep her eyes open to see the various ways in which group participants react to the exercises. This is important to enable her to help the group control arising affects and bodily sensations. When guiding individual breathing exercises in a one-to-one setting, the therapist may also close her eyes so that the patient will not feel she is being watched. Next, attention and interest are directed to what participants observe in themselves. It is possible to learn to simply wonder about and observe with curiosity any tension, pain, or restlessness in the body, as well as feelings and thoughts. This will create more space for images, thoughts, and experiences. Participants descend safely into a state of *just letting themselves be*, which requires time and peace. They can let their breath move as it wishes. This is where change begins.

> *A mother of teenage sons reported at the second group session: "I came home from the group session and we sat down for dinner. My sons curiously asked whether I can now breathe right. No, I cannot, I replied. My sons wondered why this wasn't taught at breathing school and asked what on earth we were doing there then? I said we just let ourselves be." A warm laughter burst out in the group. The pleasure of shared understanding was perceptible in the group.*

The worlds of being and doing

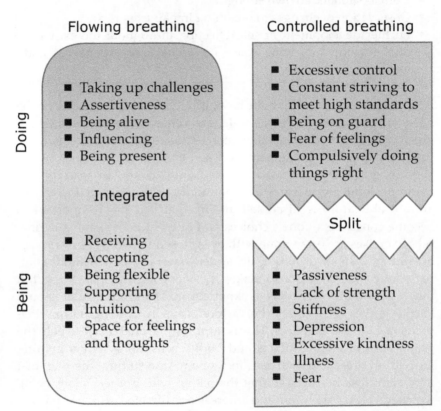

Flowing breathing

Controlled breathing

Doing

- Taking up challenges
- Assertiveness
- Being alive
- Influencing
- Being present

- Excessive control
- Constant striving to meet high standards
- Being on guard
- Fear of feelings
- Compulsively doing things right

Integrated

Split

Being

- Receiving
- Accepting
- Being flexible
- Supporting
- Intuition
- Space for feelings and thoughts

- Passiveness
- Lack of strength
- Stiffness
- Depression
- Excessive kindness
- Illness
- Fear

Breathing exercises are started by getting to know one's own breathing rhythm and way of breathing. Participants get to know how breathing feels in various parts of the body. The therapist encourages them to regard bodily sensations with compassion and curiosity. Doing and being are discussed both generally and in the context of breathing. Exhaling exercises are started with passive exhaling. *Letting go* is the key term associated with exhalation. Images are also brought into the exercises. During exercises participants observe what is happening in the body. "How does breathing feel?" Does exhalation flow freely, or does muscle tension or the feeling of having to do things right prevent this? When the patient experiences letting go, the experience of a pause after exhaling is often triggered without trying. Participants can look at this moment of rest, simply wondering about it and observing it with curiosity. Many people are astounded by how the pause gets longer and marvel at the great pleasure it brings.

Many people have a fixed idea that orthodox breathing exercises involve puffing the chest out during inhalation. This is not true. The change begins with emptying the inner space and observing the flow of breath. Active exhalation exercises open up spontaneous expression. Participants blow, hiss, use their voice and strength to exhale. Active exercises provide courage, and release joy and playfulness in the group. Participants first allow inhalation to occur by itself, then they can aim at conscious and natural breathing. The objective is for the participants to get to know themselves and their breathing and to find first-aid measures for controlling anxiety. Calming images and words are used, such as, "Just breathe calmly, no matter what happens." Increased consciousness of one's own body can later be used to create a connection between ways of breathing, muscle tension, feelings, and internal speech.

As group work proceeds, exercises are performed in pairs. The effect of interaction on the way of breathing can thus be examined. Participants can practise new ways of encountering one another. They pause to study phenomena related to space. Taking space is essential for changing the way of breathing. Space exercises are begun with body boundary exercises. Boundaries are enforced by active muscle tension, images, or an outlining exercise performed in pairs. Participants discuss how space is taken or whether it is given. The experienced space may sometimes become so restricted that there is "not even room to breathe". If this happens, a person may feel that someone is walking over him and his own experiences are invalidated. In the group, participants discuss whether it is still possible to breathe and how they can gradually learn to defend their boundaries.

Participants are generally encouraged to do breathing exercises at home, but those who are excessively striving are recommended not to do any exercises for the time being. They should practise letting go and learning to be kind to themselves. All participants are encouraged to practise observing their breathing and influencing it in normal daily situations, while in traffic, at the shops, and at the workplace. Observation is particularly useful when dealing with people or issues that are problematic—for you can always breathe.

Art postcards and pictures of nature are used to activate images. Associative cards bring up repressed feelings and stimulate open interaction. In exercises, participants are asked to make choices, such as

"Choose a picture representing how your breathing feels." Exercises reinforce participants' reliance on their own way of observing and making choices. Participants draw two images of their bodies, one at the beginning of the group work, the other one at the end. Drawings can also be made to depict breathing, fears, and a feeling of safety. Pictures are not interpreted but each participant speaks of their significance to himself and can show his pictures to the group, if he so wishes. Images are also fed by reading poems, stories, and fairy tales that can strengthen the connection between bodily experience, images, and unconscious feelings. Music used in connection with breathing exercises also creates an atmosphere filled with images and a feeling of being supported. Participants are encouraged to enjoy nature and the arts and to observe their dreams with curiosity.

Various group dynamic phenomena, such as resistance and transference to the therapist and to other group members, are examined in appropriate situations. Group therapist training or experience of working with groups is helpful when working according to these principles in groups of people with breathing disorders.

Towards the end of the group work, reactions, thoughts, and feelings arising from the imminent separation are discussed, as well as how the end of group work feels in the body. It is good to talk about how separation may activate old fears associated with loss. Ways of coping with separation are discussed. Symptoms that were the reason for seeking help may be activated towards the end of group work. Discussing all this will make participants feel better, and the phenomena can be used to help in studying and promoting change. A short-term therapy group provides a good opportunity for separation work, helping participants to face the limits of time and to take responsibility for themselves and for the possibilities for change in their life.

Summary of psychophysical therapy based on a patient case:

Examination and assessment by a physician

A middle-aged man with epileptic-type seizures was referred by a health centre to a general hospital outpatient department of neurology. At work, his vision had suddenly become blurred. In the middle of his visual field, a round opening had appeared that had started to expand. His muscles were twitching, his heart was beating, and he felt that his breathing was laboured. It hurt to turn his head. He was frightened by his symptoms.

A neurologist performed a physical examination. In addition, he asked about the patient's current situation. It turned out that the patient was under stress at work due to tight schedules, and life at home was stressful, too, because his child didn't sleep well. The neurologist considered the symptoms to be due to overbreathing and referred the patient for assessment for breathing school.

Psychologist's assessment

At the psychological assessment visit, the mechanism of overbreathing was re-examined. As part of the examination, the patient had been referred for a voluntary hyperventilation test. In the test, he had developed symptoms that were similar to those he had had during the attack. He was amazed at how such symptoms could quickly be produced by breathing. He said he had been frightened by the attack because it had brought to his mind a previous attack at his summer cottage. The fear was aggravated by the fact that his mother had died of a neurological illness. Stress at work also made the situation worse. The stress was due both to demands placed at work and to the fact that the patient demanded a lot from himself and wished to have a more challenging job. The patient was interested in breathing school and was referred for assessment by a breathing therapist.

Assessment by breathing therapist before breathing school

At the assessment visit, the patient's breathing was rapid and irregular, performed using the upper chest. His relationship to his body was watchful. His body language showed that he paid attention primarily to others. Interaction with him felt natural. It appeared to be possible to use images to describe bodily experiences. The general impression was of an open and sensitive patient.

Observations made by breathing therapist during group therapy

The patient attended the group regularly. He concentrated on the breathing exercises and actively participated in group work. Other men in the group were helpful when we practised using images. Together the men pondered and wondered about the power of images in calming down breathing when symptoms occurred. The patient listened carefully to what the therapist and other group members said. He didn't speak much about his own affairs.

Final assessment visit to breathing therapist

At the assessment visit after breathing school the patient's breathing rhythm was normal. He used his abdomen and diaphragm for breathing. He had learned to listen to and observe his bodily reactions, and he was more approving of himself. His relationship to closeness had remained unchanged. He was better able to use images. He learned from the exercises through identification.

Final assessment visit to the psychologist

The patient told the psychologist that the assessment visits had already helped him. He had learned ways of breathing and means of calming down that he applied when symptoms of overbreathing occurred. In breathing school he appreciated being given space and the choice of either speaking or not speaking about his affairs. At the end of the breathing school treatment, he was able to bring about organisational changes at his workplace that relieved his stress at work. He kept more in contact with his father, from whom he had become more distant after his mother's death. He took sedative medication rarely and a short course of antidepressants. He had started recognising his problems with self-esteem, emerging depression, and anger management. For these reasons, he sought psychotherapy for six months. Six months after the end of the breathing school treatment he was happy with his life. He spoke more about his affairs and feelings with his family and friends. Now, fifteen years later, he is still feeling fine. He says he has got a better grip on the stressors in his life and has learned to live more calmly.

CHAPTER THREE

Psychophysical regulation of breathing

Päivi Lehtinen, Minna Martin

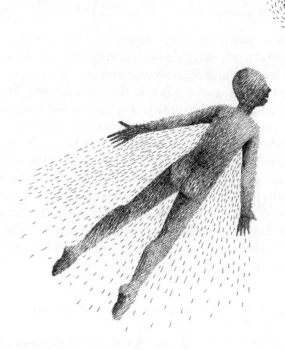

*In the world of my cells, I am capable
of doing something
I otherwise dare not
even think.*

This chapter deals with the main anatomical and physiological features of balanced and imbalanced breathing, emphasising the aspects that are psychophysically most significant.

Breathing forms the basis for life. Imbalanced breathing may be due to somatic disease but also to emotional problems. It was only when writing this book that we became fully aware of the number of psychophysical connections related to breathing that exist in bodily structures and functions. Many observations that we had made in patients or in ourselves on the psychophysical connections of breathing were reinforced. Understanding such connections may help health care professionals to understand many of the physical symptoms that were previously considered medically unexplained.

3.1. The tasks of breathing

The primary task of breathing, ventilation, is to deliver oxygen to all parts of the body and to eliminate carbon dioxide produced by metabolism and muscle work. The cardiovascular system takes care of appropriate distribution of oxygenated blood in the body. Another main task of breathing is to regulate carbon dioxide levels and acid-base balance in the body in a manner appropriate for cell function. In addition, breathing and the respiratory system have many other tasks affecting psychophysical well-being that are not always recognised. Breathing also affects many more body parts and functions than is usually thought, in fact it affects almost the whole body. (See Bartley & Clifton-Smith, 2006; Chaitow, Bradley, & Gilbert, 2002, 2014; van Dixhoorn, 2007; Monsen, 1989; Timmons & Ley, 1994.) It may not always be easy to perceive the connection between breathing, the mind, and interpersonal interaction. However, practice often helps to improve introspection.

Tasks of breathing and the respiratory system
• Breathing brings oxygen into the body and eliminates carbon dioxide produced by metabolism • Breathing is a central and immediate regulator of acid-base balance in the body • The breathing rhythm mechanically regulates the variation in heartbeat during the respiratory cycle. The heart rate increases with each inhalation and slows down with exhalation

- Respiratory movements act as a pump for gas exchange and body fluid circulation. The continuous rhythmic movement facilitates the circulation of venous blood, lymph, and cerebrospinal fluid
- The flow and pressure of exhaled air support the voice and speech
- Normal respiratory mechanics help to keep the spine and surrounding bone and muscle structures flexible
- Respiratory muscles are involved in maintaining posture and in strenuous physical work. Balanced breathing and the associated appropriate use of respiratory muscles are associated with flexibility, ease, and good coordination of movements of the whole body
- Normal respiratory mechanics facilitate digestion through rhythmic variation of positive and negative pressure. In addition, they keep the circulation in the inner organs optimal
- Breathing (rhythm, depth, use of accessory respiratory muscles) provides nonverbal information on people's current emotions, ways of expressing themselves, and personality for both themselves and external observers
- Breathing can be used to regulate emotions. Holding one's breath or hyperventilation can be used to keep intolerable feelings out of consciousness
- Calm breathing gives space for recognising and expressing feelings
- Calm breathing calms the mind and body.

People breathe individually. Many professionals find this hard to accept and may therefore try to teach a "correct" breathing technique. However, respecting individuality does not exclude the recognition that some ways of breathing are more favourable for psychophysical well-being than others. It is, therefore, an important task for the therapist to help people recognise by introspection ways that improve their well-being.

The rhythm and depth of breathing, use of respiratory muscles, and spread of the respiratory movement in the body vary. Breathing in various positions and during movement requires differing use of muscles. People normally use many different ways of breathing. Simultaneous, coordinated use of many muscles even for calm breathing reflects the normal ability of breathing to change and to react to feelings and movements. As breathing cannot be regulated by controlling each required muscle separately, it is not possible to teach a "right" way of breathing that would suit everyone. If this were done, the person would fare as badly as a centipede trying to move by moving each leg separately. To learn to calm down your breathing, you do not need to know the anatomics of respiration in detail. When guiding people, it is unnecessary to direct their attention to the use of the diaphragm or other muscles, as this often only confuses them and makes their breathing become forced and unnatural. Use of images is clearly better for achieving fluent synchrony experienced as a pleasurable feeling of "breath flowing". Nevertheless, we find it necessary for therapists to have sufficient basic knowledge of how the body works; otherwise, they might provide incorrect information or instructions preventing fluent breathing.

This book explains how to help to restore balanced breathing. *Letting be* is described as the method forming the basis for psychophysical exercises and for learning to recognise how different ways of breathing feel in various parts of the body and in the mind. Breathing patterns are learned by experiencing and by using images. People learn their own ways of being in their bodies and breathing. Such work can also be useful for patients with severe diseases, as well as after accidents and operations, when patients have to get to know their changed bodies and to look for new optimal ways of breathing.

3.2. The breathing process

Air flows through either the nose or the mouth into the pharynx, further on to the larynx, and then through the trachea and bronchi into the lungs. The inner wall of the bronchi consists of smooth muscle. The bronchi divide into smaller and smaller branches terminating in alveoli (air sacs in the lungs). Pressure changes in the thoracic cavity caused by the movements of the thorax and the diaphragm, together with the suppleness of the thoracic wall, costal cartilage, and lungs facilitate the movements of the diaphragm and thus the breathing process causing gas exchange in the alveoli.

We have learned to think that air can be obtained quickly and easily through the mouth. It has additionally been concluded that mouth breathing is appropriate because in connection with strenuous exertion more gas exchange is needed, but John Douillard, a specialist in sports medicine (1995), and John Bartley, an ear, nose, and throat surgeon (Bartley & Clifton-Smith, 2006), have pointed out that nasal breathing is, in fact, more effective than mouth breathing. Nasal breathing activates the diaphragm. Also, when breathing through the nose, air flows more easily into the lower parts of the lungs where, due to the conical form of the lungs, there is abundant vasculature and a large gas exchange area. This means that the respiratory system and the heart need to work less actively than in the case of more poorly oxygenising thoracic breathing. When a person starts to relearn his inborn skill, nasal breathing, his performance level may at first become lower because his nasal and other respiratory muscles may have become weaker for lack of use. As a result of training, the muscles will become stronger and gas exchange will gradually become more effective.

In addition, nasal breathing has other advantages. The abundant villi on the nasal mucosa warm up and humidify the air and filter viruses, bacteria, and fine particles better than the oral cavity. Nasal breathing helps the lungs stay supple and the alveoli remain patent. When breathing through the nose, the amount of inhaled air remains better under control, which helps to reduce the risk of overbreathing. Some people benefit from a nasal breathing exercise consisting of taping the mouth shut with light wound tape for the night.

Mouth breathing may provide the only possibility for getting air if there is anatomical obstruction in the nose or congestion due to allergies or infections. Mouth breathing is also common in distressed and anxious people. The connection between the mind and breathing can thus already be seen at the very beginning of the respiratory cycle. Even if the above problems are eliminated, mouth breathing may persist and thus maintain extended overbreathing. Some people get into the habit of mouth breathing even without any problems such as those listed above. This may, for example, be related to problems in body awareness, such as difficulty in being aware of one's breathing or in being aware of being in a position complicating breathing. After breathing school, one patient said that she believed her nasal cavities had felt congested due to lack of use. Her breathing gradually became easier as she started paying attention to nasal breathing. Jim Bartley (Bartley & Clifton-Smith, 2006) has observed that people with imbalanced breathing are more likely to suffer from nasal congestion.

Even though balanced breathing is experienced as continuously flowing, breathing consists of several phases. The phases include inhalation and exhalation, that is, pulmonary ventilation, gas exchange between blood and the alveoli, transportation of gases in blood, and gas exchange between blood and tissues. Gas exchange on the cellular level, that is, *cellular breathing*, is also a form of breathing.

3.2.1. Inhalation

The diaphragm is central to balanced breathing. Normal, calm inhalation starts with contraction of the diaphragm. From the diaphragm, the breathing movement spreads in a wavelike manner both down towards the pelvis and up towards the chest. The spine performs a minor rolling movement with the pelvic spine tilting slightly forward (lordosis) and the connection between the cervical and thoracic spine becoming levelled. The spinal movements during breathing are small, and may only be perceptible to a very careful observer.

The diaphragm is a dome-shaped muscle between the chest and the abdomen. It has openings for the inferior vena cava, the aorta, and the oesophagus. The diaphragm is attached to the whole thorax, ribs, costal cartilage, the area of the xiphoid process, and the vertebrae. In addition, large abdominal, back, and pelvic muscles are attached to the diaphragm in an overlapping fashion, working together with it. The diaphragm also participates in maintaining the posture. Therefore, it affects the body extensively. The diaphragm is innervated through the phrenic and intercostal nerves. Its movements are harder to recognise than those of other voluntary muscles. It is therefore difficult to influence directly and consciously. Optimal diaphragmatic respiration is thus easiest to learn indirectly. In psychophysical breathing therapy, images, movement, and voice are used as aids in various breathing exercises.

Air enters the lungs through suction. The suction occurs when the diaphragm contracts and moves down, expanding the thoracic cavity lengthwise down to the abdominal cavity, and pushing the abdominal wall out and forward. This downward movement of the diaphragm is facilitated by images of breathing down to the bottom of the abdomen. The outer intercostal muscles then contract, lifting the ribs to expand the lower part of the thoracic cavity sidewards. The muscles supporting and lifting the ribs, actually working as accessory respiratory muscles, also participate to a lesser extent. Interestingly, we have not seen the nasal muscles included in the respiratory muscles even though the nose is quite significant for balanced breathing.

3.2.2. Exhalation

At rest and during slow movement, exhalation occurs passively as the diaphragm and other muscles participating in inhalation relax and return to their original positions. The spine moves in the opposite direction to that during inhalation. The suppleness of the costal cartilage and the lungs assist exhalation. The thoracic cavity and the lungs shrink, and the air pressure in the alveoli exceeds the atmospheric pressure. Air flows out from the lungs. If the person is calm, the exhalation phase is longer than the inhalation phase. Many people have problems precisely with exhalation. Such problems are often associated with difficulty expressing feelings and tension in respiratory muscles. The significance of exhalation is explained in more detail on pages 208–220.

3.2.3. Pauses in breathing

Calm breathing with pauses helps air to get down into the lowest parts of the lungs and into the alveoli and also helps air rich in carbon dioxide get out. In normal breathing, inhalation is followed by a brief pause. If it is necessary to hold one's breath for any reason, the pause may be extended. In some breathing therapy methods, patients are advised to do this to prevent hyperventilation. In the method we describe this is not done. We have noticed that holding one's breath after inhalation may provoke muscle tension and a feeling of pressure that people with imbalanced breathing often have anyway. Instead, we strive to achieve a natural flow of breathing, and particular attention is therefore paid to letting go during exhalation, as well as to the pause after exhalation. The pause is not actually a pause between cycles of breathing but represents fading out, during which the flow continues on both mental and physical levels. During the pause, respiratory muscles relax and respiratory gases are balanced to a level appropriate for the metabolic needs.

The pause after exhalation is not always mentioned in texts on respiratory mechanics because breathing has more often been studied during stress than during rest and recovery. Better knowledge of calming systems is useful for the treatment of stress and exhaustion. For many people, the pause experienced after exhalation is a highly satisfying and relaxing moment.

3.3. Whole-body breathing

3.3.1. Accessory respiratory muscles

When the body needs more oxygen for effort requiring increased muscle work, accessory respiratory muscles are recruited to get air into the lungs quickly. Calm abdominal diaphragmatic respiration is resumed when the need for increased breathing ceases. Accessory respiratory muscles may also partly compensate for the use of the primary respiratory muscles if the latter have become weaker from disease, or if their use has been reduced by obesity, surgery, unbalanced movements or working positions, or for mental reasons. (See, for example, sleep apnoea on pages 94–95).

There are different views on the role and relative significance of accessory respiratory muscles. A large number of muscles may participate in breathing in various situations and positions requiring use of strength and in connection with various emotions.

> A patient reported that she had suffered from upper back and deep neck muscle tension for several years. She had tried various therapeutic and self-care methods. Whenever her muscles relaxed even slightly, a strong, frightening feeling of helplessness ensued. She had dealt with this to some extent in psychotherapy but still felt that she could not continue breathing exercises alone because the experience was so frightening. "I use my muscles to ward off early traumatic experiences," she said.

The main tasks of accessory respiratory muscles are associated with movement or maintenance of position. The thorax and the muscles attached to it are used to maintain the position of the head, neck, ribs, spinal structures, upper limbs, and the back. During breathing, these muscles either expand the thoracic cavity or stabilise the spine and ribs around the thoracic cavity. The primary respiratory muscles can be assisted by front and back neck muscles, shoulder muscles, muscles raising and supporting the ribs, and intercostal, chest, back, abdominal, and pelvic muscles.

Muscles participating in breathing

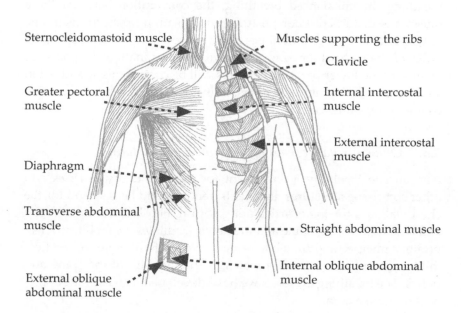

Sternocleidomastoid muscle

Muscles supporting the ribs

Clavicle

Greater pectoral muscle

Internal intercostal muscle

External intercostal muscle

Diaphragm

Transverse abdominal muscle

Straight abdominal muscle

Internal oblique abdominal muscle

External oblique abdominal muscle

Reproduced from Chaitow, Bradley & Gilbert (2002, p. 18).

Abdominal muscles are mainly active during exhalation but they also participate in inhalation. During inhalation, the abdominal muscles must be appropriately strong to provide a supportive wall against which the diaphragm can work. Weak and tense but also particularly strong abdominal muscles may hinder inhalation and the work of the diaphragm (cf. case on page 91).

The pelvic floor muscles act as a counterforce to the diaphragm. As the diaphragm contracts, the pelvic floor muscles relax, and vice versa. Appropriately strong and well-developed pelvic floor muscles bear the weight of the inner organs as the spine is stabilised. This way, muscles can lift and expand the thoracic cavity. In addition to being strong, it is important for pelvic floor muscles to be able to relax. Constant muscle tension, urinary problems, and imbalanced breathing are often intertwined.

The diaphragm, abdominal, pelvic floor, and back muscles form a flexible "box". These muscles work in a certain order. A good balance between back, abdominal, and pelvic muscles is very important for breathing. In imbalanced breathing, the cooperation between these muscles is disturbed. Poor postures and breathing pattern disorders, as well as anatomic abnormalities and diseases, may affect muscles, the order of their activation, and their mutual coordination. The passage of air into the lower parts of the lungs will be compromised and, all in all, less air will flow into the lungs. Lower back and neck pain are also common consequences.

3.3.2. Other auxiliary breathing structures and posture

Appropriate flexibility is important for the respiratory muscles and other soft tissue structures, ligaments, tendons and fasciae, and for the chest wall and the joints articulating with it. Flexibility of the cervical and other parts of the spine and the pelvis facilitates the mobility of respiratory muscles and thus breathing movements. Vice versa, the flexibility of respiratory muscles increases the mobility of the spine and pelvis. The breathing exercises we have developed increase the suppleness of the skeleton.

A therapist working with breathing should therefore pay attention to the flexibility of the spine and supporting structures, back position, patients' vertical position, and how they use their bodies. Supple movement of the spine during breathing should be looked for. Exceptional tightness, tension, weakness, or shortness of accessory respiratory muscles, again, should direct attention to how the patient breathes. In psychophysical therapy, the aim should not be to correct either posture or breathing from outside but to help patients observe these themselves. In our experience, posture and breathing may improve without physical exercises if patients can be helped to understand their situation comprehensively, provided that imbalanced breathing or posture problems have not persisted for long.

> When I was ten years old, I was sent to a physiotherapist for guidance for my posture; this was undoubtedly appropriate because my upper back posture was stooped. However, this approach did not help me. No one asked how I was or appeared to understand that by stooping I was protecting myself from mental pain. This had largely to do with the situation in my family and my relationship to my parents. More than postural guidance I would have needed an adult who understood my situation.

Norwegian physiotherapists (see Kvåle, Johnsen, & Ljungren, 2002) working according to a psychomotor tradition dating back to the 1940s have developed a model for the connection and interaction between posture, breathing, performance capacity, and muscles. They consider the twelfth thoracic vertebra as the key point. The area around this vertebra is also called the *solar plexus*. It forms the attachment point for various muscles (the diaphragm, transverse abdominal muscle, longissimus lumborum muscle, quadratus lumborum, iliopsoas, and latissimus dorsi muscles) which affect each other's tension as well as posture, breathing, and muscle work chains. The iliopsoas muscle anatomically connected to the diaphragm is an important link between mind and body. Its automatic contraction in situations of impending danger or threat makes one reflexively take a protecting position (curving the trunk), which directly affects breathing. Mere anticipation of threat may make the muscle prepare for it, and people suffering from anxiety may therefore have chronically tense iliopsoas muscles (Berceli, 2008).

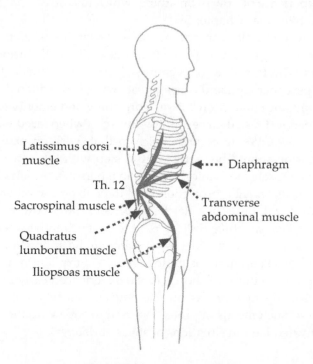

Reproduced from Monsen (1989).

A physiotherapist had noted pain in the twelfth thoracic vertebra in a patient with shoulder and back pain, who had been referred by an occupational physician. This observation gave the physician a natural opening to ask the patient about stress. The tense patient told the therapist about a crisis in his life that had been getting worse over the last couple of years. Antidepressant medication and discussions calmed down the patient's overarousal and helped him to make decisions that helped to relieve stress and restore the experience of coping.

3.3.3. Breathing and muscle tension

Kirsti Monsen, a Norwegian physiotherapist and body psychotherapist (1989, p. 26), summarises [translated for this edition]: "When breathing is relaxed and spontaneous, it flows freely through the respiratory tract, changing according to the body's internal and external requirements. Such breathing also provides the ground for good mental flexibility and basically allows feeling and showing feelings." In this book, we emphasise the experience of flow of breathing, which releases *mental breathing*, mental mobility (see Chapter Six).

Respiratory muscles can become tense if you are on guard or suppress your feelings, as well as due to or associated with various physical factors. The free flow of breath is disrupted. Wilhelm Reich, an Austrian psychoanalyst and colleague of Freud, is considered a pioneer of describing the connection between breathing and emotions. He realised that people tense their respiratory muscles when faced with threat (Boadella, 1994). We agree with Reich in that work on patients with muscle tension should be carried out in step with the patient, not by working on muscle mechanics. Tension in a person's muscles may represent necessary mental protection until the person can otherwise sufficiently deal with his issues. Reich's pupil Alexander Lowen described in his book *Betrayal of the Body* (1967) the connection between breathing and emotions in a way that has resulted in the aphorism: "Shallow breath and blocked emotions go together." We explain in more detail in many places in this book how a threat experienced early in life often remains in body memory as muscle tension and breathing with the upper chest. Such means of protection used to cope with the threat are easily activated later in situations of stress or danger.

With advancing age, a seventy-year-old single woman had begun to feel lonely. She had developed increasing musculoskeletal problems and a feeling of shortness of breath. No pulmonary disease or other physical cause was found to explain the shortness of breath. A pulmonary specialist considered the shortness of breath to result from hyperventilation, and the patient was referred for assessment for breathing school. The patient said she had had trouble breathing ever since she was a child. Therefore, she was for instance never able to run properly. She also said that all her life she had felt tenseness in her body. She associated such being on guard with her experience of her dominating mother. The patient felt she could not get married because she thought her mother would not have approved of it. Getting old, together with the increasing loneliness and decrepitude of her body made her muscles more tense and further impaired her breathing. The patient reacted to this threat similarly to the threat she had experienced as a child, that is, by holding her breath. Psychophysical breathing therapy improved her state considerably.

Tensing the muscles can be consciously utilised in methods of psychophysical therapy to control intolerably strong feelings or emerging images of trauma. However, prolonged tension of accessory respiratory muscles and their simultaneous use for breathing impede breathing and cause muscle pain. We therefore recommend this type of work only with a therapist.

Accessory respiratory muscles are automatically already taken into use when preparing for increased need for energy. This may occur either before actual physical straining or due to arising stimuli for action, such as when preparing for a performance or getting angry. Muscle tension hinders the use of the diaphragm for breathing.

We found an old source describing in concrete terms the effect of images on the physiology of breathing. William Faulkner observed as early as in 1941 when performing a fluoroscopic examination of a patient's diaphragm how mental images affected the contraction and relaxation of the diaphragm. This is how he describes his observations:

An unemployed, penniless patient with many kinds of unexplained physical symptoms first breathed superficially, his diaphragm only moving about one centimetre. When the patient was asked to imagine finding 10 dollars on the street, his diaphragmatic excursions increased to 7 centimetres on breathing. When he was subsequently asked to imagine the wind taking his money, the diaphragmatic excursions decreased again to only 1.5 centimetres (pp. 187–188).

The space available for the lungs decreases if breathing muscles are constantly contracted. The person may then experience having no space for feelings or needs in his mind, either. For his body to get enough air he must resort to chest breathing and increasing his breathing rate. Abdominal or diaphragmatic breathing effectively also ventilates the lower parts of the lungs, where there is plenty of lung tissue because the lungs are cone-shaped. It uses about 5 per cent of the total body energy expenditure, whereas breathing with the upper part of the chest uses as much as 30 per cent of the total energy expenditure (Bartley & Clifton-Smith, 2006, p. 56). Breathing with the upper part of the chest is therefore exhausting in the long term. Long-term use of accessory respiratory muscles has significant negative health effects. The multiple tasks of breathing and the respiratory organs are inadequately accomplished if breathing takes place in the long term mainly with the accessory respiratory muscles.

The following reflections by a patient show the connection between culture and breathing physiology:

> In the old days, women needed to wear corsets to be beautiful. Diaphragmatic breathing was not possible inside the tightened corset. This made breathing superficial, women suffered from a lack of oxygen and easily fainted. Corsets were loosened and breathing was restored. Today women construct the corsets inside themselves. You must be of a certain look and form, lose weight, and keep drawing in your stomach. You do exercises to develop an internal corset, and when you catch a glimpse of your reflection in a shop window downtown, you quickly draw in your stomach. What is worst about this is that breathing becomes as superficial as with a corset but it is not as easy to loosen the internal corset. It is really difficult to give up constant tension of abdominal muscles. I started noticing this when I began singing again after a long break. It is difficult to breathe all the way down. My singing teacher's instructions to breathe into my toes, and the image of a soft baby tummy helped a little. It is now easier for me to notice the difficulty of breathing also in everyday situations, such as when climbing stairs. It is hard to breathe deeply and calmly when I exert myself. I also wonder what is wrong with a world where something as natural as breathing can be so badly disturbed.

3.3.4. Psychophysical view of voice production

Breathing and voice production are closely connected. Voice production requires the cooperation of exhaling and voice-producing structures, the larynx, and pharyngeal muscles. Tension of the larynx in the upper respiratory system very commonly causes problems with voice production. The larynx is connected to accessory respiratory muscles in the upper body, such as muscles in the neck-shoulder region (Aalto & Parviainen, 1985). Methods of psychophysical breathing therapy are therefore highly useful in addition to actual speech therapy methods. They are also useful for musicians, especially for wind instrument players (Korpela, 2012) and for singers. In fact, they may make speech therapy possible in the first place. Psychophysical breathing therapy may also be an important addition to voice massage therapy (see Voice Massage in References), a method of manual treatment of anatomic structures associated with voice production that was developed in Finland.

> *A patient participating in breathing school saw a voice massage therapist because she still experienced tightness in her upper body after attending the group. She had originally been referred to breathing school by a neurologist because of dizziness associated with hyperventilation. In breathing school, she learned, for example, to better recognise occasional tension in her upper body and related to the use of her voice. Dizziness ceased, voice production improved and she even became generally more relaxed as a result of these treatments.*

In the exercise chapter (page 228–229) we describe conscious working with the pelvic floor muscles. The pelvic floor and laryngeal muscles work as a counterforce to the diaphragm. The significance of the cooperation of these muscle groups is recognised in connection with expressive and singing skills. Many people have experienced how emotional issues affect muscle work and voice production, particularly singing. An amateur singer tells about this:

> *I developed a singer's block. The hobby that had brought me joy began to bring more pain than pleasure. High notes choked my soprano throat, and anticipation of failure took the joy out of singing. Over the years I learned to associate this with problems in letting go, being seen and taking space, and with being good enough as I am. As the breathing school was coming to an end, I was asked to perform again for the first time in several years. I told myself I would go there to breathe for the listeners. I was only a mediator of music. All the notes were already there, I only needed to let them out. It was just breathing aloud. I knew how to breathe. It would not matter if they could hear the tension in my voice. I would again calmly concentrate*

on inhaling. I would let the balloon inside me be filled. I would remember the pause and let go after exhaling, that is, between phrases. There was no hurry. No one would expect me to do this perfectly. What was, was good enough. Breathing flowed within me and my voice flowed with it.

We also interviewed a professional soprano singer, who said:

Preparing a singer's instrument starts with relaxing the defence system on the front side of the body. Release any tension in the forehead, face, jaw, and neck. Wind down any unnecessary lifting of the chest, and allow the region of the diaphragm and the abdomen to soften. At the same time, place the centre of gravity in the body as low as possible. The aim of relaxation is to produce maximum resonance in the whole body. A tight and tense body will not resonate freely.

Once the instrument has been opened, a space opens in the abdomen, into which it is easy to breathe. Conscious use of the diaphragm and the lungs can be bypassed by using the image of breathing through the neck and back. Breathing will open up the sides but they need not be consciously kept open. Breathing in this position will spread out the sides of the diaphragm. The diaphragm lies flat inside the body.

When singing, exhalation must be as gentle as it is otherwise. Pressed exhalation will contract the diaphragm and squash the ends of the lungs together causing compression in the trunk. Singing represents free flow of energy and warmth. To sing, the common detrimental reaction of the diaphragm, that is, tension, must be bypassed. The aim is to let go of the need to defend oneself and thus to allow the diaphragm to work as a breathing muscle.

All the above, including the energy and warmth from the body, affect the function of the larynx. The sound of the voice is formed in the larynx. It has several layers. The lower the vibration, the more overtones there will be. The better you can open up your body and resonate all the way down, the more overtones there will be, resulting in a more perfect voice.

Even though the above examples are associated with singing, people have similar experiences of any use of the voice and any self-expression. All our courage is concentrated in exhalation and use of the voice.

3.4. Regulation of breathing

3.4.1. Nervous and biochemical regulation

The regulation of breathing is mediated by *nerve impulses* and *chemoreceptors*, that is, sensory organs responsive to chemical stimuli in the blood, and occurs in breathing centres in the brain stem, which integrate messages from various parts of the body. These regulation systems work automatically but the mind may affect breathing through both regulation systems. When a person breathes in a physiologically optimal manner, the regulation systems automatically and accurately choose, inhalation by inhalation, the way of breathing requiring the least amount of muscle work and thus consuming the least amount of energy (Jennett, 1994, pp. 74–75). This is done by varying the breathing rate and depth and the use of various muscles. The regulation of breathing is also affected by emotions and associated stimuli to act that may involve a threat or be of a positive nature. In this case breathing according to physical needs may be disturbed.

Under normal circumstances, the blood carbon dioxide level is the most significant regulator of breathing. Inhalation begins when the carbon dioxide level is elevated. Thus, when you hold your breath, the need to inhale arises from accumulation of carbon dioxide, not from lack of oxygen. Oxygen levels must be considerably decreased before they essentially affect the regulation of breathing. This may occur in the mountains or in patients with severe disease.

Chemoreceptors convey information on carbon dioxide levels and acid-base balance, that is, pH, to the breathing centres. Based on the information they receive, the inhalation and exhalation centres send orders to the respiratory muscles. If the blood carbon dioxide level is too high, normally due to muscle work, chemoreceptors recognise this and breathing increases. Muscle work exceeding the oxygen intake capacity also increases the acidity of blood through elevated lactic acid levels. In addition, breathing centres receive information on expansion of the lungs and on joint movements, for example, through peripheral receptors and from muscle spindles and tendon receptors in the region of the diaphragm and the thorax. Motor nerves carry orders to act from neural breathing centres to the respiratory muscles.

Autonomic neurofibrils from the central nervous system enter the lungs through the anterior trunk of the vagus nerve conveying calming signals and through sympathetic ganglia in the chest conveying stimulating signals. The breathing centres form a part of the reticular activation system in the brain stem, conveying information on vital functions, heart function, contraction or dilation of blood vessels and thus regulation of blood pressure, muscle tone, and autonomic nervous activity. Relaxation of the jaw muscles and the muscles around the eyes, for example, reduces the heart rate and calms down breathing (Porges,

2011). The reticular activation system thus affects total psychophysical alertness.

The neurofibrils mediating voluntary and autonomic action from the breathing centre lead to the motor nerve cells in the anterior horn of the spinal cord, from where nerve impulses are transmitted to respiratory muscles. Conscious influence on breathing is conveyed to breathing centres through the cerebral cortex, through nerve impulses from the primary motor cortex and from premotor areas. Nerve impulses from these areas also mediate the modification of automatic regulation mechanisms of breathing associated with speaking, singing, and blowing. Feelings affect breathing, and breathing, in turn, directly affects the chemical regulation system. This direct connection between feelings and the chemical system is rarely mentioned.

3.4.2. Autonomic nervous system

The autonomic nervous system helps to keep the functions within the body as stable as possible when facing various internal and external challenges. It acts through a complicated regulatory chain on smooth muscle and thus on the bronchi, blood vessels, myocardium, and glands secreting various hormones, such as stress hormones.

The autonomic nervous system is traditionally divided into the sympathetic and parasympathetic nervous systems. According to Stephen Porges (2011), the autonomic nervous system is divided into three systems regulating different functions. Normally, a sensible balance exists between these. The sympathetic nervous system prepares the body for action, for *fight* or *flight*, as necessary, that is, for extra movement and added metabolic needs. If the limbic system activates the posterior trunk of the vagus nerve, the body *freezes*. The anterior trunk of the vagus nerve, in contrast, calms the body down, thus regulating overarousal of the sympathetic system.

> *I fell on my slippery and icy home yard and felt severe pain in my back. I was quite calm and able to call the ambulance. The ambulance men asked me to stand up from the lying position, and to my astonishment I was able to do so. The men pondered aloud whether they should leave me alone at home and whether my pain would gradually subside. I vaguely felt there was something badly wrong with my body but I was not able to explain my feelings in more detail. I realised that I was in danger of being left unassisted. Afterwards I realised that I had been trapped in a frozen state. The paramedics may have interpreted my calmness as a sign of no*

particular danger. However, as my blood pressure was really low (probably in consequence of the shock), they decided to take me to a medical centre. A vertebral fracture was diagnosed there.

In human developmental history, the ability to fight, flee, or freeze was needed to survive. The body still reacts to various threats, even mental ones, as if they always require physical action or its prevention. In association with, or instead of, physical action, mental action and psychophysical means of calming down may suppress such reactions, thus restoring the psychophysical balance.

The sympathetic nervous system stimulates breathing and circulation. Circulation is activated as the heart rate is accelerated and contractility of the heart increases. Superficial blood vessels contract to allow more blood to flow into large muscles. This results in elevated blood pressure. The smooth bronchial muscles do the opposite, they relax and thus dilate the airways. Therefore, oxygen intake and the elimination of carbon dioxide increase. The availability of nutrients improves. In contrast, the activity of the digestive system decreases, with decreased motility and slower secretion in the digestive tract. When the challenging situation is over, activity of the anterior trunk of the vagus nerve restores bodily rest, recovery, and calming down. Breathing slows down, the bronchi revert to their previous state, heart rate slows down, blood vessels in the skin are dilated, improving peripheral circulation, and the digestion rate increases.

Autonomic regulation of breathing can be consciously influenced to a certain extent. It may also be useful to know that breathing cannot be completely controlled even if many people try to do so. People can hold their breath and vary its depth and rhythm to a certain extent. Loss of consciousness due to overbreathing, in the end, will trigger automatic breathing mechanisms (Jennet, 1994, p. 73), that is, people cannot be suffocated by hyperventilating even though it may feel like it. We often explain this to patients who fear that they will not get enough oxygen, assuring them that, come what may, people do get quite enough air. Activity of the sympathetic nervous system can be increased by accelerating breathing. This is easy to verify by breathing rapidly and deeply for a few minutes; effects such as increased heart rate and trembling hands will be observed. Similarly, the activity of the anterior trunk of the vagus nerve can be activated by consciously slowing down and calming the breathing rhythm and other action, as is done in the psychophysical breathing therapy we present in this book and in many other forms of therapy.

3.4.3. Effects of hyperventilation in the body

Physiologically, *hyperventilation* means ventilation of the lungs exceeding metabolic needs. Unnecessarily deep breathing or superficial and rapid breathing with the upper lungs may increase the tidal volume, leading to a physiological state of hyperventilation. Hyperventilation is a normal reaction when the body prepares for physical activity requiring exertion. It becomes inappropriate if excessive breathing continues but no physical activity is started. This may occur if feelings are experienced as overwhelming. The main consequences of hyperventilation are lowered blood carbon dioxide levels and increased pH values. Other effects occur as a chain reaction. Through various physiological systems, the effects of hyperventilation extend to virtually the whole body.

Keeping the acid-base balance within certain limits is a necessary prerequisite for cellular metabolic processes that optimally require a pH of 7.35–7.45. A change in pH level may be due to either breathing or metabolism. On the other hand, increased breathing may be a means of restoring normal acid-base balance disturbed for metabolic reasons. A patient with diabetes, for example, may develop ketoacidosis, an acidosis due to lack of insulin. Ketoacidosis automatically triggers a reaction where the patient tries, by breathing more rapidly, to reduce the excessive acidity of the blood.

Biochemical effects of acute hyperventilation in the body

- Blood carbon dioxide levels decrease
- Blood pH increases (respiratory alkalosis), that is, blood becomes too alkaline
- Dissociation of oxygen from haemoglobin becomes more difficult
- The amount of oxygen available to cells decreases
- Local and cerebral circulation decrease due to the constriction of blood vessels
- Autonomic, sympathetic, motor, and sensory nervous system activity increases
- Electrolyte activity changes in a complex manner.

Hyperventilation affects the acid-base balance after about two minutes. The body cannot tolerate pH imbalance for long. The balance is stabilised by *buffer systems* (Gilbert, 2002a, p. 65), of which respiration is the primary one and very rapid. Renal buffer systems do not become effective for several hours. Buffer stores are needed to keep metabolic variation within normal limits.

The amount of oxygen entering the cells decreases due to poorer circulation but also because haemoglobin releases less oxygen to cells when there is an alkaline body pH. Here is another direct link between the effects of breathing and emotions on basic body functions. Cells suffer from a lack of oxygen even though the amount of oxygen in the blood is sufficient. The person then often feels a need to breathe more, and this only worsens the lack of oxygen in the cells. Even professionals do not always recognise this physiological fact.

Motor and sensory nerves and the autonomic sympathetic nervous system are activated by hyperventilation. The activation of motor nerves results in contraction of skeletal muscles, muscle tension, and, at worst, muscle cramps. Tingling and numbness of the skin, for example, are due to the activation of the sympathetic sensory nervous system. Circulation decreases in smooth muscle, superficially, in the internal organs (the bronchi, and cardiac and gastrointestinal blood vessels), and in cerebral blood vessels. Hyperventilation also affects electrolyte activity (potassium, magnesium, phosphorus, calcium) and lactic acid metabolism in complex ways.

Chronic hyperventilation may easily continue for physiological reasons. Ventilation needs to be increased by only about 10 per cent to maintain chronic hyperventilation (Salzman, Heyman, & Sieker, 1963). Chronic hyperventilation may be due to continuous stress or to hyperactivity of the sympathetic nervous system associated with anxiety. However, this need not be so. Hyperventilation may continue even if the mental or physical stress that originally triggered it no longer exists or if for example the anatomic abnormality compromising nasal function has been corrected (Bartley & Clifton-Smith, 2006, p. 13). Imbalanced breathing easily becomes conditioned. Examples of experimental studies illustrating the conditioning of breathing are given at the end of this chapter. Many physicians, psychologists, and physiotherapists doing clinical work have observed conditioned hyperventilating breathing patterns after the diseases causing hyperventilation have been cured.

On the other hand, not all stress or tension is visible. People may appear balanced even if they are experiencing great mental distress.

Even less attention has been paid to the effects of chronic hyperventilation on the body's biochemistry, the primary and accessory respiratory muscles, or the skeleton than to the effects of acute hyperventilation. In chronic hyperventilation, buffer systems correct the acid-base balance. However, reduced buffer stores decrease the possibilities for balancing the effects of physical or mental stress. Carbon dioxide levels may be lower than normal, and the body may become adapted to tolerating this. It is therefore difficult for people who have been hyperventilating for a long time to tolerate the higher carbon dioxide levels associated with normal breathing. If so, symptoms may increase at first when attempts are made to restore the balance of breathing. In chronic hyperventilation, the breathing centre gradually adapts to excessively low blood carbon dioxide levels, and the body thus supports chronic hyperventilation (Gilbert, 2002a, pp. 71–72). In patients with pulmonary emphysema, adaptation occurs in the opposite direction: patients become adapted to elevated blood carbon dioxide levels.

The originally Ukrainian, later Russian, professor of medicine Konstantin Buteyko studied readaptation of the breathing centre to normal carbon dioxide levels. He became interested in the effects of excessively low carbon dioxide levels on smooth muscle activity, metabolism, and hormone activity. The breathing method developed by Buteyko has been adapted for the treatment of patients with asthma, who have benefited significantly from using the method. Buteyko's method is similar to the method we describe in this book in that it emphasises nasal breathing, exhalation exercises, and the pause after exhalation. However, the methods differ in the way they are implemented in practice. In Buteyko's method nasal breathing is practised both consciously during the daytime and by taping the mouth shut at night. Exhalation is practised by pausing a few times during exhalation and then letting go and exhaling until the end pause (McKeown, 2004).

If the symptoms of imbalanced breathing are severe, we recommend first doing exercises involving holding the breath or interrupting exhalation together with a therapist. This is because in anxious people *holding the breath* often alternates with hyperventilation. Body awareness improves when working with someone else; people learn to better recognise reactions reflected in breathing, and this makes it possible for them to constructively influence their own state.

Acute hyperventilation is often followed by holding the breath, which may in that case be a physiological means of balancing carbon dioxide levels. Holding the breath may be associated with any activity requiring a high level of attention or exertion, with holding back emotions, or with a wish to remain unseen. It may occur acutely or, depending on personality features, represent a person's deeply rooted behaviour either when alone or in interaction with others. Even in a state of mental balance, people react to emotions by changing their breathing, but in that case even breathing is restored after the stimulus stops exerting its effect. Health involves the ability to vary breathing according to internal and external demands. Nevertheless, one of the aims of psychophysical breathing therapy is to increase flowing, uninterrupted breathing.

As hyperventilation affects nearly the whole body through the circulation and the nervous system, symptoms and sensations associated with it occur extensively around the body. Recognising this will help the therapist to see a patient's various symptoms as consequences of imbalanced breathing.

Common symptoms in hyperventilating patients

- Symptoms associated with breathing: shortness of breath, sensations of dyspnoea and lack of oxygen, deep, sighing inhalation, rapid and superficial breathing
- Symptoms associated with nervous regulation of blood vessels
  a. Central nervous system: vertigo, blurred vision, double vision, other visual disturbances, episodes of unconsciousness
  b. Peripheral symptoms: tingling, numbness, and feeling cold, particularly in the fingers, arms, around the mouth, and in the lower limbs
- Symptoms associated with nervous regulation of muscles: muscle stiffness, tremor, or cramps, particularly in the fingers, arms, lower limbs, speech organs, the face, around the mouth, and in thoracic muscles
- Symptoms of cardiac origin: palpitations, tachycardia, stabbing chest pain
- Gastrointestinal symptoms: dry mouth, sensation of a lump in the throat (*globus*), swallowing problems, nausea, upper gastric pain, belching, flatulence, intestinal spasms

> • Mental symptoms: general tension, anxiety, restlessness, sense
>   of unreality, sense of panic, fear of loss of control, and fear of
>   death
> • General symptoms: fatigue, sleep disturbances.

Hyperventilation does not affect all people in the same way; symptoms and sensations may vary for many reasons. Symptoms and sensations may also be affected by factors simultaneously affecting organ systems, such as the autonomic nervous system or the person's mental state. The main symptoms purely due to hyperventilation are a feeling of coldness in the limbs, dizziness, and various visual sensations.

> *A patient suffering from severe chronic hyperventilation came to his psychotherapy session wondering why his fingers were so cold even though the weather had been warm. It turned out that he had just had blood tests that he feared.*

People are not always capable of describing their symptoms or feelings. One of the aims of the psychophysical breathing therapy we have developed is to help people observe and identify their bodily sensations calmly and accurately. It is assumed that some people have special biological features in some parts of their bodies, making them susceptible to experiencing symptoms of hyperventilation precisely in those parts. One ultrasound study showed that people who showed most contraction in the blood vessels at the base of their skull during voluntary hyperventilation were most susceptible to panic symptoms (Gibbs, 1992).

As research methods have developed further, more detailed information has been obtained on the effects of hyperventilation. Modern brain imaging methods have made it possible to confirm impairment of cerebral circulation due to hyperventilation. According to Gilbert (2002b, p. 127) various studies have found loss of concentration, memory, motor coordination, reaction time, judgement, and general intellectual functioning as a result of reduced cerebral circulation due to hyperventilation. In one laboratory study involving experimental tasks requiring attention and quick reaction, physiological hyperventilation was found to impair performance in a visual attention test (van Diest, Stegen, van den Woestijne, Schippers, & van den Bergh, 2000).

3.4.4. Connections with other body systems

Many hormones, such as thyroxine and luteal hormone, affect breathing. Luteal hormone levels are elevated during the latter half of the menstrual cycle, and this makes breathing deeper. Premenstrual symptoms (PMS), that is, tension, headache, and nervousness, are also associated with hyperventilation (Damas-Mora, Davies, Taylor, & Jenner, 1980). Breathing and relaxation therapy has been helpful for patients suffering from PMS.

Hyperventilation impairs immune function in both the short and long term. This results in an increased risk of inflammation. In addition, hyperventilation elevates blood histamine levels. This may affect symptoms of allergy. Histamine secretion is particularly problematic for patients with asthma because histamine causes bronchial constriction. (See Bartley & Clifton-Smith, 2006; Gilbert 2002a, p. 73.) We have therefore used methods of psychophysical breathing therapy to calm down patients with asthma and various allergy symptoms.

> *A pulmonary specialist had suggested that a woman suffering from numerous allergies and asthma should come to breathing school due to attacks of dyspnoea that were partly atypical for asthma. During breathing school she came to realise that her allergy and asthma symptoms became worse if she was scared by the first mild symptoms and started hyperventilating. She learned to take her symptoms more calmly and to differentiate better between symptoms due to true allergy and ones due to hyperventilation. Her overall symptoms were alleviated.*

3.4.5. Hyperventilation, diet, and digestion

Low blood glucose (sugar) levels potentiate the effects of hyperventilation on the brain. George Engel and his co-workers studied this as early as in 1947. Engel gave his subjects various amounts of glucose as they hyperventilated, and studied the electrical activity in their brains. It slowed down progressively with decreasing blood glucose levels. The brain needs a constant supply of oxygen but also a constant supply of glucose, which is necessary for obtaining sufficient energy. The brain consumes about 20 per cent of the total body glucose. Brain cells have a very low capacity for storing energy. They are therefore dependent on a constant supply of glucose within the blood (Gilbert, 2002a, p. 78). Hyperventilation causes vasoconstriction in the brain, thus affecting cerebral metabolism. People susceptible to hyperventilation, particularly, should follow a diet keeping blood glucose levels as stable as possible. Well-known consequences of low blood glucose levels include irritability, headaches, and sudden fatigue or loss of consciousness.

Many people suffering from anxiety and panic attacks have been advised to avoid coffee and alcohol. Caffeine stimulates the sympathetic nervous system and thus accelerates breathing with all the known consequences. In the short term, alcohol depletes brain glucose stores and also potentiates the effect of hyperventilation (Gilbert, 2002a, p. 78).

Other factors associated with diet and intestinal function may also be associated with imbalanced breathing. Factors connecting the intestine and mental health are being examined, and information is being sought on, for example, the effect of stress in early childhood on intestinal microbes and how changes in intestinal microbes are reflected in later health.

Regulation of the activity of the digestive system is complicated. It occurs both locally and in the central nervous system. Intestinal function is affected by many body systems that may also interact. Any effect of imbalanced breathing is difficult to verify and specify. On the other hand, as the multiple bodily effects of hyperventilation are known, it can be assumed that imbalanced breathing contributes to disturbances in the function of the digestive system. Reports can be found in the literature that people with intestinal disorders often have symptoms typical for stress and hyperventilation. Digestive disorders may be influenced by features of imbalanced breathing, such as changes in circulation in the internal organs, the autonomic nervous system, secretion of digestive enzymes, and respiratory mechanics. In addition, the function of the diaphragm and pressure variation in the abdominal cavity may be disturbed by changes in respiratory mechanics.

The irritable bowel syndrome is a common digestive system disorder that is difficult to treat. However, a trial with psychophysical breathing therapy can well be recommended for patients with irritable bowel syndrome in association with other treatment and monitoring, particularly if the patient has stress symptoms or sensations consistent with hyperventilation.

3.5. Definition of imbalanced breathing

3.5.1. The concept of imbalanced breathing

Many discussions have been held on how to define and what terminology to use for breathing that is not optimal, but not directly due to somatic disease either. Definitions and terminology are not only linguistic problems. In health care, it is important to give names to symptoms experienced by patients; otherwise, problems easily remain without sufficient attention. This also applies to research. It is difficult to study a symptom or syndrome that cannot be clearly defined.

Hyperventilation syndrome was previously almost the only term used for a breathing disorder not directly associated with somatic disease. This concept was first adopted by the American physician William Kerr with his coworkers in 1938. Kerr and colleagues used the term hyperventilation syndrome to describe a complex of symptoms affecting various organ systems that they considered to be due to low blood carbon dioxide levels and an alkaline pH. They used case reports to describe how suppressed feelings and associated anxiety preceded the emergence of symptoms. In addition, they paid attention to the vicious circle of anxiety and symptoms and to sympathetic stimulation simultaneously affecting the symptoms. It has subsequently been shown that in practice the criteria for hyperventilation syndrome are far from functioning as well as was originally thought even though, in theory, hyperventilation conforming to the physiological definition can be accurately confirmed. For example, differences have been observed between acute and chronic hyperventilation, and organic disease and hyperventilation are known to be associated in certain ways. The criterion of anxiety as a triggering factor has also raised criticism because anxiety is often not easy to diagnose in a doctor's office when a patient presents with physical symptoms.

The Dutch developer of breathing therapy, researcher and physician Jan van Dixhoorn abandoned the concept of hyperventilation syndrome (1997) because he considered it too narrow. Hyperventilation refers to just one aspect of respiration, namely gas exchange. Van Dixhoorn emphasised that respiratory movements affect the whole body. He recommended the term *dysfunctional breathing*. This term has, indeed, become more widely used in the international medical literature. Van Dixhoorn reports that, in his experience, the concept of dysfunctional breathing describes the entity better and extends the indications for breathing therapy because disturbed breathing causes other problems than those associated with respiratory gas exchange. In the literature and in health care, the term *functional breathing* is also used. For this book, we decided to mainly speak about *balanced* and *imbalanced breathing*. We believe these terms appropriately describe breathing in its many regulatory tasks.

3.5.2. Observation of breathing

Hyperventilation is often identified with visibly rapid, gasping breathing. In an acute situation, this is how it usually presents. Physiologically, hyperventilation represents breathing with an enlarged volume, and, therefore, breathing too deeply although less frequently may cause hyperventilation, as well as rapid, scanty breathing. Particularly if hyperventilation is chronic, breathing may appear calm because even one deep breath may be sufficient to maintain physiological hyperventilation (Salzman, Heyman, & Sieker, 1963).

Central features of imbalanced breathing

- No pause after exhalation
- Holding one's breath (extended pause after inhalation) with the chest in the inhalation position
- Increased respiratory rate at rest (normally ten to fourteen per minute)
- More frequent mouth breathing
- Use of accessory respiratory muscles also at rest
- Frequent sighing or yawning
- Abdominal muscles that are tense and stiff or act in the opposite way to how they should (contract when inhaling and relax when exhaling)
- Irregular use of the above ways of breathing
- Recurrent clearing of the throat
- Swallowing of air and sometimes belching
- The subtle movement of the spine on inhalation and exhalation is lacking
- Observable problems in interpersonal interaction.

It is difficult but not impossible to observe chronic hyperventilation. Chronic hyperventilation can be reliably and effectively assessed without any laboratory or instrumental tests. In a Norwegian study (Kvåle, Johnsen, & Ljungren, 2002), physiotherapists trained to treat and assess breathing observed the breathing of patients with musculoskeletal pain before and after psychomotor physiotherapy. Their observations proved quite reliable. Breathing therapy helped these patients.

Minna Martin recounts her experience of learning to observe the use of accessory muscles and how she uses this skill in practical clinical work:

When I received my training in physiotherapy we spent a lot of time observing each other, watching positions, moving, muscle work, structures, etc. In addition, we learned to make observations by palpation. The development of observation skills formed a central part of learning to work as a physiotherapist. However, it is not easy to learn to observe breathing. We need to learn to pay attention to quite subtle signs. I developed this skill guided by my mother, who had worked as a general practitioner for decades. My children had respiratory infections when they were small. I learned to notice the use of accessory respiratory muscles by watching my children breathe. Depression of the supraclavicular fossa and intercostal spaces are signs of the use of accessory respiratory muscles, and it was often possible to see hard pumping in the abdomen, too. When watching closely, I could also see the muscles surrounding the nostrils work. By peeking under the child's shirt I could see when it was time for the child to inhale steam to expand the bronchi.

Later on, these observation skills were useful in my clinical work as a psychologist. Hyperventilating patients with panic disorder show quite similar changes to little patients with infections. Of course, as a psychologist, I don't peek under people's shirts. In addition to breathing, I observe tenseness in neck muscles, deepening of the supraclavicular fossa, and the area of the nostrils. Patients themselves are not always conscious of the signs of overarousal or changes in breathing. In this case, I may ask a question like "I wonder what is happening now?" or "Do you find any change in how you are feeling now?" Through physical signs we get to discuss what is happening here and now.

3.5.3. Imbalanced breathing and health care

Imbalanced breathing is quite common, and people suffering from it use a lot of health care services. The symptoms are often dismissed as imaginary, or they may be extensively investigated in various specialties. It may be said that the symptoms are not dangerous and the patient will just have to learn to live with them. In some cases, this may be sufficient. It is difficult to get any accurate figures on the prevalence of imbalanced breathing because it is difficult even to define it.

The Nijmegen Questionnaire (van Dixhoorn & Duivenvoorden, 1985) is a useful screening tool for both practitioners and patients. It has often been used in multinational studies. Physicians and patients often only concentrate on one or a few symptoms, and imbalanced breathing as a factor combining the symptoms may not come to mind. A score of 23/64 has been considered a significant cutoff in the Nijmegen Questionnaire. Patients receiving higher scores have been found to have imbalanced breathing. However, it is good to remember that the list of symptoms does not differentiate between acute and chronic hyperventilation. Patients with chronic hyperventilation often have fewer symptoms than those with an acute hyperventilation attack. In addition, the questionnaire clearly describes symptoms produced by the sympathetic nervous system. Caution should be taken when applying cutoff scores given in screening lists with symptoms for clinical work. Patients may have symptoms requiring examinations or treatment even if their scores do not meet the screening limit. Patients mark on the form how often they have the following symptoms.

Scores

0 = Never
1 = A few times a year
2 = Monthly
3 = Weekly
4 = Daily or nearly daily
  • Chest pain
  • Feeling tense
  • Blurred vision
  • Dizzy spells
  • Feeling confused
  • Faster or deeper breathing
  • Short of breath
  • Tight feelings in the chest
  • Bloated feeling in stomach
  • Tingling fingers
  • Unable to breathe deeply
  • Stiff fingers or arms
  • Tight feelings around mouth

- Cold hands or feet
- Palpitations
- Feelings of anxiety.

As close observation of breathing requires particular training, it would be useful for health care institutions to have available clear laboratory or instrumental tests that could prove patients' symptoms to be due to imbalanced breathing. Today, both physicians and patients are used to confirming diagnoses by laboratory and/or instrumental tests. In the case of breathing, this is difficult because breathing may change quickly for physical or mental reasons. Laboratory methods, such as the hyperventilation provocation test combined with capnography, can no more than confirm the suspicion that symptoms are due to or affected by imbalanced breathing.

In psychiatry, little attention has been paid to imbalanced breathing and its consequences. Breathing problems are considered to belong to anxiety symptoms, and no attention is paid to the bodily consequences of imbalanced breathing. The significance of imbalanced breathing has been discussed mostly in connection with panic anxiety. Studies show that patients fulfilling the criteria of panic disorder often have low breath carbon dioxide levels even between attacks (Wilhelm, Gerlach, & Walton, 2001). This suggests chronic hyperventilation. Patients with hyperventilation attacks often fulfil the diagnostic criteria of panic disorder. Clinical experience has shown that many patients and patients with many types of psychiatric disorders may have imbalanced breathing because imbalanced breathing is often associated with stress and anxiety. Many patients might therefore benefit from paying attention to and calming down breathing, as well as from psychophysical breathing therapy appropriate for the patient or patient group. Patients with generalised anxiety who are afraid of disease, for example, may benefit from knowing that their odd symptoms in various parts of the body are due to imbalanced breathing and that calm breathing will alleviate them.

It is naturally most important to diagnose somatic diseases which may have the same or similar symptoms as imbalanced breathing. Diagnosis is complicated by the fact that patients may suffer from both somatic diseases and imbalanced breathing, and that the latter may be a stress reaction to the disease or some other problem. It would be good for primary health care practitioners to recognise the effects of imbalanced breathing in the body, to take these into consideration when examining the patient and to study any mental stressors, as well. It might then not be necessary to refer the patient to specialised care. On the other hand, differential diagnosis may in some cases be very difficult and examinations in specialised care may be necessary.

A middle-aged man had started using health centre and hospital emergency services because of dyspnoea, palpitations, and chills that began at night. Ten years previously, he had been diagnosed with allergy to certain raw vegetables and fruit. He had previously done well despite his allergies by avoiding allergens and taking antihistamines as necessary. Then, he and his wife had driven to their summer cottage to get some respite from caring for four ailing people, his and her parents. While staying there, he had woken up one night with physical symptoms, of which dyspnoea was the most significant. The day before, he had mowed the lawn and eaten a vegetable casserole. He suspected that the possibly mouldy grass and the vegetables he had eaten had caused the symptoms he interpreted as allergic. Within one and a half months, the patient used emergency services a total of seven times and was admitted to a general hospital ward twice. The symptoms were suspected of being due to an anaphylactic reaction, and he was given cortisone and adrenaline in addition to the antihistamine he had already been taking. The symptoms were made worse by this treatment indicated for an anaphylactic reaction because adrenaline increases sympathetic nervous activity.

They finally started suspecting hyperventilation behind the symptoms because arterial blood samples showed an alkaline pH and accelerated breathing and tension in the neck-shoulder region was noted. In addition, symptoms were found to be alleviated by calming down the patient's breathing. The patient was referred to consultation by a pulmonary specialist and to allergy tests. The tests did not provide any new information. The pulmonary specialist referred the patient for psychiatric consultation and assessment for breathing school. In a more detailed interview the patient was found to have, in addition to dyspnoea and cardiac sensations, other typical symptoms of hyperventilation, such as tingling and numbness. His spouse had also noticed that the attacks began with accelerated breathing. In addition, it was difficult for the patient to be in places with a lot of people that were difficult to get out of. He also easily got out of breath when moving. He was given the psychiatric diagnosis of panic disorder including agoraphobia.

After breathing school and six months of psychotherapy, the patient's state and performance capacity improved. When he learned to better observe and ponder over his feelings and thoughts, the attacks nearly disappeared. He became more conscious of the mental factors triggering the attacks and no longer considered his allergies as causing the symptoms. He no longer got out of breath inappropriately when moving. By using psychophysical first-aid measures and, rarely, anti-anxiety medication he was able to cope with attacks of anxiety and hyperventilation that still sometimes occurred.

3.6. Conditioning of ways of breathing

3.6.1. Role of breathing in the physiology of fear conditioning

Breathing is of central importance in reaction to emergencies. Christopher Gilbert, a clinical psychophysiologist, describes (2002b, p. 122) how the modification of breathing in a dangerous situation ultimately depends on many kinds of information reaching the brain: "vocalization (a cry for help, a shouted warning, perhaps a growl), preparation for exertion, the need to freeze and become perhaps less noticeable, the need to maximize sensory acuity by stilling the body, the need to either remain calm or to return to a baseline state of calmness". These needs are often contradictory. Therefore, breathing often varies in anxious people. They alternately hold their breath and hyperventilate.

Rational brain (neocortex)

Emotional brain (limbic system)

Primitive (reptilian) brain

The breathing centre has connections not only to centres regulating vital functions but also to the limbic system in the brain, that is, structures in the anterior and middle parts of the cerebrum, linking the cerebrum with the brain stem. The limbic system is important for the regulation of emotions and many autonomic functions. It has a central role in implicit conditioning, or conditioning occurring with the help of unconscious memory (LeDoux, 1996). The voluntary effect is mediated from the primary motor cortex and premotor areas through the cerebral cortex.

Everyone has experience of reacting physically in a threatening situation before becoming conscious of the danger. This often happens when driving a car. Sensations may have continued for a few seconds or more before the threat triggering the reaction becomes conscious. The delay is explained by implicit memory that need not be conscious. It also explains quick bodily contingency reactions based on conditioning. Brain imaging studies have confirmed that the conscious mind may be unaware of the action of the emotional brain, that is, consciousness and the cerebral cortex are bypassed. Implicit memory associated with ensuring survival is located in the amygdala. Explicit, conscious, memory is based on the activity of another part of the limbic system, the hippocampus (LeDoux, 1996).

The amygdala has numerous chemical and neural effects on the body systems associated with emergency actions, that is, triggering of stress reactions to cope. When the system works well, the amygdala triggers action. Further action will require instructions from higher reasoning centres in the cerebral cortex. The prefrontal area of the cerebral cortex may control reactions originating deep in the brain. It may prevent outbursts of rage, eliminate fear, and generally hold down feelings. Overaroused people bypass the chance of assessing the situation realistically and regulating it by calming down. A strong emotional reaction originating from deep in the brain will then lead to an automatic, quick fight or flight reaction. The ability to calm down and to assess the situation calmly will suppress the reaction. However, such action always requires a slow process of changing the reaction. In other words, it will take more time to learn ways of calming down than to condition the emergency reaction. Moreover, even at best calming down can only alleviate sensations caused by panicking and will not magically wipe them away, as many people wish.

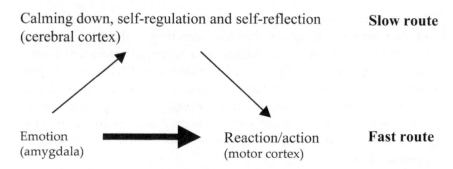

Calming down, self-regulation and self-reflection   **Slow route**
(cerebral cortex)

Emotion   Reaction/action   **Fast route**
(amygdala)   (motor cortex)

In humans, memories stored in the amygdala are particularly associated with the assessment of social signals and, as in other mammals, also with the observation of danger or situations evoking fear. Numerous early, conditioned fear reactions are stored in the amygdala. Gilbert (2002b, p. 121) says that "The amygdala reigns over the body like an ever vigilant watchdog, with its permanent archive of stimuli associated with danger combined with its primitive repertoire of emergency actions." The storage of emotional experiences depends on their strength. The stronger or more significant an experience, the more permanent a trace it will cause in the limbic system (LeDoux, 1996). However, studies summarised by Dębiec and LeDoux (2009) have shown that even well-consolidated memories may be altered.

> *At the first visit, a therapist discussed childhood experiences with a pregnant woman fearing delivery—how the woman had been afraid when her father hit her mother. When discussing this, the woman's shoulders rose, her neck muscles became visibly tense, and breathing became shorter and quicker. She only noticed these reactions herself when the therapist drew her attention to them. This made it possible to note how automatic such preparedness was. It was difficult for the mother-to-be to imagine surrendering to delivery, to her body directing the process, and to receiving help, as necessary. Delivery finally went uneventfully and was a positive experience for the mother.*

3.6.2. Breathing and smell conditioning

Multiple chemical sensitivity is problematic and, in its mild form, quite common. Little is known about the mechanisms behind it. Breathing offers an interesting viewpoint on both the occurrence of sensitivity and its treatment. Multiple chemical sensitivity can be an example of conditioning of breathing. Reacting to an unpleasant smell from a potentially dangerous chemical by breathing superficially so as to prevent the chemical from entering deep into the lungs is a way of protecting the body. However, superficial breathing may persist even in the absence of the original exposure. This may occur particularly if the exposure was frightening or the person was otherwise stressed and hyperventilating.

Multiple chemical sensitivity refers to reacting to smells to which the person has not been shown to be allergic by normal mechanisms of allergy (see for review Graveling, Pilkington, George, Butler, & Tannahill, 1999). After being exposed to one agent, a person may also react to agents that are not chemically related. These people do not get used to smells, as people with no hypersensitivity do. In challenge tests, patients have described largely the same symptoms as those that occur as a result of overarousal and hyperventilation. Conditioning of breathing has been studied experimentally in young and adult animals and in humans in association with various types of stimulation. Studies show that changes to breathing are easily conditioned according to the principles of classical conditioning. Conditioning studies in humans are limited by difficulties in measuring breathing and by ethical considerations.

The following are some examples of research on smell and breathing conditioning. Two-day-old mice (corresponding to human foetuses) were separated from their mothers for one hour and thus placed in a situation provoking anxiety (Durand et al., 2003). When they were readmitted to their mothers, their breathing became accelerated by overarousal. Conditioning was examined by using lemon scent as a conditional stimulus just before the mother came in. After only two exposures, the breathing of the test mouse babies was accelerated by lemon scent alone. In adult mice and rats, notably more repeats of conditioning are needed to produce a reaction.

The results of the mouse test support studies describing the reactions of human foetuses and neonates to many stimuli and the very readily produced conditioning of stress reactions in babies. We have plenty of experiences of adult patients who say that they have had breathing problems ever since childhood without any somatic disease being found.

In another study, smell conditioning was studied by artificially changing the subjects' breathing to physiologically resembling hyperventilation and simultaneous exposure to unpleasant smells (van den Bergh, Stegen, & van de Woestijne, 1997). In the control situation, the subjects' breathing physiology was kept normal. The unpleasant smell caused more respiratory symptoms if it had originally been presented with the subjects in a physiological state of hyperventilation. However, conditioning had only occurred in subjects assessing themselves as more neurotic. The subjects also developed symptoms when they were presented with other unpleasant but chemically unrelated smells, even if they were not hyperventilating.

It is logical to ask whether these hypersensitivity reactions could be alleviated by sensitising the body to them, as is done with allergies. Usually, avoidance is the only treatment recommended for hypersensitivity symptoms. In our view and experience, some smell-based hyperventilation reactions could be unlearned by recognising the connection with body memory or automatic thoughts and learning a new reaction model in a sufficiently safe therapeutic relationship where fears associated with exposure can be discussed. We have some positive experiences of the suitability of psychophysical breathing therapy for patients with hypersensitivity to smells.

> *A painter whose hyperventilation attacks had started at his workplace had decided that they were due to the smells there. His view was reinforced by noticing that when he opened the door to the workshop and was exposed to the smells there, he could not breathe. This created a vicious circle. He was examined at a general hospital but no significant somatic disease was found. Due to suspected hyperventilation he was asked to participate in breathing school. He learned to relax and recognise connections between his mind and body. When he went to his workplace, the smells triggered a change in breathing rhythm, but the symptoms were alleviated when he simultaneously spoke to himself in soothing words and calmed down his breathing. He did not develop an attack; you can always breathe even if you are anxious. Ten years later the patient was still working in the paint shop.*

CHAPTER FOUR

Imbalanced breathing in connection with health problems

Päivi Lehtinen, Minna Martin

Sometimes, a memory of safety is enough.

In this chapter, we describe the most common direct or indirect connections between imbalanced breathing and health. Imbalanced breathing potentiates symptoms, thus perpetuating the problematic situation. This is very common in states of overarousal, such as stress, anxiety, and pain. In addition, through stress reactions, conditions such as physical illness or surgery may contribute to the development of imbalanced breathing patterns and aggravation of symptoms.

Psychophysical breathing exercises can also be used for problems with underarousal in depressed and exhausted people. Depression is not usually the main reason for seeking psychophysical breathing therapy but, in our experience, breathing therapy has reduced symptoms of depression. Williams, Teasdale, Segal, and Kabat-Zinn (2007) have also successfully applied psychophysical methods for the treatment of depression. Even though this book is not about actual depression, we hope to help readers understand how to help patients suffering from decreased vitality (energy) and underarousal.

Underarousal_____Overarousal

Balanced breathing supports self-regulation

Observations concerning breathing and other physical sensations are important because they help to guide our activity and seeking of balance if we know how to utilise the information. We can observe which part of our body feels warm or tense and whether our breathing is calm, shallow, or vigorous. Such observations improve our self-knowledge and ability for self-reflection. Donald W. Winnicott (1951, 1987), an English paediatrician and psychoanalyst, has emphasised the significance of such experiences: a true experience of the self is based precisely on physical sensations, on the body being alive as experienced through heartbeat and breathing. Therefore, improving the ability to observe both physical sensations and changes in mood is pivotal in psychophysical breathing therapy. Participants pay attention to what is happening in their bodies and create space for experiences. Through self-compassion and reassurance they learn not to let their sensations lead to impulsive panicking. Such a stance will help the person to simply wonder about his experiences instead of being frightened by them. Kabat-Zinn describes a similar way of working in his books (1994, 2013).

Effects of stress, anxiety, pain, physical disease, and surgery
• Activation of stress reaction and fight or flight reaction • Muscle tension • Changes in breathing: overbreathing, holding the breath • Anxiety and fear • Activation of assimilated, possibly problematic interactive models • Being on guard in interaction • In the case of protracted symptoms, formation of rigid mental structures.

4.1. Stress

4.1.1. Positive stress

Stress is a factor that triggers many disturbances. The creator of the stress concept, endocrinologist Hans Selye (1974), considers stress as the body's general response to any challenge, whether positive or negative, physical or mental. Selye calls positive stress eustress (becoming more alert) and negative stress distress (becoming overwhelmed). Being positive, eustress is experienced as making the body and mind more alert. This makes our potential available for use; we want to push ourselves voluntarily, learn new things, and put everything we can into what we are doing. We learn such curiosity, enthusiasm, and seeking of challenges in interactions where our abilities and potential are recognised and we are urged and encouraged to face new issues. We receive support in our learning as necessary, and later enjoy the feeling of succeeding on our own.

Characteristically for eustress, we experience the level of stress as appropriate, that is, not an excessive burden on the body or mind. Another characteristic of eustress is that we can utilise our resources to reduce stress. People experiencing positive stress are typically able to react rapidly to the stress and seek the necessary changes instead of pushing themselves and clenching their teeth to cope. These skills strengthen the ability to cope with stress, which will protect against negative stress. Excessive stress consumes our resources without resolving the stress-inducing situation. In real life, eustress and distress often vary and situations may involve both threatening and positive challenges. Our assessment of which type of stress we are experiencing depends on our previous experiences and our attitude to them.

Bodily stress can be triggered by many physical stimuli, such as heat, cold, pain, thirst, low blood sugar, or disease, as well as by mental stress. Triggers of mental stress, on the other hand, may be more difficult to define and there is no comprehensive description available, so far, for this complex psychobiological phenomenon. Nevertheless, many causes of mental stress are familiar to modern people: challenging relationships, excessive stimuli (noise, traffic, being bombarded with information from TV and information technology, background music), rush, time pressure, a competitive, performance-centred lifestyle, lack of sleep, etc. People often maintain stress by demanding a lot from themselves or by repeatedly putting the needs of others before their own. Stress thus means that we assess the demands on us and our resources and find them to be out of balance. Stress is a natural reaction to trying to cope with a physical or mental burden. The problem is that people will not always listen to the warning signs and try to cut down on stressors soon enough.

These traffic lights can be used to distinguish between positive stress and stress that is becoming negative:

You are stressed

when you feel that there are more demands than you can physically or mentally handle

Sufficient resources
- A small amount of stress keeps you alert
- You have sufficient leisure time to recover

Maintain the same system

At the edge of your resources
- Mind and body in state of alarm
- Stress symptoms

Place matters in order of importance

Running out of resources
- Exhaustion
- Your situation requires total reassessment of your life

Seek professional help

4.1.2. Negative stress

For a while, stress may help us to cope with demands. However, if it becomes prolonged or if we need to face several stressors at the same time, the risk of various physical and mental diseases will increase. Anyone exposed to stressors for a long time is in a constant *fight or flight state* without the chance for recovery. In that case, stress-related cortisol secretion and long-term activation of the sympathetic nervous system increase. Constant secretion of stress hormones has detrimental, cumulative long-term effects on various organ systems. It weakens the immune system, increases blood coagulation, destroys neurons in the hippocampus, impairs glucose metabolism, affects the cardiovascular system, and disturbs mood, memory, and ageing of brain tissue. The interaction between stress and disease works in two directions—stress contributes to the outbreak of many diseases, and disease causes stress, reduces available resources, and thus impairs stress tolerance (Korkeila, 2006; McEwen, 1998).

The relation between breathing and stress also works in two directions. Increasing stress causes imbalanced breathing. In prolonged stress, overactivated breathing persists. We rarely come to think of how much stress imbalanced breathing causes. Constantly imbalanced breathing causes disturbances that are either biochemical in nature or result from respiratory mechanics. When a person receives training in breathing, she may be astonished at the difference made by her improved breathing pattern: she no longer feels tired but more alert and relaxed. Calming down of breathing thus notably promotes stress control, both by calming down the mind and by influencing physical stress responses.

Activation of rigid, persistently negative conditioned reactions is typical for prolonged stress. Such reactions may make a person continue working with clenched teeth and performing even after depleting his resources or, alternatively, may make him passive and inactive. Some people try to cope by performing and trying to keep everything firmly under their control. The problem is that one cannot control a living connection to oneself, others, and the rest of the world. Repeated experiences of not being able to influence stressors may also lead to *learned helplessness* (Seligman, 1991). In that case a person no longer tries to influence stressors even if he has the chance to do so. Learned helplessness has severe effects on the body. It has been found that what is destructive for the immune system is precisely a prolonged experience of lack of control, not the stress as such. The very thought of "You can always breathe" will protect us from stress and create an impression of being able to influence our situation. Stress may sometimes have insidious effects: it may gnaw at our immunity even if we do not realise we are stressed. In addition, a pessimist's way of life often involves neglecting oneself: it is no use taking care of yourself because things will turn out badly anyway. Learned helplessness will thus lead to increased malaise and stress. On the other hand, a small amount of pessimism (realism) is not detrimental and may even protect us from trouble.

Some individuals react to helplessness by attempting to replace it by aggressive fighting. In psychophysical breathing therapy we often see people finding it hard to set boundaries to protect themselves from excessive stress. In addition, they often have problems in expressing disagreement or anger. They may not dare at all to express feelings that they feel are forbidden, and may thus also avoid any use of physical strength associated with such feelings. Caution may become the pervasive hallmark of life. Alternatively, disappointment or disagreement may even be expressed too forcefully, violating other people's boundaries. Psychophysical breathing therapy can be used to seek constructive solutions for difficulties in self-regulation and self-expression. Assertive expression taking one's own rights and needs into account can be learned in interaction in an environment allowing feelings of being tired and limited.

4.1.3. Recovery from stress

Recovery from stress can be regarded as finding a suitable balance between being and doing, and as the ability to integrate perseverance and letting go. It is the ability to recognise the individually appropriate level of challenge and need for rest, and to listen with a particularly keen ear and appreciation to bodily messages. In addition, it is the ability to experience work, every now and then, at least, as playful and creative. However, it is well known from clinical work that for many people life involves constantly having to perform and that stressed people do not recognise their stress even though, in the eyes of outsiders, their situations appear highly stressful.

Perseverance and letting go in scale pans

Balance is a combination of
perseverance and letting go

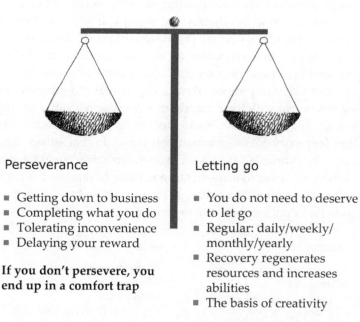

Perseverance

- Getting down to business
- Completing what you do
- Tolerating inconvenience
- Delaying your reward

**If you don't persevere, you
end up in a comfort trap**

Letting go

- You do not need to deserve
  to let go
- Regular: daily/weekly/
  monthly/yearly
- Recovery regenerates
  resources and increases
  abilities
- The basis of creativity

**If you don't let go, you will
work with clenched teeth**

If you are not capable of persevering, you will fall into a comfort trap, that is, you cannot maintain your activity unless you receive immediate reward. On the other hand, if you are not capable of letting go and just being, you will work with clenched teeth.

At his first breathing school lesson, a private entrepreneur was shocked to hear the therapist say that he could just let himself be. The very thought of just being threatened his work ethic. A private entrepreneur cannot just be. He stopped attending the school after the first lesson.

One can get used to stress and, in that case, it will be more difficult to influence. People vary greatly in the extent to which they are capable of recognising or describing bodily problems or seeking help for them. As paradoxical as it may seem, after breathing therapy a person may report more symptoms than before. For example, she may only recognise tension in the neck-shoulder region in psychophysical therapy. If she has always been tense, she may consider it normal. People rarely know that calm breathing might alleviate pain in the shoulder region. Not only may stressed people have problems in recognition, they may also "treat" themselves by making changes more likely to promote dysphoria, such as stopping exercising, reducing time spent with their friends, or increasing alcohol consumption (Martin & Kunttu, 2012). Small amounts of alcohol may relax but increasing doses and frequency of consumption will stimulate sympathetic nervous system activity (Korkeila, 2006). People often wish they could have a sensible solution for stress management, something to remove the pressure. Stress will not ease off without changes to one's life and self-reflection. It is essential to find a balance between experienced stress and one's resources.

Means

Making your burden more reasonable:
- placing your tasks in order of priority
- taking heart and discussing things
- asserting yourself

Means

Strengthening your tolerance:
- relaxation
- physical exercise and diet
- seeking support

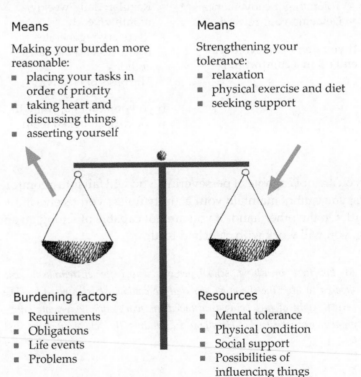

Burdening factors

- Requirements
- Obligations
- Life events
- Problems

Resources

- Mental tolerance
- Physical condition
- Social support
- Possibilities of influencing things

4.1.4. Physical exercise, breathing, and recovery

Of the most common means of managing stress, exercise is considered a rather effective way of unloading its burden. It has extensive effects on mind and body and works rapidly—starting exercise may show as improved well-being within as little as a fortnight (Korkeila, 2006). However, one mustn't overdo it. Excessive exercising may maintain stress instead of alleviating it. Overtraining in athletes may thus represent a combination of exhaustion and imbalanced breathing. Following exercise recommendations is not simple for all stressed people. For people tending to hyperventilate, physical exercise may be unpleasant because it increases symptoms related to imbalanced breathing and the resulting alkalinity of the blood. Overbreathing during exercise also increases muscle tension and the person's condition will thus not improve because rest and recovery remain insufficient. He may need to learn to breathe calmly before starting to exercise. For many people unaware of their breathing problems and muscle tension, combining the mindset and methods of psychophysical breathing therapy with exercise instruction would thus serve to prevent problems and help them become more balanced. In sports medicine, attention has been directed to how nasal breathing may promote performance and health even during strenuous exertion (cf. page 29). For people exercising actively, breathing exercises may provide the chance to learn to stop and to acquire patience. Psychophysical breathing therapy will also provide competing athletes with the chance to balance stress and tension (Tuomola, 2012).

A study by van Dixhoorn in patients with myocardial infarction (van Dixhoorn & Duivenvoorden, 1999) showed that physical performance as part of the patients' rehabilitation improved when breathing therapy was added to the rehabilitation programme. A five-year follow-up also showed improvement in the patients' cardiac health as measured by physiological parameters, and a decrease in the prevalence of cardiac diseases and in health care costs. In the Netherlands, breathing therapy has been adopted as a part of rehabilitation of patients with myocardial infarction.

Psychophysical breathing exercises could be utilised more in day care centres, at schools, and in physical exercise for children, as illustrated by the following examples:

> In a day care centre, children were calmed down by using mental images while they were lying on a mattress. Another group of children learned

to calm each other down by kneading each other's backs with the palms of their hands. A teacher, who had worked with her breathing in her own therapy, said that she learned to calm down a restless secondary school class by her own breathing: "Previously I might have raised my voice, now I just breathe. I have found it to be much more effective than getting all worked up."

Getting support from one's relatives is another important means of managing stress. Throughout life, intimacy, touching, calming down together, sharing, and putting things into perspective are among the most important means of restoring balance. In addition, various hobbies, such as singing, gardening, or taking part in cultural activities will help. One factor connecting all these is calming down of breathing. We may not be aware of it, but when we are feeling safe, calm, experiencing pleasure, touching, another person's presence, warmth, having time for ourselves, easing up, our breathing gets deeper and calmer. Or on the conscious level: by breathing calmly we can find our way out of the cycle of stress.

Many helpers think it is their task to support people in achieving better stress tolerance and improved performance. In psychophysical breathing therapy, we think in the opposite way: we do not want to teach people to tolerate more stress but to lower their tolerance of stress by reacting to stressors more rapidly. It is not always about reducing the amount of what we do but learning calmer and less demanding attitudes. Self-compassion is the mental equivalent of soothing breathing.

4.2. Anxiety

Words and expressions for breathing or shortness of breath reflect the close connection between the mind and breathing. The Greek word *psykhe* and the Latin word *spiritus* both mean soul, mind, and breathing. In Finnish, the word *ahdistus* (anxiety) refers to both mental anxiousness and difficulty in breathing. The two often coexist, making it difficult to find out whether the symptom is related to a bodily disease or to mental anxiety alone. In any case, mental anxiety, like other feelings, is experienced in the body as well, depending on the severity of anxiety and one's capability of detecting what happens in the body.

4.2.1. Necessary anxiety

Anxiety, too, can be seen as a part of the biological fight or flight system. It prepares us to recognise threats within the mind that, for one reason or another, cannot yet become conscious. It also helps us to protect ourselves against external dangers. This type of anxiety is called *signal anxiety*. According to the Finnish psychoanalyst Veikko Tähkä (1993), signal anxiety is of great importance for a person's mental development. Anxiety is a force that makes the mind move. At best, it makes us utilise and develop short- and long-term resources. Therefore, anxiety is of great significance for our well-being. We should not strive to get rid of it right away but learn to listen to what we can learn about ourselves through anxiety.

4.2.2. Unbound anxiety

Anxiety may take the form of signal anxiety representing a transient experience of vague threat. In this case the anxiety is optimal for balance and tolerable. However, if basic confidence and the ability to regulate anxiety remain defective, a person may not be able to tolerate much anxiety or use the anxiety constructively. She may not have had a soothing, compassionate other, who helped her to handle and regulate excessively intense feelings or tension. In such cases anxiety may become overwhelming in stressful situations. Unbound and unaddressed anxiety may cause a feeling of suffering and lead to severe overexcitement or inactivity. However, the anxiety may also serve to protect from even more difficult feelings.

Anxiety may appear in attacks, as in people with panic disorder. In a panic attack, a person feels he is losing control of both mental and bodily functions, which is frightening and anxiety provoking. At worst, fear of complete loss of control may lie at the heart of the panic attack, and fear of severe diseases and death are also common. According to Diamond (1987), becoming helpless is frightening because it reminds one, often unconsciously, of moments of helplessness experienced in childhood when no suitable compassion or help was available.

People suffering from panicky anxiety often experience their feelings as shameful and frightening (Shear, Cooper, Klerman, Bush, & Shapiro, 1993). Feelings experienced as overwhelming that are present in the background may trigger a panic attack. People may strive to avoid forbidden or shameful feelings by emphasising the bodily sensations associated with panic attacks: "Everything would be fine if only I didn't have these symptoms." On the other hand, a threat of panic and catastrophe is associated with the bodily sensations. Catastrophic thinking is often associated with unconscious feelings experienced as negative that are about to surface. Similar bodily sensations in other connections may not give rise to fear or catastrophic thinking. In breathing school, we repeatedly hear how deep feelings of shame are and how strongly shame is felt in the body. Shame is relieved by the experience of being accepted as you are, of being allowed to "just exist". Self-compassion forms an important tool of emotional regulation here, helping to subdue the experience of shame.

If one's ability to tolerate anxiety is deficient, external means of controlling and avoiding anxiety become important. It is typically hard to tolerate being in places or situations difficult to escape or where you "must" be. A person who suffers from panicky anxiety may also experience human relations as overwhelming and therefore start to avoid social events.

People with poor anxiety tolerance build up a strong and rigid defence structure. It is common to use extensive, strong rejection and even conscious suppression of feelings as defence mechanisms. Excessive kindness as a defence mechanism is familiar to us particularly from groups of middle-aged women and worriers. Strong defences impoverish these people's feelings and restrict their lives. They do not recognise anxiety as a warning sign of threatening danger and thus cannot find constructive means to adjust or defend themselves. Only the overpowering strength of panic forces them to feel anxious (Baumbacher, 1989). Joyce McDougall (1989) has observed that some people defend themselves by appearing as normal as possible, as if they were entirely without inner conflicts or mental problems. She describes these people as "pseudonormal" or "normopathic".

If a person is not capable of experiencing anxiety, overbreathing may become a surrogate for mental anxiety. Overbreathing will then act as a mechanism wiping away thoughts and feelings. In her book *Theatres of the Body: A Psychoanalytic Approach to Psychosomatic Illness* (1989, pp. 123–124), Joyce McDougall describes her patient Tim's psychoanalysis, illustrating this psychophysical means of protection.

> One day, as he continued complaining that life is meaningless,
> I told him that everything he had recounted thus far made me

keenly aware of the existence of a sad and embittered little boy within him who had buried the lively part of himself with his dead father and who doubted, therefore, whether his existence could be meaningful to others. He seemed to take it for granted that his wife, his mother and his analyst were indifferent to the survival of this unhappy child.

After a stunned silence Tim replied, "This idea—that somehow I don't exist for other people—affects me so deeply, I am almost unable to breathe." He sounded as though he were on the verge of tears and remained silent, breathing heavily, until the end of the session. I eagerly awaited the next analytic hour. After his usual mute 10 minutes, Tim began, "I'm tired of this analysis and your eternal silence. Nothing ever happens since you never say a word. I should have gone to a Kleinian!" All trace of the previous session had vanished! Later, I was able to understand that at the very moment Tim began to have trouble breathing, he was already expelling from his mind and body the memory of my words along with their psychological and physical repercussions—that is, their affective impact.

A person who has difficulties regulating her feelings may use all the means of protecting herself listed above and even that may not be sufficient, but she may experience her feelings as intolerable. If we are incapable of calming ourselves, feeling self-compassion, or setting ourselves boundaries, of regulating or understanding our experiences, feelings may take the form of uncontrollable, impulsive action either against the self (self-destructive behaviour) or against others (violent behaviour).

Bodily reactions provide distance from the source of anxiety, and normal functioning may initially be preserved. The person will consider her panic disorder purely as a disease and not experience the attacks as related to the world of her experience. This means that she protects herself mentally, either by fending off from her consciousness feelings that are too anxiety-provoking and have manifested as bodily reactions or by not feeling difficult feelings in the first place but only having undifferentiated bodily experiences.

In our experience, it may sometimes be possible to connect to the causes of anxiety quite quickly; defining somatic symptoms as resulting from imbalanced breathing and, thus, taking such symptoms seriously and considering them understandable often facilitates identifying the anxious feelings behind them. It is valuable for an anxious person to have the chance to see a helper tolerating his feelings. When the helper is capable of breathing calmly and communicating through his very existence, "Don't worry, you are allowed to experience things as you do," space is created in the patient's mind for experiences that were previously impossible.

In a safe therapeutic relationship, bodily sensations, particularly those related to breathing, can help to detect anxiety. Through such sensations, patients may learn to ask themselves, even when they are alone, what happened, what they are actually feeling, and what may be bothering them. After getting to know themselves, many people have found that the body is often wiser than the mind. Physical symptoms may, at best, help to increase self-understanding (Broom, 2007). Many people who have been through psychophysical breathing therapy have started utilising this knowledge. After learning to recognise and name beginning symptoms, they have developed means of tolerating or preventing beginning anxiety attacks. If, however, the emphasis in the therapeutic situation is on removing symptoms, this may confirm the patient's experience of the symptoms being more dangerous than they are and of the need to get rid of them quickly.

> An engineer sought help for severe dizziness, dyspnoea, and hand tremor threatening his ability to work. Clinical physiological studies had shown problems in the regulation of breathing. He started breathing school saying: "An engineer's logic says if there is a fault in breathing, it must be fixed." Attempts had been made, in vain, to treat him in psychiatric units but this did not help because he did not recognise his mental problems. Breathing school was useful for him. In partner exercises, his symptoms were activated: his hands cramped and started shaking. The engineer's logic worked again. He sensed that there were feelings behind his symptoms that he did not recognise. He started wondering about any connection between his symptoms and human relations. A connection had been created between the mind and body. After breathing school he continued in individual psychophysical therapy for five years. He became more conscious of his problems, and even after fifteen years of follow-up he was well and had made progress at work.

Breathing can also be manipulated consciously up to a certain point to shut the difficult feeling out of one's consciousness or to get attention.

A female patient who had received insufficient care from her parents said that even as a child she had learned to get at least transient attention from her parents by becoming dizzy through deliberately overbreathing.

4.2.3. Interaction and anxiety

Various interactive situations often arouse mild or transient anxiety, tension, or fear (Rochat, 2009). It is completely normal for situations differing from everyday life to arouse the mind and body, as well as breathing, to enable us to respond to increased challenges. Such anxiety or arousal may be caused by situations such as a public appearance, a job interview, or a party (Martin, Heiska, Syvälahti, & Hoikkala, 2013). Along with stress experiences, feelings of excitement are among the most common experiences of psychophysical imbalance. For example, about one in three Finnish university students reports anxiety when speaking in public and about half of them stress. For some students, anxiety in social situations may be considerably stronger, causing significant restriction of life and difficulty in proceeding with studies, coping at work, making friends, or dating. Anxiety may present as extensive unease associated with many social situations or as more restricted fear associated only with certain situations perceived as challenging, such as fear of speaking in public or eating with other people. For some, even casual meetings with people they know may arouse fear (Kunttu, Martin, & Almonkari, 2006). Perception of threat occurs particularly in association with feelings of shame, inadequacy, and worthlessness felt in company (Rochat, 2009).

Social anxiety depends on many interrelated factors. It is related to general sensitivity and sensitivity to bodily sensations, and to experiencing overwhelming feelings. These are associated with imbalanced breathing, which people rarely recognise as being connected with symptoms of anxiety (Martin, Heiska, Syvälahti, & Hoikkala, 2013). Many worriers say that they have been sensitive and shy ever since childhood and, therefore, withdrawn from relationships and social challenges. Sensitivity as such does not cause shyness or anxiety. It is more important how a sensitive child or young person is treated (Aron, 2003). Experiences of interaction affect the development of shyness, social anxiety problems, and associated muscle tension and an imbalanced breathing pattern. Imbalanced breathing is a consequence of stress experienced in a social situation, on the one hand, and of defending oneself from feelings of shame, on the other hand. Such a response pattern may be conditioned in human relations, families, peer relations, and school environments fostering insecurity. For some people, feelings of social anxiety are potentiated in connection with changes in life and associated unconscious insecurity and stress. Such changes may include going to school or changing schools, moving house, or natural developmental transitions, such as puberty. The beginning of social anxiety symptoms may also be associated with traumatic experiences (Rochat, 2009). For children and adolescents, being bullied, the parents' divorce, or a parent's heavy alcohol consumption or mental health problems may represent such traumatic experiences. In consequence of such experiences, a child or young person may get into a state of excessive chronic alertness, and may also interpret other social situations arousing insecurity as signs of danger. Increased anxiety is often also the result of increased demands experienced at school, in studies, at work, or during leisure time. However, it is often people themselves who have demanding or even merciless attitudes to what they do, both towards themselves and towards others.

Worriers use their physical sensations and feelings as information about assumed attitudes of other people towards themselves. They try to hide from other people their symptoms and their perceptions of themselves. Nevertheless, flushing, sweating, or hand tremor may be visible and thus threaten to "reveal" the anxiety. The person is afraid that others will react negatively to such symptoms and tension. Out of fear and shame, he or she may start to avoid socially challenging situations.

The tendency to withdraw, to try to be invisible, and to swallow and cover one's feelings often appears as cautious and superficial breathing. Overbreathing reflects anxiety associated with the situation. The internal experiences of many people with social anxiety problems and their attempts to defend themselves are also reflected in their posture.

People suffering from social anxiety often remain alone with their problems. At school, they may have been allowed to pass a course without giving a presentation or a speech. Alternatively, they may have been forced to give a presentation without support or constructive feedback. These methods will not help to solve the anxiety problem. Social anxiety may be alleviated by compassionate and encouraging human relationships, assisted training, and learning ways to soothe oneself, such as calm breathing patterns.

4.3. Pain

4.3.1. Significance and alleviation of pain

The capacity to feel pain is a life-preserving ability that protects us from dangers. Everyone knows from experience what their reaction is to sudden pain: immediate inhalation followed by intensive exhalation. If this is not followed by action, overbreathing may ensue. Modern analgesics have brought great pain relief. In acute pain, sufficient analgesic medication makes you feel better in many ways, promotes recovery by facilitating movement, and prevents the pain from becoming chronic. But in addition to medication, other means are needed if pain is severe and long lasting. Our most significant means of regulating pain is associated with an interactive relationship that is calming, nurturing, and comforting and allows us to soothe ourselves later on when experiencing pain.

Acute, severe pain often involves imbalanced breathing, accelerated breathing or holding one's breath, or both. In connection with a painful procedure, experienced nurses and doctors may tell the patient to "breathe calmly" or to "remember to breathe". People often push against pain, trying to put it out of their minds. If you suffer from pain, people often say "forget it" or "ignore it". Such phrases do contain a partial truth: directing your attention away from the pain will help you to cope somewhat. Denial, again, usually increases the experience of pain and resulting stress. Various types of relaxation, breathing, mindfulness, and mental training have been shown to be useful in the regulation of pain.

Overbreathing is a useful impulse, when you are in sudden pain. It will have been expedient in earlier stages of evolution, in particular since it speeds up the ability for fight or flight, as necessary. In addition, overbreathing is associated with the alleviation of acute pain. In ritual ceremonies and in connection with torture, overbreathing is often utilised to alleviate pain. Breathing therapy is naturally quite significant in the physiotherapy of patients who have been tortured (Hough, 1992). In an acute situation, overbreathing acts similarly on both physical and mental pain, having an anaesthetic effect on both. However, if overbreathing continues, pain will be experienced as more severe.

> *I underwent a painful procedure. I had not realised that it would feel so unpleasant and did not know I could prepare for it by taking preventive analgesic medication. In the actual situation, my breathing was first*

blocked for several seconds and then accelerated for a long time. I felt severe pain several hours after the procedure. A few years later the procedure was repeated. I then noticed the first changes in my breathing already when thinking about making the appointment. I took preventive analgesics for the procedure. In the waiting room I concentrated on soothing myself by breathing slowly. The procedure was painful but this time pain didn't take control over me because I breathed evenly, concentrating on long, calm exhalation. I was surprised to see the significance of breathing for pain control, even though I did have similar experience from giving birth. I just had not known how to adapt those skills to a different situation.

4.3.2. How pain becomes chronic, and the consequences

When pain is prolonged and becomes chronic, a series of mental and bodily conditioning reactions begin. These maintain a vicious circle of pain. Long-term pain may develop if the source of pain cannot be eliminated or because physical and emotional pain is processed in the same brain area and the source of pain is thus displaced (Eisenberger, 2012). Somatic pain may lead to mental pain, depression, or vice versa. Depression in connection with chronic pain may be due to losses associated with pain and impaired functional ability. The difficulty of constructive processing of the experienced loss leads to "displaced sorrow", that is, depression.

If the pain signal is not eliminated, the person becomes sensitised and conditioned to it. The signal becomes more intense in order to make her eliminate the source of pain, for example by changing her behaviour. A "pain memory" is created, that is, pain is experienced even in the absence of the original stimulus (Eisenberger, 2012). In that case, neural pathways suppressing pain do not act normally. It has been found that people with such inaccurate pain often have disturbances in their attachment. They may not have been able to assimilate "the other" soothing their emotional and physical pain and may thus even later more easily be overwhelmed by an uncontrolled experience of pain.

The experience of pain activates unconscious internal interactive models. This is reflected in, for example, how we seek help and our attitudes to ourselves and our symptoms. We learn how to react to pain in interaction. We assimilate how our parents reacted when they themselves experienced pain or how they reacted to us when we hurt ourselves or fell ill. If we have become used to thinking primarily of others and putting our own needs second, we dare not ask for help in dealing with pain because we assume others will need help even more. The ability to reach the internal soothing other is central for regulating the experience of pain, keeping calm, and soothing and comforting oneself. Self-compassion is like a kind, internal caress to soothe the pain.

4.3.3. Breathing, posture, and pain

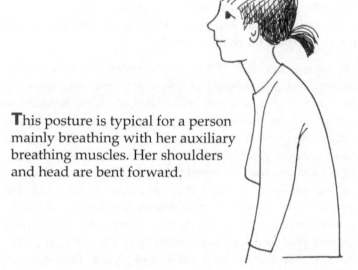

This posture is typical for a person mainly breathing with her auxiliary breathing muscles. Her shoulders and head are bent forward.

If a person breathes chronically with his upper chest, his posture will gradually change, his head and shoulders moving forward. Such a change in posture may occur for physical, ergonomic, or mental reasons, or all three simultaneously. Imbalanced breathing may be one reason for stress symptoms in people working with a poor posture on a computer. If the head is pushed forward and the auxiliary breathing muscles are subject to excessive strain, the posture will also disturb the dynamics of the muscles around the jaw joint. This will lead to occlusion problems and cause headaches (Bartley & Clifton-Smith, 2006; Hruska, 1997).

In a study with college students involving cellphone text messaging, Lin and Peper (2009) found that all twelve subjects showed significant increases in breathing and heart rate as well as in skin conductance when texting. Most of them also felt hand and neck pain. One wonders what their health will be like after fifty years!

Changing of conditioned movement patterns and working positions will take time because a change also needs to take place in the person's relationship to his body and body language. The relationship may have become very controlling and negative or passive and evasive of responsibility. If so, a change of position will require a therapeutic relationship, while ergonomic guidance alone, for example, will not be sufficient. For a permanent change, the patient needs encouragement to increase her ability to observe herself. She may then learn to become conscious of herself in relation to gravity and her vertical position and to breathe appropriately in various situations. The results are often good if the patient sees the need for change herself:

> After the breathing school I felt the need to improve the quality of my life in other ways too. I took a course in Alexander technique and consequently lay down on the floor daily with a pile of books under my head. In addition, I started neck and shoulder exercise classes. After a few months, I had an X-ray of my neck taken because I knew there was some erosion there. I had indeed taken good care of my neck: there was a wedge-shaped opening visible between vertebrae that showed that my neck had been tilted forward and had now become straighter. It was now important to continue taking good care of the condition of my muscles. At about that time, I had a wonderful experience: I saw that the streets in my hometown were really beautiful. I had not noticed their impressive proportions. My new posture really felt good, and the change was not only physical. I still sometimes have neck pain but now it serves to remind me to hold my head up!

4.3.4. Pain and muscle tension

Little is known about long-term imbalanced breathing associated with prolonged pain and there have been few studies. Patients with chronic pain often breathe with their upper chest, using their auxiliary breathing muscles more. Auxiliary breathing muscles are mainly meant for short-term use for movement and maintenance of posture. Prolonged use leads to changes in the muscles, causing pain and reducing muscle strength. Breathing becomes shallow and focused on inhalation. Laboratory studies have shown that patients with chronic pain have a low exhaled air carbon dioxide content, that is, their bodies are in a state of physiological hyperventilation (see Wilhelm, Gevirtz, & Roth, 2001). In practice, we have found patients with chronic pain to have superficial, imbalanced breathing.

Many of our patients with breathing symptoms suffer from severe, vague pain in the upper body. They are often worried by the symptoms and associate them with cardiac symptoms. Health care professionals do not necessarily understand the origin of such pain, either. The pain may be dismissed as being due to tension, and its connection with imbalanced breathing may not be explored. In many cases, muscle pain in the upper body is due to long-term inappropriate use of auxiliary breathing muscles.

> *Muscle pain was not the first possibility to occur to me. Particularly as muscle pain is mainly considered to be due to stress or tension. This was quite intense chest pain. I asked my husband to press at the point of pain, and he had to press really hard. Gradually the pain subsided. The symptoms were often quite vague: once the right side of my face got sort of paralysed for a while. Now I know this was related to overbreathing.*

A classic test by Friedman from 1945 supports the connection between the use of breathing muscles and muscle pain. A tight bandage was placed around the abdomen and lower ribs of healthy subjects. They started experiencing shortness of breath and, in a couple of days, developed chest pain that grew worse on exertion. The pain stopped when the bandage was removed. Another group of subjects had chest pain to begin with but no cardiac disease. Bandages were placed around their chests so that they could not breathe heavily using their chest muscles. The pain subsided but recurred after removing the bandage when the subjects again started using their upper chest muscles instead of the diaphragm for breathing.

We have successfully applied the phenomena described in the test in psychophysical breathing therapy. Placing bean bags of two or three kilograms on the chest helps to move breathing with auxiliary muscles downward. In many people, the weight and the resulting experience of body boundaries and of getting stronger increase the feeling of security. Work done by auxiliary breathing muscles between the ribs and in the neck area decreases. These effects together help increase the person's awareness of the movement in diaphragmatic-abdominal breathing. Bean bags are frequently used in our groups, and the meaningful experience has motivated many of our patients and students to make bags for themselves to calm down their breathing at home. Their minds then also calm down. We think that the bean bag also acts as a transitional object activating and strengthening the ability to calm down and thus enhancing the feeling of security.

> *A therapist lent a patient who had suffered from anxiety since his childhood heavy bean bags to take home. After three months, the patient brought up*

the use of the bags. He said he had used them every night when going to bed. He said he fell asleep faster, slept more peacefully, had more peaceful and interesting dreams, and no longer had constant tension and pain in the neck and shoulder region, a heavy feeling in his chest or a lump in his throat. Meanwhile, of course, his situation had been discussed, too, but he himself felt that the use of the heavy bean bags had gradually changed his way of using his upper body muscles.

Muscle tension may have both physical and mental causes. The mental causes are discussed in many connections in this book. There may be many kinds of physical stressors: congenital ones as well as ones due to musculoskeletal disease, trauma, or ageing. Stressors may also be associated with overweight or strain on the body due to working positions, sports, or the use of mobile devices. Imbalanced breathing may persist, become conditioned, even if the original stressor no longer exists. Long-term use of auxiliary breathing muscles may also cause pain through blood vessel or nerve impingement.

Chain reaction due to breathing predominantly with auxiliary breathing muscles in the long term

- The first reaction is increased muscle tension: this affects muscles, muscle fasciae, tendons, cartilage, joints, and ligaments
- Muscle metabolism gradually changes: constant contraction of muscles and fasciae is associated with lack of oxygen, inflammation, or irritation
- Decreased flexibility of joints and ligaments further hinders breathing
- Movements change
- Trigger points are formed
- Nervous overreaction develops
- This leads to decreased elasticity of the lungs, which further hinders breathing
- This results in increased susceptibility to, for example, many musculoskeletal diseases.

(Modified from Leon Chaitow, 2002, pp. 87–93.)

Development of trigger or reflection points is one of the physiological phenomena related to inappropriate long-term use of auxiliary breathing muscles that probably explains many peculiar pain symptoms.

Trigger points are defined areas in the tissue that can be stimulated to produce pain distant from the point of stimulation. Pain caused by trigger points due to overuse of auxiliary breathing muscles may occur extensively in the body. For example, pain due to tightness of muscles in the throat and neck region may be felt in the forehead, eye and ear regions, jaw joints, maxillary sinuses and teeth, as a lump in the throat, or even as tingling in the fingers.

Trigger points are a phenomenon known in medicine but in health care they are only rarely linked with respiratory problems through overuse of muscles. Chaitow, an osteopath (2002, pp. 99–104), Bartley, an ear, nose, and throat surgeon, and Clifton-Smith, a physical therapist (2006), regard trigger phenomena as very significant sequelae of prolonged imbalanced breathing. (See also Richter & Hebgen, 2008.)

The following figure describes the complex connections between muscle pain and breathing.

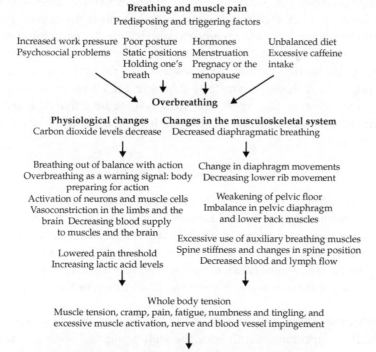

Breathing and muscle pain
Predisposing and triggering factors

Increased work pressure Poor posture   Hormones   Unbalanced diet
Psychosocial problems   Static positions Menstruation   Excessive caffeine
                         Holding one's   Pregnacy or the intake
                         breath   menopause

Overbreathing

Physiological changes   **Changes in the musculoskeletal system**
Carbon dioxide levels decrease   Decreased diaphragmatic breathing

Breathing out of balance with action   Change in diaphragm movements
Overbreathing as a warning signal: body   Decreasing lower rib movement
preparing for action
Activation of neurons and muscle cells   Weakening of pelvic floor
Vasoconstriction in the limbs and the   Imbalance in pelvic diaphragm
brain Decreasing blood supply   and lower back muscles
to muscles and the brain
                          Excessive use of auxiliary breathing muscles
Lowered pain threshold   Spine stiffness and changes in spine position
Increasing lactic acid levels   Decreased blood and lymph flow

Whole body tension
Muscle tension, cramp, pain, fatigue, numbness and tingling, and
excessive muscle activation, nerve and blood vessel impingement

Aches and pains of the head, masticatory muscles, neck, shoulders,
chest, and lower back, and bladder, intestinal, and gastric problems

Modified from Bartley and Clifton-Smith (2006, p. 76)

4.3.5. Psychophysical treatment of muscle pain

Many professionals working with muscle problems, such as physio-therapists, osteopaths, and voice massage therapists, pay attention to breathing problems and deal with their consequences in muscles, muscle fasciae, and joints. Breathing exercises, relaxation, and mus-cle manipulation change muscle dynamics and normalise the function of pain pathways. For the effects of treatment to persist, it would be important for people with chronic symptoms to have the chance of par-ticipating in psychophysical breathing therapy. Patients with breathing problems may need breathing therapy, muscle and joint manipulation, psychotherapy, and medication. The combination of various types of treatment and the correct timing of each treatment are decisive for success.

In psychophysical breathing therapy, people are taught a new kind of approach to pain and tension: calm breathing will relieve the symp-toms. Directing the attention to breathing may help the patient to con-centrate on other things. The idea of an internal soothing caress will help to relieve the pain and muscle tension and comfort the pained mind. When the patient learns to breathe calmly despite the pain, the chances of recovery will be notably improved. He may learn to recognise and study pain, bodily tension, and restlessness through breathing. He learns to exist with the pain instead of avoiding it. He may also use other images to influence his experience, such as imagining that he is breath-ing into the pain and visualising the pain leaving the body as he exhales.

4.3.6. Labour pain, fear of delivery, and breathing

> When giving birth, I let myself be carried by the flow, just let it happen. I concentrated on what I had been instructed to do, "Keep your hands open and your jaw relaxed." I kept swinging my hips, leaning against the babycare table. I used my voice to support exhalation. This made it easy to breathe in deeply and calmly all the way down even when in severe pain. I thought that calm breathing would help the baby on its hard way out.

It all starts in the early stages of life, in the womb and when new-born. It is important to influence the well-being and feeling of safety of the parents, and the mother in particular. Being supported by people breathing calmly will essentially improve the mother's and child's chances of maintaining, strengthening, and learning balanced breathing patterns.

Overbreathing due to pain is a well-known phenomenon in connection with childbirth (see Brownridge, 1995). Overbreathing may have various causes, not only the pain associated with the widening of the birth canal. Breathing needs to be increased during the expulsive stage, and one may easily breathe more than physically required. Overbreathing may be due to mental anxiety with various psychological causes: fear of loss of control, of inability of the body to give birth, or of repetition of previous difficult experiences from giving birth, or worry about becoming a parent. Unfavourable experience from early interactions and associated fears of not being met with empathy may also be reflected in fears of childbirth. For this reason, the mother may not dare express her distress. Overbreathing during childbirth causes the same physiological chain reactions in the mother and the foetus as overbreathing in general, resulting in a relative lack of oxygen in the tissues. Lack of oxygen may also result from holding the breath. If the baby is poorly or if the placenta is not working well, the effects of overbreathing and stress hormones may be harmful to the baby. In addition, contractions may slow down and labour may be prolonged.

Anaesthetics are very important for alleviating labour pain but the mother needs other help, as well. Giving birth is very often strenuous. To be able to calm down, concentrate, and breathe as required in each situation, the mother needs someone to support her and the security and help provided by a midwife and sometimes also a doctor. In Finland, a spouse or other trusted person is usually present to support the mother giving birth.

> When giving birth for the first time I used all my strength to work against the pain and against the movement of the baby through the birth canal. This may have represented an unconscious effort to cancel the birth and to repress images I associated with it. I refused to be in the vertical position and stuck to the idea of getting epidural anaesthesia. When epidural anaesthesia was given, contractions ended and had to be intensified by intravenous medication. Labour was prolonged by several hours. I was not far from panicking, and I was certainly far from breathing calmly.

It is natural to feel nervous or, to some extent, afraid of delivery. Fear of pain and loss of control are often the topmost reasons for fear of giving birth. Mothers with intense fear often wish to have a caesarean section.

They may need special support to help them deal with the fear of giving birth and to assess which method of delivery would be best for the well-being of the mother and the child being born. In addition to making delivery easier, treatment of the fear of delivery aims to improve the well-being of the mother and her family both during and after pregnancy, amongst other things by examining the content and the intensity of the fear.

Mothers have sometimes been found to suffer from quite profound fears of delivery. The body "remembers" experiences that were too early or too painful to put into words. Observations made on the mother's breathing patterns may lead to the issues causing the fear. Asking about the history of breathing problems or sensations associated with imbalanced breathing will shed light on the problem. In this context we can bring up the change of breathing in stressful situations and speak about the soothing effect of calm breathing in these situations and when in labour pain. In addition to examining fear, it is important to calm the mother down and to increase her feeling of safety in a situation where no one can guarantee that things will proceed uneventfully. The mother can be reminded that should anything go wrong with delivery today the mother and the baby can be helped in many ways. In most cases everything goes well and the beginning of new life and motherhood is a joyful event. Many women are afraid that they do not know how to give birth or that they might damage the child through their inability. Speaking about the fact that childbirth is inherently an event guided by biological processes has eased the fears of many women.

If the fear of delivery is strong, an elective caesarean section may be performed. In Finland, the choice of procedure ultimately depends on the course of the delivery and on the condition of mother and child during its course. It is often possible to encourage a mother fearing delivery to give birth vaginally. Mothers who have received help for their fear of delivery are often afterwards happy with both themselves and the personnel if they have had the courage to give birth vaginally or at least to attempt it. It is important that the mother does not feel that the risks of delivery are being understated. Making an appointment to contact the mother after delivery will also add to the feeling of safety. In addition, the mother's safety can be increased and the father's fear of his spouse's delivery can be alleviated by seeing the father as well as the mother before delivery.

In addition to the help of the nurses, midwives, and gynaecologists—the most important people to help the mother with her fear of delivery—individual psychophysical therapy or psychophysical antenatal classes can be offered for further treatment. These forms of treatment involve breathing exercises, relaxation, mental training, and discussion of fears. In mothers who have taken classes applying such principles, childbirth has proved to be more rapid and safer than is generally the case in primigravidae.

4.4. Somatic disease

Overbreathing may be biologically directly associated with somatic disease. It may compensate for excessive acidity in diabetes, kidney, and liver diseases, guarantee the supply of oxygen in heart failure and in many lung diseases, and trigger an asthma attack. Overbreathing may also be due to brain damage. Somatic diseases may be associated with imbalanced breathing in other ways, too.

As disease depletes physical and mental resources, the mind cannot necessarily process the associated stress, and the body will reflect this in breathing, as well as in changes caused by the disease. As somatic disease worsens the patient's condition, she may first try to improve her functional ability by increasing inhalation. If she is physically too weak to function, a physiological state of hyperventilation will occur, unless she is suffering from insufficient ventilation due to disease.

A somatic disease may be worrying and threatening. In addition, many somatic diseases, associated examinations, and treatments will cause pain, which may lead to imbalanced breathing. Changes to breathing and activation of the sympathetic nervous system may, in turn, complicate examinations and therapeutic measures. For example, drawing of blood samples or insertion of an intravenous line is difficult in patients with "poor blood vessels", and repeated needle pricks may be needed. Supporting and calming down patients through breathing exercises, images, and a safe therapeutic relationship may facilitate also these therapeutic measures.

Disease and sickness may alter the mental balance for many reasons (see Broom, 2007). A somatic disease may also prevent balancing physical exercise that is important for mental well-being. Changes may occur in interpersonal relations that are hard to adapt to.

It is often difficult to distinguish symptoms of disease from those caused by functional breathing problems. However, it is important to try to do this. Diagnosis and treatment of somatic diseases will be easier if the effects of imbalanced breathing are recognised. Worries about somatic symptoms may be alleviated by explaining that some of the symptoms are caused by stress and imbalanced breathing. Factors causing stress can then be understood and the threat of being ill can be alleviated. For some people, it may be sufficient to discuss the situation, to provide various forms of breathing therapy or at least pay attention to breathing and provide first-aid instructions for it. However, first aid and increased understanding alone are not always sufficient, as is shown by the following case example. A period of breathing therapy may be needed to provide more space for calming down and learning something new.

> *A fifty-year-old female patient had had a mild myocardial infarction and been treated appropriately but her cardiac symptoms still persisted. The patient consulted a doctor many times and had many examinations but no medical explanation was found for her symptoms. Finally, she was referred for psychiatric consultation, where her somatic symptoms suggestive of overbreathing and her personality and situation were examined more extensively. Panic disorder was diagnosed. The patient was matter-of-fact and sprightly, and did not present with any anxiety or depression. She had always considered it important to keep her problems to herself. There had been no one to listen to her problems when she was a child.*
>
> *Having a myocardial infarction turned out to have been difficult for reasons she had not recognised. She felt it shameful to feel ill when no explanation was found for her symptoms in medical examinations. Just before having the myocardial infarction she had returned to work after a long period of sick leave due to breast cancer. The need for further sick leave due to the myocardial infarction was a great disappointment for her. Discussing these stressors made the patient feel better but was not sufficient. She did not seek any further somatic examinations but her symptoms continued. She was referred to breathing school, where she learned to calm herself down whenever she started having chest pain. She also started to recognise her depression and the reasons for it. The breathing school had given her help for such processing. She now accepted antidepressant medication that had actually been recommended for her before. Her new self-image allowed vulnerability and being needy.*

The following case example describes the interaction between structural weaknesses in the body, stress, working positions, and breathing problems. A forty-year-old dairy farmer with health care education had all her life suffered from coughing and sinusitis, problems with her voice at times, and back pain. As structural weaknesses she had a narrow nasal cavity and atopic mucosa and her vertebrae were unstable. Due to her educational background, she was able to make accurate observations of her breathing and of the effect of her physically strenuous work on her health. Finding these connections and observing and treating them required visits to several health care experts, physicians, and therapists and improvement of the patient's powers of self-observation.

> When inhaling I felt as though I had a tight bandage around my ribs. It was hard to breathe in deeply and calmly. Breathing became more difficult after I had strengthened my transverse abdominal muscle to support my back, as I had been instructed to do by my physiotherapist. I noticed that using my lower abdomen heavily for support further compromised my breathing, which became superficial and short. Proper breathing was also hindered by my stiff thoracic spine and various degrees of vertebral subluxation complex. I easily develop vertebral subluxation complexes in my thoracic spine and need to release them daily by doing various kinds of reaching and twisting movements. Nerve impingement is sometimes severe enough to cause pain in the thorax and make deep breathing downright painful.
>
> Pain makes it difficult to consciously breathe calmly. When I have back pain, I focus all my attention on keeping the pain away and forget about calm breathing. Breathing is also complicated by haste, stress, and anxiety. It becomes broken and superficial. When, during a hectic day, I try to relax for a moment and take a nap, I notice that my heart is pounding and that I am all tense. Making a conscious effort to breathe calmly sometimes helps.
>
> Various awkward positions hinder or compromise calm breathing, for example my daily working positions and sleeping position at night. When milking cows I squat down low, and when I clean a cow's udders I reach my arms up diagonally and find my breathing to be broken and shallow. Due to my back, I need to sleep on my side. In that position I feel as if my shoulders are cramped, and free movement between my thoracic spine and ribs is prevented.

4.4.1. Asthma

Asthma provides an example of how physical and mental factors related to disease may aggravate or even cause an asthma attack through overbreathing. In respiratory diseases such as asthma, chronic bronchitis, or chronic obstructive pulmonary disease, airway obstruction restricts the flow of air in the bronchi, causing disturbance in gas exchange in the pulmonary alveoli particularly on exertion and, during attacks, also at rest. Asthma is a disease with long-term bronchial inflammation predisposing to bronchoconstriction. During symptoms, the patient's bronchi react readily to many irritants, such as dust, allergens (agents causing allergy), cold air, and physical and mental stress. Anxiety disorder is diagnosed more often in patients with asthma than in the general population (Korkeila, 2007; van Lieshout & Macqueen, 2012).

Patients with asthma often tend to overbreathe when the bronchi are constricted during attacks. This way, they try to intensify their breathing. Due to narrowed bronchi, the feeling of shortness of breath may be more intense than warranted by the true need and possibility for ventilation. It is therefore difficult for many patients to distinguish between symptoms of overbreathing and asthma. Psychophysical breathing therapy helps to develop the ability to make this distinction (see case report on pp. 36–37).

Overbreathing with excessive ventilation results in drying and cooling of the airways and makes them more sensitive to irritants. This is made worse by breathing through the mouth, which may be associated with anxiety. A vicious circle may develop, with every consequence of overbreathing, such as the contraction of smooth muscle due to lowered blood carbon dioxide levels and the resulting further contractility of the bronchi. Chronic overbreathing impairs the immunologic defence and may aggravate the symptoms of asthma by this mechanism, too (Stäubli, M., Vogel, F., Bärtsch, P., Flückiger, G., & Ziegler, W. H., 1994). Excessive increase in breathing is common in people with undiagnosed and unmedicated asthma and several other pulmonary diseases. Imbalanced breathing increases the symptoms in patients with asthma. In addition, it may lead to excessive use of asthma medication.

The above situations predispose patients with asthma to conditioning experiences, and even a slight change in breathing may then be interpreted as a beginning asthma attack. Therefore, even before physical exertion the fear of an asthma attack may cause overbreathing, which in turn may lead to an asthma attack in connection with the physical exertion. Unfortunately, people may avoid exercising for this reason. In exercise-induced asthma, the bronchi are constricted on exertion even if the patient does not overbreathe. Therefore, correct timing of medication is important. A conditioned reaction to allergens may develop, in which case any agent, smell, or even impression reminding of an allergen may cause an asthma attack. Patients may therefore falsely interpret a bout of overbreathing as an asthma attack caused by allergy. And, of course, a person with asthma, often distressed by the asthma as such, is no less susceptible to anxiety and stress caused by other factors. The opposite is, in fact, rather the case.

An overview of asthma breathing exercise programmes as accompanying treatment strategies to complement traditional pharmacological treatment has recently been published by the English authors Thomas and Bruton (2014). According to this overview, in many asthma patients pharmacological treatment is not sufficient. The authors present breathing exercise programmes which research has shown to be effective.

4.4.2. Hypoventilation

Chronic hypoventilation represents a disturbance in alveolar gas exchange or insufficient ventilation. Ventilation or exchange of air in the lungs is inadequate and as respiration cannot remove carbon dioxide sufficiently, it is accumulated in the body. The subsequently increased partial pressure of carbon dioxide in arterial blood causes symptoms such as daytime fatigue, wooziness, dyspnoea on exertion, sleep, memory, and concentration disturbances, and increased heart and respiratory rates. Rapid, ineffective respiration, use of auxiliary breathing muscles and reduced chest mobility are typical for such situations. However, they do not improve ventilation. This state is the opposite of hyperventilation but may look like it. Distinguishing between hypo- and hyperventilation is challenging but important for the patient's treatment.

In respiratory physiotherapy it is important for the patient to practise appropriate breathing in various situations and positions, to learn expectoration methods that they can use themselves, as well as exercises maintaining and improving chest mobility and maintaining muscle condition. Some psychophysical breathing exercises will help these patients greatly.

4.4.3. Diabetes

Overbreathing may be related to diabetes through a biological mechanism. The following case example shows how hard it may be to distinguish between symptoms of hypoglycaemia (low blood sugar) and overbreathing triggered by anxiety.

> *A twenty-year-old man was referred to a psychologist because of poor control of blood glucose levels. He had moved from his childhood home to his own place and felt insecure. When jogging he often had attack-like symptoms, feelings of weakness, dizziness, anxiety, and breathing problems that he believed were due to hypoglycaemia. He had adapted his insulin dosage and meals in advance for jogging. However, to play it safe he took a snack with him and ate it as symptoms occurred. This relieved the symptoms but his blood glucose was high when he returned home. His sensations were discussed in more detail. He was asked to breathe calmly and not to eat while jogging. On follow-up his blood glucose was found to remain normal. A general feeling of insecurity and the fear of not being able to manage his disease when living alone caused bouts of overbreathing. He interpreted his sensations as symptoms of hypoglycaemia. He only recognised his anxiety on closer discussion of his situation.*

4.4.4. Sleep apnoea

Sleep apnoea is an increasingly common health problem. There are many known risk factors. The pharynx may be structurally narrow and the neck short but the main risk factor is obesity leading to accumulation of fat in the pharynx and thus making it narrower. This impedes the passage of air, causing sleep apnoea and resulting lack of oxygen. After sleep apnoea and the resulting hypoventilation, the patient will compensate for insufficient oxygen intake by overbreathing. Disrupted sleep and lack of oxygen cause daytime fatigue.

A patient who attended breathing school had for many years used a CPAP (continuous positive airway pressure) device to help him to sleep at night. He came to breathing school because he also had breathing problems during the day. The therapy helped him with his breathing problems and also allowed him to connect emotionally with his early losses. We have no information about his later life.

> *I have drawn the conclusion that I am a lousy breather. I can hardly let air out. At night, I have fifty-nine sleep apnoea events per hour, that is, only one minute of uninterrupted breathing per hour. I would like to know how many times I need to inhale to keep alive. I have been keeping alive by one miserable minute of uninterrupted breathing per hour.*

The flow of air, breathing, stops because I have been left alone, rejected.
I am unprotected, in distress. I have not been taken care of, cared for. My
boundaries remain undefined, anger cannot find its way out but hurts.
I cannot connect with other people, I remain outside. Words will not
come out of my mouth, my needs, wishes, and desires remain untold and
unheard.

In addition to problems related to pharyngeal fat tissue, obesity may mechanically hinder natural movement of the diaphragm during breathing, and the diaphragm then gradually gets weaker through lack of use. Breathing then mainly occurs with auxiliary breathing muscles and becomes superficial. This is a particular disadvantage during REM sleep when chest muscles normally relax and the diaphragm is used for breathing (Coffee, 2006).

Oddly enough, little attention has been paid to how patients with sleep apnoea breathe during the day. In the daytime, patients with sleep apnoea probably have similar problems to others overexerting their auxiliary breathing muscles. It is usually unknown how the patient used his respiratory muscles before he developed sleep apnoea. All symptoms of patients with sleep apnoea are often attributed to lack of oxygen during the night and associated daytime fatigue. We do not wish to underestimate either the commonly known risk factors or the impact of night-time sleep apnoea and poor quality of sleep on the patient's quality of life and health. However, a more comprehensive approach to breathing might open up new aspects and treatment approaches.

Like Coffee (2006), we believe that chronic hyperventilation may be one of the risk factors for sleep apnoea. Sleep apnoea may thus represent a manifestation of prolonged and possibly unconscious stress. If so, we can ask what the factors were that led to imbalanced breathing and development of overweight in the first place. Poor sleeping is known to increase obesity. Patients with sleep apnoea may long have breathed in a way that stresses the body, by excessive use of auxiliary breathing muscles. Development of overweight may also be associated with unaddressed anxiety. There may be other problems in the background, as is discussed in this book.

We have treated anxious patients with muscle pain, who at the end of treatment have reported that the symptoms of sleep apnoea experienced by them or noticed by their spouses ceased with the end of anxiety and the normalisation of breathing mechanics that probably occurred in that connection. In addition to other treatment, many patients with sleep apnoea may benefit from psychophysical breathing therapy.

4.4.5. Functional pelvic floor disorders

The most common disadvantages of functional pelvic floor disorders are inability to hold urine, faeces, or air, or difficulty expelling these. This may be associated with dysaesthesia, pain, fear, or anxiety. Incontinence may occur when walking or pushing or during sexual intercourse, or unnoticed without advance warning in any situation. Patients may have several symptoms concomitantly or mixed forms of symptoms.

They may also suffer from either numbness or increased sensitivity of the pelvic floor. Functional pelvic floor disorders are often associated with aches and pains. Vulvodynia (pain in the female genitals) presents as pain and/or smarting in the area of the external genitals. It may involve mucosal problems such as dryness or inflammation. Pain on intercourse and vaginism (spasms of the vagina), involuntary muscle spasms, or tension and vaginal pains interfere with normal life. Tenderness in the lower abdomen and pain radiating to the pelvic or hip area are also typical. Sometimes the pain is known to arise from the bladder, uterus, intestine, lower back or nervousness. The cause may be anatomic or physiological. However, the cause cannot always be identified.

Pelvic floor muscles are partly subject to voluntary control. They have many important tasks. They support the urethra, vagina, rectum, and viscera from below, forming a "floor" for the pelvis. They work together with the diaphragm and the deepest abdominal and back muscles. They are highly important for sexual function and pleasure. Pregnancy, childbirth, hormonal changes, gynaecological operations, ageing, and overweight put a strain on and affect these muscles.

The functioning of pelvic floor muscles can be measured with an EMG device. In our approach, breathing and use of the body are also observed during measurement. Muscle work is targeted at the pelvic floor, aiming at freely flowing respiration and optimal use of the body. Hurry, tension, pain, fear, anxiety, overbreathing, and irritation of the bladder or intestine often increase muscle tension at rest. By calming down breathing, the resting tension can be lifted, reducing the experienced tension and pain. Breathing exercises are used to learn to relax the pelvic floor when inhaling and to strengthen the support of the pelvic floor when exhaling, by drawing the coccygeal bone towards the navel. Identifying and strengthening the body boundaries is essential for giving the pelvic floor the necessary support. This will enable the patient to picture the pelvis as an integrated whole.

It is not uncommon for psychophysical treatment of pelvic floor problems to reveal the presence of severe mental problems. This gives the physiotherapist a natural opportunity for referring the patient for assessment of the need for psychological treatment. Pelvic floor disorders are so common that the psychophysical treatment methods we describe will be very useful in health care.

CHAPTER FIVE

Breathing in interpersonal encounter

Minna Martin, Maila Seppä, Tiina Törö

To protect and take cover,
to be the source,
a shady corner and a seed,
and all this yet
carefully protecting yourself.

Breathing patterns develop in early interaction. Breathing becomes an important means of mental and physical self-regulation, and breathing problems reflect experienced deficiencies in interaction. Throughout life, human relationships play a significant role in regulating breathing—and, vice versa, breathing influences the regulation of affects. If we experience human relationships as safe, we learn to override automatic fear reactions arising from deep in the brain and to deal with our anxiety. We can then examine what we experience with understanding and develop self-compassion and means of calming ourselves, allowing breathing to flow freely. On the other hand, if we experience a lot of fear, shame, tension, anxiety, or other difficult affects in connection with interpersonal interaction, various imbalanced breathing patterns may be conditioned to express the fight or flight reaction in the body (Bourne, 2015; Gerhardt, 2004). To be able to influence our breathing patterns we thus need to understand the invisible and nonverbal patterns of human relationships and emotions woven into our bodies, muscles, and breathing (Siltala, 2002).

The concrete breathing exercises presented in this book arise from the topics discussed in this chapter, that is, early interaction and encountering the self and others. We therefore suggest that the reader does the breathing exercises while reading both this and the exercise chapter. This will provide an in-depth understanding of the exercises, and doing the exercises will make it easier to understand why precisely the concepts chosen for this chapter are essential for breathing.

5.1. Being and breathing

5.1.1. Body memory forms the basis of our existence

Early in life we do not yet have a language to express the pleasure or anxiety we experience. Therefore, we use the whole body for communication, including breathing. The body will later remember and faithfully repeat what we have learned in this preverbal phase. Through *body memory* (Rothschild, 2000), our early experiences are thus reflected in our breathing patterns as adults, for instance in the way in which we breathe in reaction to overwhelming situations.

Early undifferentiated bodily experiences form the basis for the preconscious memory structure and function of the mind. The conscious mind that later develops and can be shared verbally is based on the body memory and bodily skills. The preconscious basis of the mind cannot develop by itself, without work and interaction. The earliest form of work a little baby does is sucking the mother's breast and breathing actively in-between. Active work as a factor in building the mind and maintaining balance remains significant throughout life (Lehtonen et al., 2006). To counterbalance work, even a little baby takes breaks, wondering, listening, and recovering. The parent needs to be present at these times (Beebe, Knoblauch, Rustin & Sorter, 2005; Stern, 2004). This interaction builds the baby's live preconscious mind, creating space for images and experiences of pleasure, and affecting bodily functions (breathing) and emotional behaviour throughout life.

We learn *implicit communication* through ways of touching, tones of voice, facial expressions, various rhythms, and details of breathing. The significance of implicit communication, which takes place largely on the preconscious level, is associated with survival and processing of experienced stress (Stern, 1998). We thus learn the basis for self-regulation even before learning to use language. Disturbances in non-verbal communication and in mediating self-regulation skills from nurturer to child are associated with later problems: stress reactions learned early, and associated breathing patterns, are later automatically activated in threatening situations.

The term "body memory" may be partly misleading because we do not experience our earliest experiences as remembering. The experience might be more appropriately called *implicit relational knowing*: the other person is what I feel he is. We may realise that recollection is relative: "This is what I remember but my memory may be wrong." But implicit relational knowing (Lyons-Ruth, 1998) is quite fixed, it is neither questioned nor reflected on. Bodily experiences, such as the sensations mediated by breathing patterns, only reinforce this. Due to the nature of such "knowledge", reaction models learned early are often learned without sufficient scope for understanding and without the ability to observe what is happening inside or wonder what one's way of experiencing things might be related to. On the contrary, body memory works automatically, as a reflex, without conscious choice. It is not guided by the more highly developed cerebral cortex but reactions occur deep in the brain. If a person interprets a situation as threatening, the "primitive" reaction mode quickly leads to over- or under-regulation of bodily functions, further leading to distorted perception. If a person is afraid of being rejected, he may be quick to over-interpret messages from the environment as rejection. If a person carries in his being and bodily reactions adverse memories of his earliest interactions with others, he may unconsciously invite other people to recreate familiar interactive experiences. At worst, the response of the environment may be that "You get what you ask for" (Gerhardt, 2004).

But body memory does not only mean remembering problematic experiences; positive bodily experiences may also be remembered from early life:

> In a dancing lesson, I stopped to observe how pleasant it was to reach my hand up towards the ceiling and follow my hand with my eyes. My side stretched, and the sole of my foot felt comfortable against the floor. I wondered at how such a simple thing could feel so pleasant. In my mind, I saw a baby reaching out to touch her mother's face. How utterly pleasant it can feel to know how to reach out!

People may eliminate good body memories from their mind and thus not be able to use such memories as resources. They may do this to protect themselves from disappointment or other difficult feelings. In a good enough therapeutic relationship, early body memories return to form a driving force together with increasing images, feelings, and more memories. In psychophysical breathing therapy, we aim to revive positive early physical experiences. In a breathing exercise, people can experience the same restfulness and protection against emptiness as under the protection of an early nurturing relationship. This will create space for images and their own genuine feelings.

5.1.2. Images and the experience of existing

Images are among the main targets and tools in psychophysical breathing therapy. By images, we mean emotionally charged pictures of oneself or others. They arise from various bodily sensations, associations, and feelings. Through images, the mind gradually develops a live picture of the self and other (Gerhardt, 2004; Siltala, 2002). If we fail to develop the ability to create and maintain images, we will be exposed to stress and anxiety. To endure loneliness, being separate, and other difficult situations and emotions, we create soothing, supportive, and self-compassionate images. Listening to breathing may be an excellent tool for finding such approving, compassionate presence.

Differentiation of images of oneself and others signifies psychological birth as a separate person (Mahler & Bergman, 1975). Nevertheless, detachment from the early relationship always results in a conflict that remains throughout life. Accepting anxiety means stepping into emptiness. Giving in to the feelings then emerging will create a silence representing pure existence. Our relationship with nature, with products of creative arts, fairy tales, and dreams are our guides on these excursions. Too sudden separation from a parent, due to death or sickness, for instance, will leave the child insecure. It is then important to strengthen basic confidence particularly when parting (Winnicott, 1951). One of Maila Seppä's patients made a suggestion for building a bridge over the pit of anxiety:

> At the last session before the holidays, my therapy patient brought a cassette asking me to record something. He said this would enable him to reinforce his image of me for the duration of the break. I was confused by the surprising request and about to refuse but then I said I would tell him a story if one came to mind. At night, in the dark, a story started to emerge, and I recorded it on the cassette. Listening to it in the morning I was astonished by the contents and by the long pauses and slow rhythm of speech. After the holidays, my patient said he had listened to the cassette every day when driving. He did not remember anything about the contents because he had been listening to the pauses and the melody of my speech. Later on, we came back to the contents.

Images thus provide a resource for calming down, and for processing and describing our experiences and feelings animatedly in words, too (Winnicott, 1951, 1987). In this chapter, we present the concepts related to images that are most important for psychophysical breathing therapy.

The earliest experiences between mother and child are stored primarily as basic bodily and physiological experiences but also as images. This dual understanding represents one of the early ways in which children perceive themselves and their surroundings (Siltala, 2002). Thus, the earliest images are *body images* of themselves and their caregivers and are based on sensations. An image is created of how they are able to use their bodies, how the body feels when moving and breathing. The image also covers the appearance of the body, its surface, mass, inner spaces, and orifices. As it is not easy to learn to control the orifices or to perceive the body boundaries, feelings of fear or shame may affect such images unconsciously even in adulthood and be reflected in breathing (Hägglund & Piha, 1980). One aim of psychophysical breathing therapy is to clarify the body image and to create pleasurable body images. In addition to breathing exercises, tools such as drawing body images, picturing body boundaries, and verbal metaphors as a symbolic expression of bodily experiences may be used.

Preconscious images based on sensations form generalised memories of experiences, or *representations*, memories of how to be or how to breathe with another person, of the other person's facial expressions, and of emotions related to such situations (Stern, 1985). The body image and such representations form the basis of images associated with *object relations*. These images of a reciprocal relationship form the basis for emotional self-regulation, influencing our choices, behaviour, and attitudes both towards ourselves and in interactive situations. The images arise in relationships in early childhood and do not disappear with time. We constantly develop new impressions of ourselves and others but early images that are partly unrealistic exert their influence in the background. They appear particularly strong in reactions to stress or threat. For example, we can feel helpless when we fall ill or get into a conflict, even if we are otherwise independent. People attending breathing school have the chance to commune with their early experiences by utilising the concept of the *inner child* (Harris, 1969). Through this concept people can, for example, achieve a living connection with pain experienced as a child, but also recognise playfulness in themselves. By "inner child", we mean a person's image of himself as a child (in the past) or of the child in himself (in the present). Images of the self and the other influence various bodily rhythms and guide breathing patterns. Breathing patterns conditioned in early relationships are activated and act as a radar or a compass telling us how we actually experience things. Breathing reacts faster and more genuinely; the conscious emotional experience may be created with significant delay.

During personal development, the inner world of images and the outer reality approach each other but will never become exactly congruent. We can never give up all unrealistic images or accept the outer world or ourselves completely. This does not mean experiencing a conflict but a normal tension between the inner and outer realities. The *potential space* created between the inner world of images and the outer reality will relieve the tension. By potential space Donald W. Winnicott

(1951, pp. 135, 144–148) meant a state of mutual understanding and care, where the two parties create *good enough* images of each other (Winnicott, 1951, p. 95). The image is created and maintained by mirroring and matching up, through faces, expressions, looks, voices, breathing, touching, and rhythm. It is essential to develop a feeling of being on a sufficiently similar wavelength and compatible. When two people meet in the potential space, their experiences also meet. New ways of imagining or acting may be developed. At best, in the potential space, when the other person is looking at us or supporting our breathing, we may experience a feeling of relief, release of stress, and compassionate comfort, as well as of being seen and understood. In addition, the potential space is a space facilitating balanced breathing: in a good enough relationship there is space to breathe. It is a favourable prognostic sign for breathing therapy if such compatibility can be experienced at the assessment visit already. Many breathing school exercises were created through such creative encounters.

The potential space will keep internal and external realities both apart and interactive. We can reach the external reality and simultaneously have a living connection with our internal images. In breathing exercises, the aim is to create such a working experience. Tension created by frightening or anxiety-provoking images or by various sides of the self can be examined through breathing exercises or, alternatively, through working with mental representations. Art postcards or other pictures can be chosen to represent images of oneself, and we can examine, for example, whether it is possible to accept in ourselves the polarities of helpless and capable, fearful and courageous, shy and curious. A similar experience integrating various sides of the self or contradictory feelings may also be achieved through other creative work:

> When improvising in a dancing class everyone was asked to work on a physical or mental problem, for example, by moving in a way relieving backache. I wanted to work on my anxiety in performance. I was going to give a lecture to a large group of physicians. In advance, I saw my audience as demanding and myself as very small. When dancing, I sought both movement representing insecurity or even dread and moving like a self-confident queen. Something strange happened during the class. Instead of anxiety, I felt titillating anticipation. The image of firm ground beneath my feet arose. It represented self-confidence.

Based on his thoughts concerning potential space, Winnicott (1951, pp. 1–34; 1987) also developed the concept of the *transitional object*. This means the ability to create potential space within the mind and to calm down with the help of your own images. At first, babies will only calm down when being held by their parents, and anxious patients will only feel safe when seeing the therapist. Later on, babies can fall asleep holding a bedtime toy, for example, and the image of the soothing presence of a nurturer will calm them down. Anxious patients will calm down at home when doing breathing exercises learned in good interaction. Adults may find security in an amulet, a wedding ring, or a soothing sentence they can say to themselves, such as: "Don't worry, everything is fine." These symbols remind them of the safety felt in an important relationship. When dealing with imbalanced breathing, it is important for recovery to re-establish the ability to have an internal dialogue restoring soothing images, self-compassion, and a feeling of safety.

5.1.3. Permission to be

People reacting adversely with their breathing are particularly sensitive to other people's feelings and needs and may therefore lose contact with their own experiences. However, with appropriate support it is possible for them to regain the ability to consider their own needs (Aron, 2003). This is a central field of work in breathing therapy. Through breathing and a mindful approach, participants in breathing therapy are able to recognise their own rhythm and sensitivity and thus to start getting to know their boundaries as well as their own space, desire, and will. The experience of "being allowed to be as you are" represents the very essence of being genuine (Winnicott, 1951, 1987).

True self

Winnicott (1951, 1987) created the concept of the True Self which he described as the individual, *genuine personality* that develops and becomes stronger in sufficiently supportive circumstances.

The basis of the True Self is physical. It begins with general sensations of one's body being alive, based on feeling one's heartbeat or breathing, for example. This represents the primary experience of being, being allowed to be what we are. Play is another representation of such a state; when playing and in our images we are allowed to feel anything possible. Creative activity arises from these experiences. Winnicott has said that only the True Self can be creative and only the True Self can feel real.

Such development is not always possible, and psychological growth may be prevented. If a parent projects excessive anxiety into the relationship and this is frequently repeated, the child may need to protect himself from his and his caregiver's anxiety or anger by adopting a *false personality* structure (False Self). To be accepted, the child may strive to become what he assumes the parent or carer wants him to be. This phenomenon is particularly apparent among people who tend to react adversely with their breathing. Over-adjustment leads to falseness that protects the True Self like a wall. Children who are neglected and left too often to soothe themselves will develop muscle tension for their protection. People whose boundaries are repeatedly violated may also end up doing the same themselves. Muscle tension and holding the breath become means of taking care of ourselves and maintain the illusion of being able to keep things under control without mental work. Emotions that cannot be controlled by tension are swallowed during the pause in breathing and thus fended off. But tension that impedes breathing will not bring relief and will instead increase the feeling of threat and the need to control. In addition, it will prevent interaction in encounters with others.

Excessive adaptation represents both a disturbance in early interaction and a prerequisite for coping. People showing excessive adaptation surrender to external demands by giving up their own way of experiencing—"Don't worry about me, I'll be fine". They perform, keep busy, do the right thing, and please others. No matter how they try, they will not feel satisfied but lack joy in life. This may be difficult to correct because the environment will misunderstand adaptation as positive: people adapting excessively will be experienced as lively and easy. At the other extreme, "difficult" and unadaptable people will feel that everything matters and no one understands or is capable of helping. Unadaptable people watch their boundaries and interpret any attempt at contact and even constructive feedback as an attack.

It should be remembered that we are all incomplete and false at times. We should be aware that it will take a lifetime to find the True Self. We will never be finished, and development will never end.

Desire and will

Desire is closely associated with emotions and drives. Will is more conscious action related to the ability for reflection. Desire cannot be controlled, told to disappear, or to be suppressed but it cannot be allowed to flourish unlimited, either. At best, one's own will, a constructive choice, will create boundaries to limit desire. True freedom arises from positive choices, from being capable of deciding when to say "yes" or "no" to ourselves or to others.

Desire is related to being gratified but no gratification can be maintained endlessly. Even the most satisfying experiences lead sooner or later to some degree of disappointment, dissatisfaction, or feeling of imperfection. In the course of their development, people learn to tolerate these as natural experiences belonging to life and existence. Imperfection becomes part of the basic nature of being human. Sufficiently good begins to be enough. This is not easy to accept, though, and for this reason some people fervently strive to solve the problems associated with human existence, suffering, and conflicts due to desire by "auxiliary means" that in turn bring about further problems. Pauses in breathing and swallowing of impulses are common ways of smothering desire. As muscles are used to control breathing, emotions, and desire, chronic muscle tension is very common.

The body with all its tension carries many existential conflicts. The solution cannot be found outside the self, such as in massage or correct breathing techniques, even though these can provide transient relief. Neither is relinquishing desires causing conflicts the solution for achieving peace of mind and well-being. Desire is an expression of our life force, and attempts to relinquish it will lead to apathy and loss of joy in life. "Don't worry about me, I'll be fine" epitomises the attempt to fend off our own desires and the inability to mourn what cannot be achieved. Instead of denial we should examine the relationship between desire and clinging, not denying the desire but not depending on it, either. Desire should be given space to breathe, and the person desiring should be encouraged to examine the nature of his desire (Epstein, 2005). Only when people can be honest about their desires can they be present and alive. Breathing will then also become easier.

It is not easy to find out what our true desires are; people tend to experience conflicting desires over and over again. The question "What do I really want?" may give rise to a feeling of desolation due to a feeling of emptiness: no one has understood me or provided security. The need to be comforted and cared for remains throughout life. Adults may find comfort through self-compassion. In an attempt to become free of desire people may ask: "What do I really want?" If the answer is: "I want some space of my own," and the wish is fulfilled, instead of relief they may experience a feeling of emptiness which they try to escape by busying themselves, eating, or watching TV. They are not capable of trusting that the emptiness will be filled by itself and that life will support them; that even in an empty space they can breathe safely and, being with themselves, they will not face immediate danger.

Desire lives in the body. It is no wonder, then, that some people breathe shallowly. Breathing deep down into the pelvis will cause desire and vitality in the body. For many, the sexual feelings that then arise are frightening and forbidden, and they feel that the desire in the body therefore needs to be restrained. People are often "cut into two in the middle", that is, the breath does not dare or is not capable of reaching down to the pelvic floor. Breathing is aborted by muscle tension holding back desire. Overtrained abdominal muscles may reflect an unconscious effort to take control over the body with its irrational desires. The body is like a little child in front of a stern parent, it must be disciplined and obedient. Sexuality is a basic force of existence and a prerequisite of life. In many cases, breath-holding stems from underlying denial or prevention of sexuality.

Even though many taboos from the past decades can today be examined and discussed, modern permissiveness and the possibility for free love have not eliminated fears related to sexuality and desire. Sexual freedom is seen as the freedom to do anything, but it is equally important to have the freedom not to. Real freedom can only be found through respecting oneself and others, through conscious choices, and spontaneous self-control. What we desire is not always necessarily what we need. Performance-centred sex compulsively seeking orgasm can be considered a most thoughtless waste of natural forces, or mental hyperventilation expressed in the body. Instead of naturally building up a person's energy reserves through fulfilment, it depletes the reserves.

The key to well-being may be simple: desire recognised in peaceful existence and observed as being our own will open up an awareness of a conscious choice between doing and not doing, our own will and space.

Boundaries and space

In early relationships, we build the partly preconscious basic experience that regulates how we can be and occupy space in relation to others. Early models for the experiencing of space include strategies operating on an implicit level that have allowed us to regulate our feelings, react appropriately to others, stifle or express our wishes and needs. Breathing and muscle tension play central roles in such regulation. Muscle memory forms the basis for the experiencing of space inside and around us. Children maintain their integrity by protective movements that may cut off breathing or constrict it. This forms the physical basis for anxiety. In addition, from the very beginning breathing and bodily functions involve images and words that together form the automatic programme regulating the experience of space (Hägglund & Piha, 1980).

When describing the breathing space inside us, we say that we breathe superficially or deeply, fill or empty the space, blow out or draw in air. The rhythmic use of the internal space in breathing and its involvement with the experience of the self form a central experience of life that everyone shares. It is therefore understandable that the basic problem involving space arises in connection with breathing. The lungs are, after all, concretely a living space within us.

At the bottom of breathing, in the psychophysical reality, there is the repeatedly arising question in relation to the environment, "Do I even have space to breathe?" and, behind this, the unconscious, mute question, "Is there space for my breathing within me?" The conditions of existence are addressed in the following questions: "Am I allowed to become visible and speak about myself and my feelings? Am I allowed to decide what I want to express and to whom? Am I allowed to keep my secrets?"

How people occupy space is reflected unconsciously in the way they breathe and interact. The experience of space can be seen in corporality, that is, in how people live in their bodies, in their homes, whether they dare to physically fill a space of their size, be as tall and wide as they are. Therefore, posture truly expresses how a person takes up space, which is in turn associated with the self and the boundaries of the self. A person's posture, his relation to the ground, his vertical position and way of breathing are formed during life. They depend on the way he uses his body, his muscle balance, the variation in oxygen demand, external circumstances, and the images and emotions arising in him. An inner feeling of bursting represents an attempt to eliminate or avoid a threat. If we find the environment unpredictable or demanding, our muscles become tense.

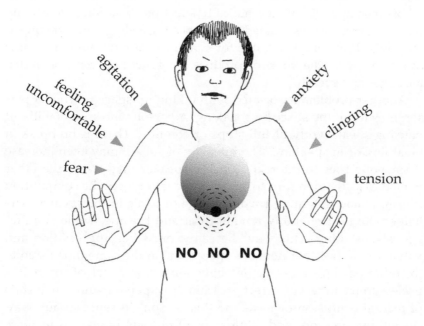

If a person has not learned to be conscious of, or value, his own thoughts, physical sensations, or feelings, it is natural to live according to other people's wishes. In the words of a physiotherapist participating in the training:

> *If there is no space—nothing will be enough. No force can make me visible unless there is space. If, again, I demand space greedily, no attention, no applause, and no success, however visible, will be sufficient.*

Sometimes it feels as though our words do not reach the listener, are not taken seriously. The problem may be in confusing mixed messages. We may say "yes" or "no" but our body may communicate the opposite. When we say "NO" emphatically, we take up external space, breathe out towards the other person. We thus define our space and express our physical and mental boundaries. For words to become flesh and to resonate, we must start by taking possession of our body. We learn to recognise what is happening in our body. Observation of breathing is a good means for this. By breathing close to another person, we become conscious of how accurately we read each other's non-verbal messages. They automatically affect our breathing. Perceiving our own territory is associated with respecting feelings and listening to ourselves. Breathing is a guide for genuine communication; falseness can be heard in the voice or produce a conflict between non-verbal messages and speech.

Another problem associated with taking up space is when a person tries to fill the space by speaking. A person who speaks without pausing speaks without full stops or commas. There is no break in breathing or in speaking. The intensity of speech may even increase if someone tries to interrupt. Such a speaker may tempt the other person to jostle for a turn to speak. If the latter loses the competition this may inadvertently provoke a state of panic in the speaker. The helper should preferably remain calm and breathe, while simultaneously listening. This way she can express her appreciation and valuation of the other person's speech and at the same time listen to the other person's message reflecting anxiety and lack of space. It is useless to try to teach correct breathing to a person who is in a state of mental confusion or to define this person's essence in any way. A soothing presence and reinforcement of boundaries will increase the person's feeling of safety and therefore his ability to regulate his own space.

Pumping breathing may also represent anxious protection of space. A woman reflected on her experience of space as follows: "When I breathe in and out and in without a break, I construct a barrier, a boundary that no one will cross." A space is always limited, whether it is an internal experience or an external tangible measure in relation to another person. Differentiation, integration, and clarification of the body boundaries are basic prerequisites for individual identity. The reality and integrity of the body image, that is, the ability to identify with one's own body, are a core aspect of *identity*.

Defending of a person's own territory begins when a child at the negation stage uses determined expressions such as "This is mine" or "I don't want to". Puberty is the second opportunity for finding, training, and reinforcing the self. The climacteric is said to provide the third opportunity for this, and this can be seen in groups of middle-aged women. Such groups often discuss the impossibility of defining their own needs between the needs of their ageing parents, children, and grandchildren. Pressure increases, the space is restricted, and the body starts crying for help. The most significant results of breathing school cannot be measured because the changes occur in relationships within families. Learning to say "no" may at first produce skirmish at the boundaries. We have heard families wonder "What kind of a school is mum going to? She's become so cross." Energy is needed to set boundaries and for the various feelings then arising. Getting hurt or disappointed or guilty all require work.

It is not always easy to perceive one's own boundaries and we do not necessarily have what it takes to do this. Even at best, the learning process may take several years. It is quite common for people to resort to black and white alternatives in boundary issues: I will either resign or defend myself aggressively. Alternatively, a person may accuse others or start feeling guilty and get depressed. None of the alternatives is satisfactory because deep down we want both to have our needs met and to be considerate to others, that is, have a living interaction with others.

The truly limited scope of life can only be realised when we stop and no longer flee from our own or someone else's crossness or disappointment. Stopping means consenting to the feelings raised by boundary issues. Becoming aware of our boundaries is a moment of seeing the facts and ourselves. It means consenting to being separate. This experience often leads to facing our fears and also to mourning. Sorrow arises when we give up old breathing habits and old ideas. Change begins with amnesty and forgiving ourselves. When we thus find ourselves, being alone and separate will be easier to tolerate. When we find it permissible to be separate and different, to have our own desires and will, boundaries in relationships will grow stronger. Boundaries do not signify complete separation and isolation. There is harmony: being both separate and connected to others. The space thus obtained is both internal and external. The internal space makes it possible for our voice to be heard. We become visible, existent, and ourselves.

Images of the self reflect the individual's
relationship to the environment (body memory)

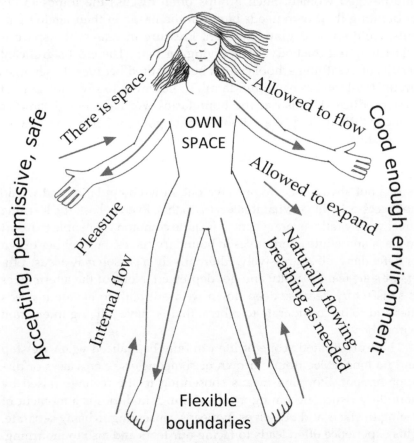

5.2. Effect of soothing presence on breathing

5.2.1. The soothing other

An anxiety, hyperventilation, or panic attack in an adult reflects the
experience of missing an internal soother and compassion. It is as if the
inner child falls into chaos, losing the ability to calm down, compre-
hend what is going on, and breathe sufficiently calmly. Some patients
with panic attacks remain indoors and do not even go shopping alone
for fear of symptoms.

I cannot control what is happening to me. My thoughts fly back and forth and I feel I will end up in chaos, falling apart. If I try to concentrate on breathing or close my eyes, I immediately get anxious. I have to move and I cannot calm down. The symptoms control my life. I get panic attacks constantly and therefore prefer to stay home rather than go out among people. I hate my body which gets to decide what I do. This is why I might just as well neglect or maltreat it.

Feelings related to laboured breathing make patients anxious. They then like to talk about their symptoms and seek quick means of controlling them. In the current world of emphasising performance, people develop deficient tools for understanding themselves and for recovering. Another person and live interaction are needed for the required safety: a parent to calm down the child, a spouse to calm down the partner, a midwife to calm down the woman in labour, and a doctor to calm down the patient. Only the ability to calm down will make it possible to study the emotions and images created inside.

Adults may try to live as if they were independent of support by other people. However, such experiences of the self are usually transient and mere illusions of independence rather than the reality. The need for care never disappears, only changes its form. When stressed, anxious, helpless, or otherwise in distress, most people need support from others to achieve balance. The significance of the soothing other may be seen in the work of a dental assistant, for example, as was reported by an oral hygienist:

A dental assistant has the opportunity for observing the patient's breathing and, through this, his fears. The assistant is in a side role during treatment, assisting the dentist and promoting the creation of a trustful relationship between patient and dentist. Many people are afraid of dental procedures. Patients presenting for tooth extraction, in particular, are always afraid. Changes in the breathing of a frightened patient may be seen in subtle bodily functions or may take clearer physical expression. Patients often do not wish to speak about their fears directly and they do not necessarily recognise them, either. The dental assistant may help the patient to cope. An understanding attitude is essential. The dental assistant must act confidently and calmly. By speaking slowly and at a low pitch, moving smoothly, and avoiding clattering the instruments she can help to create a safe atmosphere. Instruments are not shown to patients but patients are told how the procedure will proceed. The assistant can stroke a shoulder or hold a hand, as necessary. In one unit, patients were given toy crocodiles to squeeze during the procedure. This calmed down even adult patients. Sometimes patients may start to clearly overbreathe. If they cannot be calmed down, it may be necessary to interrupt the procedure, and this is expensive. It is therefore important to restore the feeling of safety. Calming down should always start with oneself. I concentrate on feeling calm and breathing slowly. Hurry is our worst enemy: it is hard to calm down when in a hurry.

The soothing other is not always available. Everyone has experiences of being left alone, some significantly more than others. If you have reflected sufficiently on your experiences of being left alone, they may become resources; through their own early experiences of being left alone parents may be able to empathise with their children. When singing a cradle song, parents who have internalised safety can, by the melody of their voices, communicate empathy and safety: "I understand you, I have been through this, too, but we will be fine together ..." Hope arises from the parent's ability to carry both of their feelings. In a shared experience of calming down, the parent's voice, singing, touch, mood, and deep and calm rhythm of breathing create potential space for processing emotions. Calming down together remains an important body memory feeding self-compassion throughout life. Even in adulthood, functional self-regulation means stopping to revive the memory of this shared existence, to listen to what is the matter with myself and how I actually feel. When people pray alone in bed at night or breathe calmly as learned with a therapist, they try to reactivate the feeling of calming down together.

5.2.2. Non-verbal and verbal communication

In the beginning of a child's development, *non-verbal communication*, that is, touch, and voice rhythm and melody, is most important. The emphasis then gradually shifts to visual communication. In the second and third years of life, it starts shifting further to *verbal communication* (Gerhardt, 2004). People who are aware of themselves can retain throughout life a living contact with bodily, rhythmic, and visual expressions of experience. Verbal expression of emotions developing beside non-verbal communication substantialises our mental experiences. The regulation of emotions, such as calming down and safety, is mediated to the other person by these means (Ogden, 1994).

Touch and intimacy

The fluid surrounding the baby in the womb and the mother's body with its movements provide the baby with its first experiences of touch. Being nurtured by the parents, being held by them, and closeness colour childhood and form the primary means of soothing and expressing understanding. Touch increases the activity of the soothing autonomic nervous system and curbs physical stress reactions. The pituitary gland secretes oxytocin, a hormone associated with pleasure and calming down, slowing down and deepening breathing, lowering the pulse rate and blood pressure, relaxing muscles, and calming down the activity of internal organs (Uvnäs-Moberg, 2003). Reactions are directed towards others, affection and trust are reinforced, and fears alleviated. Touch provides the body with rest, the mind with space, and encourages us to face new challenges. In early childhood, no one is capable of doing this alone; it is precisely the experience of calming down together that reduces stress. In the presence of the other person, physical and emotional states may form understandable experiences that we can learn to influence ourselves. Touch is closely intertwined with breathing: being held and a tender, soothing touch will calm down breathing. Lack of touch or sudden rough touch, on the other hand, impede breathing and are associated with an inability to balance stress by calming down. The need to be touched remains throughout life.

> A man came to the meeting of a group of middle-aged people and said he had cried after the previous meeting. With the help of a breathing exercise done in pairs he had realised how long he had yearned to be touched. A discussion arose about the loss of touching. "A child is nurtured, young lovers touch each other, but later in adult life, as the most active sexuality withers, there may be no touching left." In breathing school groups with middle-aged participants, people often yearn to be touched caringly.

Touch is a useful means of exerting a conscious therapeutic influence. When breathing is examined, patients may say in advance that they do not like to be touched. Nevertheless, during examination therapists should touch their patients with calm hands and help them thus to perceive their breathing. If the patient finds it possible to calm down during examination, touching between him and the therapist may become natural. In somatic health care, as well, patients can in many cases be naturally touched in connection with examination and treatment, thus alleviating fear and anxiety caused by disease and examination.

> In my work as a physician when performing electroneuromyography (ENMG), I noticed that touching made patients feel safe and increased their trust in me. Before performing needle ENMG, I would therefore examine my patients, touching them with my hands, and help them take the appropriate position for the examination. This helped me to perform painful examinations without problems.

People often benefit from encounters on many levels—tactile, emotional, and verbal. It is central for therapeutic touch to respect the other person's boundaries, separateness, uniqueness, and space, to adjust between sufficient intimacy and a suitable distance. At best, touching offers safety, calming down and comfort and alleviates discomfort, tension, and pain. Distance, on the other hand, reinforces professionality, neutrality, boundaries, and the right to self-determination. Control of physical touching requires particular concentration on the images that such touching brings about (Muurimaa, 1997).

Principles of respectful touching while listening to the other person:

- First of all, the touch must be neutral
- Listen to the "silent information" mediated through your hands
- Sense what is concrete: how does it feel underneath your hand?
- Sense temperatures: cool, cold, warm, hot?
- Sense how you use the weight of your hands
- Sense whether your hands move slowly, rhythmically, or hastily, or whether they remain still
- Sense how it feels to breathe
- Pay attention to the images arising in your mind
- Pay attention to the thoughts moving through your mind
- Pay attention to the feelings arising in you.

Touching is not always possible, and it is not suitable for every form of therapy. Understanding may also result in not touching. However, the lack of touch between health care provider and patient is not always associated with respect but with an avoidant culture, with hurry, increasing use of computers and equipment, and changing therapeutic practices. It is good to remember that touching is part of good interaction and an expression of caring. If touch is not applied as a tool, patients' early images of being bad may be reinforced and feelings of shame may thus be activated.

> *I was on a course where we were supposed to practise assisting another person's breathing by touching and various types of pressure. During an exercise my partner ended up giving me only verbal instructions. I became confused and could not bring myself to ask why he did the exercise this way. I wondered what was wrong with me, why my partner did not touch me as instructed. Was I repulsive or did I appear not to tolerate touching? After considering this I came to the conclusion that interaction depends on both parties. It was possible that the fault was not mine alone. I was grateful for this experience which helped me understand how it is to be a patient—is this the way patients feel if they are not touched when they expect it?*

It is often emphasised that if the patient is deeply traumatised touching should be avoided. This may be an important guideline, for example when dealing with patients who have been sexually abused. Their treatment should at least be begun by other means, and progress should be slow. On the other hand, there are situations where good treatment of traumatised people may require touching. The bodies of patients with self-mutilation or eating disorders, for example, may sometimes virtually cry out for nurturing touch. A safe and soothing touch may help to construct a new kind of body image and relationship to oneself. As treatment proceeds, it is good to discuss with the patient the images and emotions caused by touching. Education, experience, and supervision are important for the necessary professional skills when dealing with the most difficult patients. In addition, therapists should have sufficient experience of being touched in the context of their training.

Holding, touching, and intimacy are paths to connection but insufficient as such. In addition to concrete touching, a symbolic experience of being touched, or understood, through gaze, smile, voice, and words is needed. Concrete and symbolic touching together make the patient feel good: the brain grows, better connections are created in the neural network, and the body and breathing calm down.

In the exercise chapter, there are touching exercises on pp. 199, 204, and 205, and the "breathe for the other" exercise reflecting intimacy is on pp. 234–236.

Voice and hearing

Hearing is one of our earliest senses. The baby in the womb has a rather well developed hearing as early as in the fourth month of pregnancy, and towards the end of pregnancy he will remember quite well what he has heard. Hearing the mother's voice after birth will reinforce the baby's basic trust. For the baby, hearing the mother's voice represents being concretely touched: the mother's voice will resonate and vibrate in both of their bodies, massaging the mother herself inside but also the baby. The mother can thus use her voice to calm down, relax, and comfort them both.

Tone of voice and manner of breathing are seamlessly connected. We first learn the emotional language of non-verbal tones mediated by voice and breathing. Learning an actual language is important but will occur only later. The ability to observe and express tones will be preserved throughout life. For example, another person's mood may be transmitted through his tone of voice or way of breathing (Goleman, 2006). Children and sensitive adults are particularly prone to observe changes in these (Aron, 2003). With positions, facial expressions, and the nature of eye contact the whole body supports non-verbal vocal expression and attention to it. Posture and use of voice together reveal how comfortable a person feels. In a reserved, tense body the voice is soft and superficial, the resonator remaining deficient. Some people learn to protect themselves by using a squeaky style of speaking that puts a strain on the larynx and keeps breathing quite superficial. A body that feels safe and is conscious of its physicality is flexible and resonates with the person's own voice while breath can flow freely.

Parents feeling sufficiently calm can soothe their agitated babies by using their voice to resonate with the baby's mood, breathing, and voice melody, thus expressing that they understand what the baby is going through. Parents may imitate babies' expressions and use a moaning voice to say "Oh dear, you are so hungry." However, mere imitation is not sufficient but sensitive parents will encourage babies to gradually calm down by lowering their voice, "There, there, here is some milk for you, don't worry, everything is fine." Parents calm their tense babies by breathing calmly, rocking the baby, smiling, and using many other bodily messages. Both feel relieved when the baby calms down (Gerhardt, 2004). Similar elements can be found between therapist and patient. In the company of anxious patients therapists often instinctively empathise with the patients' mood, may knit their brow, lower their voice, and invite patients to calmer interaction. Simultaneously, the breathing and posture of both become calmer and more relaxed.

The exercise chapter discusses the significance and training of voice and expression on pp. 217–220. There is a listening exercise on p. 196.

Eye contact and visual communication

Facial expressions and eyes are important for the maintenance of existence: "He sees me, therefore I am." From the very beginning, talking face to face is a top emotional experience (Stern, 1985). Even newborn babies prefer watching faces. Therefore, parents and babies spend a lot of time talking face to face, smiling, and making eye contact. People who have just fallen in love become immersed in a similar experience when looking into each other's eyes. When a child sees a smile on the parent's face, he knows that the parent is experiencing pleasure and, in response, his own nervous system tunes up to pleasure. Biochemical changes associated with pleasure promote the growth of the "social brain" creating interneural connections. A positive look and approving interaction remain important promoters of growth and change throughout life (Schore, 1994). A restraining look and saying "no" are also necessary for the safe development of children, while a disapproving or contemptuous look stimulates the secretion of stress hormones (Gerhardt, 2004). This can be felt in breathing, as well: such looks impede breathing. At worst it may feel as if a look could kill.

Mothers look at their babies most of the time, and babies regulate the contact by looking away. Many therapists may recognise the very same thing in their relationships with their patients. Mothers (or therapists) may sometimes find it difficult to respect such an interruption in contact. The mother may be discouraged, interpreting that the baby does not like her, or she may try to force herself into the baby's space by forcing the baby to maintain contact on her conditions. If it is not clear how a look should be interpreted or if the interpretation does not fall anywhere close to the interpreter's internal experience, it may be difficult to express feelings or to respect the other person's expressions of boundaries and space. Boundaries are often unclear and are expressed in a subtle manner, such as in a look. We have found this type of experience rather common in people with breathing disorders. Tense people hold their breath and avoid eye contact, defiant ones breathe fast and stare, "trespassing" into the other person's area. Calm breathing and a soothing, approving look, on the other hand, create potential space and an experience that everything is fine.

> Two of my therapy patients had different ways of making eye contact. One stared unblinking with her big eyes. She often wanted to move her chair so close to me that I could not extend my legs. I felt uncomfortable and noticed that my breathing space grew narrower. When we got to talk about this, it turned out that as a child the patient had not felt entitled to be separate and have her own space.
>
> Another patient looked at me rarely and evasively, usually only taking a quick glance. I believe that he probably saw my silhouette at the periphery of his visual field. However, I noticed that he listened to me carefully. It was extremely hard for this patient to trust anybody. It was hard for him to have the courage to perform breathing exercises because he feared he would need to be in more contact. Exercises were therefore always performed with eyes closed.

Eye contact represents symbolic touching, encountering, respect, and presence. It is a route to compassion and empathy associated with the activity of *mirror neurons* in the brain (Hari & Kujala, 2009). There are several such systems specialised in mirroring emotions. Mirror neurons are visuomotor neurons reacting particularly to visual and acoustic perceptions. They transform reactions as if automatically to motor patterns appropriate for the situation. If implicit interaction works, the activity of mirror neurons facilitates direct identification with the other person and, in this case, no words or other agreed symbols are needed as in verbal communication. We sense in our bodies the other's intentions, movements, way of breathing, and emotions as well as any consequences of these for us. The activity of mirror neurons thus forms the basis for interaction, imitation, empathy, and the creation of images. Early images are largely based on feedback from other people's voices, faces, and body language.

In learning or treatment situations, for example, helpers use their mirroring system to understand the other person's situation (Beebe, Knoblauch, Rustin, & Sorter, 2005). As the relationship is reciprocal, changes in the helper's situation are also reflected in the other party: a strained helper's breathing will change, affecting the patient. A music teacher describes such subtle connection between interaction with his pupil and breathing:

I noticed that my seven-year-old pupil's breathing became laboured during music lessons. I thought I had given him assignments that were too difficult, and after several lessons I wondered what I could do to ease the situation. The lesson was towards the end of the day when I often felt tired. I decided to breathe really calmly, and consciously continued breathing in this calm manner all through the lesson. It was amazing that the pupil's breathing problems ceased during that very lesson and never recurred! Later he also started speaking to me more than before. Children react easily to teachers' expressions, gestures, and touch. I wonder if the pupil in this case felt more relaxed when I was calmer.

The exercise chapter discusses the significance of the direction of the look in the inhalation exercise on p. 225. See also the intimacy-distance exercise on p. 236, chair exercise on p. 237, territory exercise on pp. 238–239, and fighting exercises on pp. 239–240.

Significance of emotions and language for expression

Self-regulation and emotion regulation are essential for health. Emotion regulation means the ability to regulate over- and underexcitement to establish a suitably neutral state with room for self-reflection. Functional regulation of emotions therefore means being prepared to associate reason and knowledge with emotions and bodily sensations and vice versa (Gerhardt, 2004; Goleman, 2006). It also represents the ability to tolerate emotions, to apply and express them flexibly. Emotions are conveyed primarily by non-verbal communication. They are sensed in experiences of rhythm and tempo and felt and observed in ways of breathing (Knoblauch, 2000). This can be heard in the voice, its volume, tone, and melody. It can be observed in the ways of looking, touching, and moving and seen in facial expressions and body positions. If a parent is sufficiently attuned to her child's needs and recognises his emotional states, she can translate the child's non-verbal messages into verbal expressions (Beebe, Knoblauch, Rustin, & Sorter, 2005). This way the child gradually learns to express his feelings verbally and, as he grows, he can learn to apply reason to enable him to see things in proportion. But there is always a physical aspect to the regulation of emotions; even adults cannot calm themselves down solely by using reason or by thinking positively, and it is not possible to calm anyone down by reminding him that it is no use being nervous. It is often more useful to try to breathe calmly.

If a person does not learn to share emotions or speak about issues, some needs will remain unconscious. He will not learn to name his emotions, and others will not be able to read unexpressed thoughts. At the same time, both parties may learn to protect themselves from emotions and be unable to understand them. Only shared experiences provide the ability to understand meanings and to use varied means of expression for self-regulation and self-reflection (Gerhardt, 2004). Nearly everyone has experienced this; we feel better and we can be understood when we get something off our chest that has been bothering us. Learning self-regulation depends on the other person's empathy and reflective skills, his ability to make sufficiently correct observations and interpretations of his own and the other's feelings and situations. Compassion and affection are the main balancing factors here. Through these, parents/therapists can control their anxiety and remain separate in relation to children/patients. This facilitates acceptance of the other even when he is "totally impossible". Still, all parents and therapists know that this is not always easy. It is particularly difficult if the parent or therapist has not had the chance to process her negative feelings constructively. Parents may lose their temper, hiss "Shut up" or tell the child to go to his own room. This way children learn, instead of functional regulation of emotions, to over- or under-regulate their emotions and to protect the parent from the parent's own difficult feelings.

Breathing as a tool for self-regulation, self-expression and self-reflection

Self-regulation is breathing between these poles

Control ——————————————————————————— **Spontaneity**

Living images
Consciousness
Conscious and responsible expression of emotions
Flowing, balanced breathing

Overregulation ——————————————— Underregulation
Social anxiety   Volubility
Inhibition   Boundlessness
Constricted breathing   Accelerated breathing

Fear or shame
Images of badness
Repression or denial of images or emotions
Breaks in breathing and physical symptoms

Reciprocal *over-regulation of emotions* denotes a requirement for yourself and for others not to show emotions. Those concerned may rely on knowledge and reason alone and presume that if they expressed their emotions, they would be rejected. They try to avoid mistakes and do the right thing from the other's point of view. Some (many people with social anxiety, for example) do not show their emotions at all, some (those who try to please) make a distinction between positive and negative emotions. Avoiding the expression of emotions requires making an effort that will insidiously deplete resources; immune activity is also weaker in people who repress their emotions. These people will not seek support but adopt the model of coping alone, which further reduces their chances of coping with stress. They may appear calm. However, difficult emotions will not go away by being repressed. The body therefore remains alert and overexcited and breathing is uneven (Gerhardt, 2004).

If interpersonal interaction is conflicted and easily provokes anxiety, it may lead to unrestricted emotions, that is, *under-regulation of emotions*. Many children under-regulating their emotions tend to experience a fear of being rejected, learn to overemphasise the significance of emotions at the expense of reason, and exaggerate the expression of negative emotions to get attention. They may have parents whose behaviour is difficult to predict and whose expression of emotions is inconsistent. Such parents may at times be upset if the child is needy, clinging, or difficult, making it even less possible for the child to calm down because he gets no help from the parent. Instead of sharing emotions appropriately and making experiences meaningful, feeling bad appears as frightening overexcitement in the body. Calming down is then impossible for both. If the parent shakes the child when furious, the child will not learn to calm himself down (Gerhardt, 2004).

People who under-regulate their emotions may also split between different difficult emotions or those they consider forbidden for themselves. They split shame, anger, and fear from being needy or helpless or needing comforting. They may then express anger even when, inside, they secretly wish to receive compassion. Those who under-regulate their emotions are often very faithful to their own feelings but find it difficult to compromise or take others into consideration. It is difficult for them to transfer or delay satisfaction, and they are therefore easily disappointed.

Under-regulation of emotions is often considered clearly bad behaviour, while over-regulation may be considered civilised. However, it is good to remember that both lead to physiological stimulation activating the sympathetic autonomic nervous system, add to muscle tension, lead to imbalanced breathing, and may with time increase malaise. Processing and regulation of emotions form a whole with the regulation of breathing. If we do not learn how to deal with emotions and images as a child, it is later hard to form a harmonious whole of our own experience, thoughts, images, emotions, and physical sensations. If we do not deal with mental pain, it will be expressed as physical symptoms, in body language.

5.3. Mental obstacles to interaction, self-reflection, and breathing

Problems in interpersonal interaction are reflected in difficulty breathing calmly. Difficulty breathing calmly, on the other hand, affects how we experience a relationship. Imbalanced breathing and ensuing unpleasant physical sensations may be unconsciously experienced as indicating that the relationship is not going as wished, that something is wrong. Space and prospects would be needed to realise what is happening here and now with the other person and to understand the connection of all this with our own experiences. This chapter describes common problems associated either with emotions or with ways of thinking that place obstacles to balanced breathing.

5.3.1. Fear and shame

Early strong and repeated experiences of fear and shame are often associated with the development of breathing problems. During such emotional experiences, balanced breathing is prevented.

Fear

Fear causes the strongest physical sensations and emotional reactions. Most information is processed without crossing the perception threshold. The amygdala in the brain triggers the fight, flight, or freeze reaction (Bourne, 2015; Gerhardt, 2004). For this reason, many experiences of fear are simply part of us and we do not question them even as adults. We instinctively start paying attention to the facial expressions of people around us and looking for hints of whether we are safe or in danger, whether we should fight or take flight. On the other hand, many people say they experience panic in shops and when standing in the queue to the cashier, freezing and not daring to look around at all. We advise them to calm their breathing, to turn their heads calmly and to find other objects of interest apart from stimuli feeding panic, automatic thoughts, or immediately ensuing sensations.

To learn to regulate emotions, it is important for children to experience fears together with the parent or carer, for example when reading fairy tales or checking together that there are no monsters in the cupboard or under the bed. By facing fears together, soothing images can be created and the ability to cope independently with our emotions can develop. The protection built together with the parents thus becomes a part of the developing safe separateness and the ability to cope even in frightening situations. Building a sturdy protective wall against fears may at first seem like a good and functional idea. However, if the protective wall is too thick, it will keep us prisoner of our misunderstandings and prevent us from getting support. Excessive recognition of dangers will not protect against fears, either. Children may be afraid of the dark because they mistakenly consider harmless objects to be monsters. Frightening images are thus intensified. Children who have performed courage exercises with their parents will dare to switch the lights on and see. This will also strengthen the idea that it is permissible to get support and that you can shout for help if you need it. Those who seek support and apply their own courage are lucky because their self-reflective ability will develop to facilitate getting rid of fearful images. Those who hide below the covers and do not even dare to breathe are worst off—they will remain prisoners of their imagination (Borysenko, 1988).

Many adults, too, hide from their fears. The more people get wounded in interaction, the deeper inside they will hide their fears. The fear of getting wounded again will make them take cover. They will repress their feelings, direct their thoughts elsewhere, occupy themselves with other things, and fend off and avoid the issue. Some people are so effective in this that they do not notice their fears or helplessness at all. Their apparent lack of fear and insecurity, their complete self-confidence, may even be considered something worth striving for. However, fears do not disappear if they are pushed aside. Fear will make our body tense and rigid, and we thus create a protective armour around ourselves. Breathing will change, further reinforcing the uncomfortable sensations in the body and in interpersonal interaction. Anxious breathing will reinforce strong feelings of fear, further increasing the need to take cover. The relationship between fear and breathing problems was well described by a breathing school participant in her feedback:

> Due to fear and oppression, I learned as a child already to hold my breath and to be tense. When I was scared, I tried to become invisible so as to avoid becoming the target of mental or physical violence. With time, this bodily reaction became automatic, and even as an adult I react to other people, particularly authorities, with fear and by constricting my breath.

Fear is a central feeling worked on in breathing therapy to make it possible to endure and handle it. We work back and forth on the *safety—fear* axis, alternately reinforcing the feeling of safety and working through fears. Breathing plays a central role in such regulation. Calm breathing and the words "Don't worry, everything is fine" speak to our early experiences of fear. This work recreates the ability to calm down and improves the ability to apply safe images in anxiety-provoking or stressful situations.

**Breathing as a tool for self-regulation,
self-expression and self-reflection**

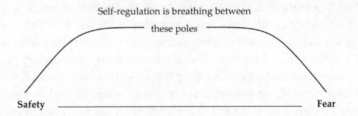

Self-regulation is breathing between
these poles

Safety   Fear

Recognising and accepting positive and negative emotions
Integrating images of good and bad as parts of the whole
Flowing and balanced breathing

Shame

No one can avoid shame, it is a part of life. Shame is important for becoming socialised and recognising boundaries, but it is equally important to recover from shame. To recover, we need support from others and a feeling of being compassionately supported.

Shame is an emotion that can be detected in children as young as three months old. It is a reaction to disappointment and to a lack of approving presence and reciprocity. If the parent does not respond to the baby's attempts at approaching her or approaches the child without the joy of reunion on her face, the baby may start to try and fend for himself and attempt to put on a brave face or, in contrast, turn his face away becoming immobile (Ikonen & Rechardt, 1993; Rochat, 2009; Stone, 1992). Another significant phase in early development is associated with setting limits and saying no. To be able to control her child constructively, the parent should first be able to calm herself down, to feel self-compassion, and to recognise and defend her boundaries, as necessary. Having developed such abilities herself the parent can teach her child to develop the same abilities that are necessary for the regulation of emotions and for reflective ability. All of these skills regulate each other. In other words, if boundaries are set for a child insensitively, without trying to calm the child down and without empathy, the child trying to assert his will may experience himself as bad and shameful. Even later, making mistakes or failure to connect may trigger shame, and this is more likely the more the person has been exposed to experiences of shame and not received support to get over it (Ikonen & Rechardt, 1993).

Reciprocal regulation abilities

Ability to think reflectively
Ability to regulate emotions
Ability to recognise and set boundaries
Ability to be compassionate towards oneself
Ability to soothe oneself

Shame is involved in many ways in the interaction between parents and children but it may be difficult to recognise. Shame is easy to recognise if people humiliate each other or laugh at each other's lack of skills. An attempt to avoid shame may be more difficult to recognise. If boundaries are not set and everything is acceptable, children may go a long way without once hearing the word "no", which would be necessary for good enough parenting. Children will by no means be spared shame if their parents are overly kind, afraid of oppressing, or fail to say no in the name of freedom. Children will then remain alone with their shame because they will not recognise it and therefore cannot process it. This may lead to their growing up into adults without boundaries, incapable of recognising or experiencing healthy, protective shame. People without boundaries will often sooner or later go too far, and they may then fall into a deep experience of shame without any means of tolerating the hard feeling or calming down.

Shame experienced as overpowering will make the person shut his mouth, swallow his words, and wish that the earth would open up and swallow him. This will depress breathing and sever the connection to the right to be, to the person's own feelings and needs. An alternative to inaction is turning against yourself:

> The experience of shame is as if I attacked myself cruelly. In my mind I curse everything I said. At the same time, some other side of me curls up to protect myself. I draw in air, cut it through midway and grunt with pain as if someone had punched me in the stomach. I feel totally awful. I lose my right to my actions and my existence in one go.

A person feeling shame is often not good enough for himself even if he tries to do everything perfectly right. He may perform, avoid spontaneity and self-expression, and imagine that by controlling himself he can avoid repeated experiences of shame. He may therefore withdraw from relationships and live in an enervating state of tension. For some reason, the parents of a person feeling shame were not able to accept him as a child as he was and thus to support his growth. A child observing the needs of his parent learns to be ashamed of being needy. The parent may also project onto the child characteristics that she cannot tolerate in herself.

> It took a long time for me to realise that there was shame behind my panic experiences. I protected myself from the shame and preferred to develop physical anxiety rather than become aware of the shame. I was ashamed for being so difficult. When I was a child, if I acted up, I was told to go into

my room. I learned to be ashamed of expressing negative feelings, and even
as an adult I considered myself bad if I made the mistake of expressing my
dissenting opinion. Now I am learning to understand that I am entitled
to my opinions. And even if someone thinks I am difficult or annoying,
I have the right to that, too.

For some people, it is shameful to have symptoms and to seek help. People with social or panic anxiety are afraid of disclosing their symptoms to others, or they may be ashamed of not even knowing how to breathe. These people have told us in their feedback how significant it was to be received as they were in a group or at an individual visit. "You can just let yourself be" is like coming home to a state of approval, wiping away all conditions and requirements for a moment. In such an environment, it is possible to share the shame, and the immobilising effect of shame can be corrected when you receive empathetic support.

5.3.2. Vicious circle and automatic thoughts

Vicious circle

Emotions, ways of thinking, interpretations, and images affect the functioning of the autonomic nervous system, secretion of stress hormones, and thereby vital functions, such as breathing, heart function, and blood pressure. Relaxing, positive, and empathetic images calm down vital processes. Anxiety laden images may stimulate breathing, and depressing images may make breathing shallower (Bourne, 2015). The reciprocal effects of the body and mind are comprehensive and work both ways: unconscious or conscious changes in breathing may change both physical and mental experiences.

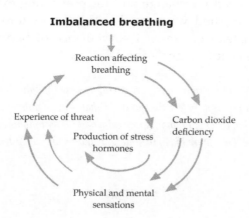

The factor triggering a change in breathing is most often unconscious. In some people, it may be a mental image or an over-whelming or unacceptable situation that provokes anxiety. In others, symptoms may be provoked by physical factors, such as pain, cold, a smell, or an unexplained, worrying somatic symptom. The trig-gering factor may cause a conditioned response affecting breathing. Overbreathing occurs and, furthermore, a chain reaction of other physical and mental sensations intensifying the breathing reaction; this, in turn, leads to a decrease of carbon dioxide. Even mild symp-toms of overbreathing may feel extremely unpleasant and frighten-ing, activating *catastrophic thinking*. People may be afraid of serious disease or believe that they cannot cope with the situation. Nega-tive interpretations add to worry, fear, and anxiety, and this intensi-fies physiological reactions and symptoms of overbreathing. Such learning is often associated with observing and watching one's own sensations with concern, and noticing the slightest changes in them. Finding new evidence supporting their fears accelerates catastrophic thinking, thus completing the self-perpetuating *vicious circle*.

People who tend to worry are not too worried about the present moment but about past events or future challenges. This way they maintain a state of overexcitement and anxiety. This often represents an unconscious attempt to restore a feeling of safety and balance. A worrier who tries to take every possible thing into consideration imagines that then nothing threatening can happen. But we can-not control life, and the effect is often quite the opposite: worry-ing increases symptoms. The vicious circle need not be repeated if we learn to observe our sensations calmly and see them as a sign that there is a need for change and for preventing exhaustion. The approach and method we have developed therefore teaches calm observation instead of worried surveillance of bodily sensations. The difference is quite significant.

> *After the end of a group, one participant reported having just as many somatic symptoms as before the group. "What is quite different is my atti-tude to the sensations. I remain quite calm and the symptoms do not upset me as before. I am more likely to simply wonder about what has happened now."*

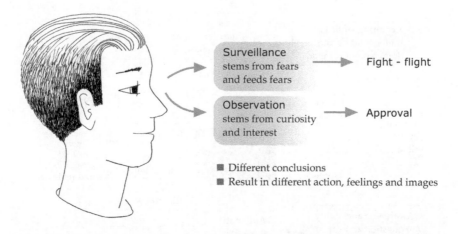

A person may realise that he is in a vicious circle but not be able to find his way out without help. Recognition of fears is the first step towards stopping the constant worrying. It may sometimes help to visualise the situation by drawing the circle on paper. Relief, "This is exactly how I experience it", may be the immediate reaction. Visualisation of the vicious circle may provide an opportunity for a new kind of assessment: "Looking at the situation afterwards, does anything come to mind that you could do to help yourself?" Hindsight can be applied to help the person to learn something new. Solutions are generally easier to find if we can visualise the situation more clearly and distance ourselves from it. We can find our way out of the circle through soothing breathing, calming internal speech, or new kinds of approaches and new ways of acting. In people who have unpleasant symptoms, the immediate urge may be contrary to what will really help. For example, the vicious circle of overbreathing needs to be broken, contrary to what panicking people feel. They may feel that they cannot get enough air. This makes them gasp for more, and this, in turn, will aggravate the symptoms. To break the circle, they should concentrate on exhaling calmly and try to find the pause after exhaling. People may sometimes unconsciously already have found ways of calming themselves down or alleviating their symptoms. It is important to reinforce their own, natural ability for finding relief.

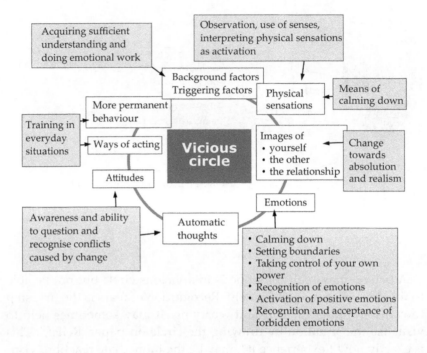

Automatic thoughts

To outsiders, what goes on in an anxious person's mind may sound unreasonable. Anxious people often believe that their thoughts always represent the truth. They increasingly refer to the products of their own mind without questioning or examining them curiously. Their self-reflective abilities are deficient. *Automatic thoughts* are the immediate flow of thought on the conscious and preconscious levels. They affect emotions and moods even if people are not completely aware of them. If people do not sufficiently question their thoughts or if they do not discuss with others thoughts arising in the vacuum of their mind, and receive feedback, automatic thoughts carry a high risk of distortion.

Automatic thoughts are typically concise, in telegram style—"I must" or "I cannot". Short as they are, these expressions involve an immense amount of emotion or associations with fear and panic, for example. Associations arise quickly, with no time for questioning. It is difficult to assess the truth of thoughts if you accept them at face value. The most detrimental characteristic of such thoughts is that they are experienced as absolutely true. To relax our thoughts, we can slow down our activity or apply various timeout methods: "Stop, think, breathe—before you act or judge yourself."

Imbalanced breathing

What am I thinking? *Automatic thoughts arise*	What am I feeling? *Anxiety and depression are* *activated*	What is happening in my body? *A stress reaction is activated and the* *conflict is expressed physically*
<ul><li>should</li><li>need to</li><li>have to</li><li>is necessary</li><li>must</li><li>I'm not good enough</li><li>I'm behaving wrong</li><li>I'm no good</li><li>I'm a failure</li><li>It's awful</li><li>It's terrible</li></ul>= blaming oneself or someone else	<ul><li>guilt</li><li>shame</li><li>helplessness</li><li>worthlessness</li><li>anger and defiance</li><li>fear</li><li>shock</li><li>panic</li><li>despair</li><li>depression</li><li>emptiness</li><li>stagnation</li></ul>	<ul><li>increased control</li><li>being on guard</li><li>muscle tension</li><li>reduced breathing capacity</li><li>fight/flight/freezing</li><li>numerous physical symptoms and sensations</li><li>working with clenched teeth</li><li>problems falling or staying asleep</li><li>passiveness and lack of strength associated with depression</li></ul>

Denial as a coping method

- no mental images *- negative or unrealistic* * thoughts*	*- no connection with one's* * feelings*	*- no recognition of bodily warning* * signs, body trying to cope alone -* * and falls ill*

Balanced breathing

| I recognise what I want
and do not want

I may think:
It is<ul><li>sad</li><li>unfortunate</li><li>regrettable</li></ul>It would be<ul><li>nicer</li><li>better</li><li>desirable</li><li>possible</li></ul>I forgive myself and
others. | <ul><li>allowing disappointment</li><li>recognising feelings of sadness</li><li>compassion and empathy towards oneself and others</li><li>self-confidence</li><li>awareness of one's own boundaries and of being separate</li><li>softness</li><li>optimism</li><li>being unreserved</li><li>being alive</li><li>joy</li><li>energy and power</li></ul> | <ul><li>deepening and facilitation of breathing</li><li>calming down and relaxation</li><li>experience of being alive and of flow in the body</li><li>tolerance and moderation</li><li>increased strength</li><li>approval of change</li><li>experience of being capable</li><li>experience of usefulness of the body</li><li>strengthening of boundaries</li><li>space and permission to be as you are</li></ul> |

In psychophysical breathing therapy, the table of automatic thoughts has been useful for visualising the connection between mind and body. People are often relieved to recognise themselves there. It gives a basic introduction to the workings of the mind.

We believe that automatic thoughts represent only the surface of the workings of the mind, like the tip of an iceberg. They are the result of other automatic processes rather than the actual reason for any symptoms. They are preceded by even less conscious generalised images of the self and others, etched into the mind. The image of another person looking at you with contempt may lead to your thinking, "I am no good." Images, on the other hand, are preceded by automatic alarm reactions programmed into the body in early relationships. This means that even before experiencing the feeling of being an object of contempt, the body reacts and breathing may be affected. Therefore, problems cannot be solved simply by concentrating on changing thinking. More comprehensive work is needed to reach and rearrange unconscious bodily experiences and images.

5.4. Mindful presence in a breathing therapy relationship

People working in helping professions often have plenty of clinical experience and knowledge of theories of well-being. However, they rarely have much knowledge of the experiences and histories of their patients. Only through getting to know their patients can they find a common wavelength and insight into the meaning of their patients' problems. The helper and the patient will study and observe together the symptoms and experiences, trying to visualise the underlying factors.

It is good to realise the significance of transference and countertransference in a therapeutic relationship. Transference is when we maintain what was learned previously, repeating it and redirecting it into a new relationship. Countertransference refers to the counterfeelings activated in the other person as a result of the transference. Transference is a natural and necessary form of learning and acting. It happens in relationships, with friends, between teacher and student, superior and subordinate, doctor or therapist and patient—that is, everywhere where people are in close emotional contact. The familiar role that we seek in the other is thus a part of our own personality structure. Mistaken predictions usually change and become modified as we get feedback and further information. Rigid, "cemented" attitudes and experiences associated with implicit memory that we cannot examine consciously are most problematic. They are "true" for the individual. The often problematic ways of breathing represent such locked and unconscious ways that are easily activated in any new situation and sometimes transferred in interaction to form a part of the other person's counterfeelings.

> *I was talking with a patient who appeared to be in a good mood. Suddenly I felt as if someone had punched me in the stomach. My diaphragm became tense, breathing became superficial, and I noticed that I became reserved. I observed this, awaiting with interest what would happen next. The direction of the discussion suddenly changed, and a moment later the patient was mad because in our last session I had posed a question related to his childhood, which he did not want to discuss. It is interesting how my body foresaw the topic and the change in the patient's mood. I was also left wondering whether by my previous question I had touched on something very painful. This later turned out to be so.*

Many forms of treatment and therapy utilise the transference phenomenon in helping the patient to learn new things. The interaction between helper and patient brings to light phenomena related to the patient's early experiences in relationships. This provides the helper with useful information about what the patient has not been capable of telling and with which he has no self-reflective relationship yet. However, we should remember that a therapeutic relationship is not affected only by the patient's but also by the helper's experiences. A therapeutic relationship is therefore always individual and unique. It is important for the helper to be sufficiently familiar with her own emotional reactions and their background, as well as with the connection between the mind and physical reactions. When working with people, it is imperative to accept the fact that work will expose you to experiences and emotions that are by no means always pleasant. Recognising your own emotions, ways of reacting, and historical experiences is important for being able to approach situations arising with patients non-defensively and to examine them with the necessary openness.

Common pitfalls in helping work and work with breathing

- **Wanting to understand too soon.** The helper "knows" what the problem is. She teaches the patient to learn the "correct" way of breathing to eliminate his problems. If the helper talks about mental experiences and interprets breathing too soon, she may bring about resistance to change

- **Rushing to do things.** The helper comforts, gives advice, takes sides or "lectures" about the correct way of breathing instead of listening calmly
- **Interrupting the topic.** The helper interrupts the patient's flow of speech, does not understand how the patient's mind moves, does not hear the patient's internal dialogue. Describing the other person's mode of speech always affects his way of breathing
- **Interest in external events.** The helper becomes interested in details and events without hearing what moods the story arouses. The helper pays attention to the patient's use of respiratory muscles without listening to how he experiences his breathing
- **Withdrawal.** The helper does not give feedback on what she has heard and understood. Appropriate information on breathing and its disturbances will calm the patient down and alleviate his fear
- **Accepting the "invitation to dance" and reacting.** The helper reacts and is provoked, taking a role maintaining negative images offered by the patient instead of recognising what is happening and utilising it.

A disruption in the relationship may occur if the helper sticks tightly to her methods and does not yield to the patient's needs. A helper sitting quietly may listen actively but may not express her thoughts or emotions sufficiently for the patient. The patient may experience the helper's non-verbal messages as inexpressive. If empathy does not come across to the patient, his mirror cells will be "frightened". This may bear out the old model of being left alone and the experience of having no support. On the other hand, a helper who actively takes sides and invades the patient's space through non-verbal communication may confirm his experience of how impossible it is to guard his boundaries. The patient may feel that his own thoughts are not sufficient. Someone else will always know more, be more creative, wiser, and better. Different patients need encountering differently, and helpers should be sufficiently flexible for this.

In the parent–child relationship, the adult has greater responsibility for fixing any disruption in interaction; in a therapeutic relationship naturally the helper. Development in either role is not always easy: we may need to be confronted with our own incapability. But the ability to learn from mistakes is one of our most valuable resources. There is no need to be a perfect parent or helper, sufficiently good is enough. It is challenging to accept the other person's right to be different, to have different opinions, different ways of life, and different values. An equal relationship tolerating difference and respecting separateness will help both parties to become stronger. The helper is at best just an assistant, the patient being the best expert on his own situation.

When working with breathing and physical experiences, early experiences can often be observed flickering on the screen. This can be the way a person speaks about himself or about others or the way he encounters the helper, or his way of protecting himself by changing his breathing or other non-verbal expression. To be able to understand one another, we unconsciously try to synchronise our mental and physical rhythms. By tuning herself to listen to any messages from her own body the helper will get information on the patient's situation or experiences and may find the way to the patient's emotional experiences. At best, the helper's physical responses will faithfully reflect the patient's emotions, even unconscious ones.

It is important for the helper to give the patient space and to trust his abilities. This is the essential change that takes place in professionals who have received breathing school training: they often report improvement in their ability to give space. However, giving space does not mean being silent or leaving patients alone in their learning process because patients may often be unable to find their way to new types of resources. Correctly timed information and guidance will calm patients down and reinforce their feeling of being heard. Being listened to attentively by someone else will activate not only conscious thinking and acting but also a comprehensive experience derived from the basic mental matrix. To grasp the experience we must concentrate on listening; that way we can discover the atmosphere behind the words and its effects.

In a good enough relationship, the helper will neither demand dependence on herself nor push the patient to become independent or to proceed too quickly. Considerately listening to the patient's rhythm, the helper will observe, express empathy appropriately, and try to create a calm and safe atmosphere. Empathy involves listening, sensitivity, and receiving and accepting the most painful and shameful experiences. The therapist needs to tune in comprehensively—not just listen but receive with her whole body.

In a helping relationship, the two parties should allow the development of sufficient synchrony, that is, fluent non-verbal interaction. A good interactive relationship can thus be compared to the experience of flow. It is mental breathing between two people. The entirety of gestures, positions, eye contact, tone of voice, breathing, speech rhythm, and touch is essential for the compatibility of interaction. If there is sufficient compatibility and "breathing" between the two, non-verbal messages will continue in harmony even if there are pauses in the conversation or if the two sometimes talk at the same time. Thus, the aim is not to have faultless interaction. The experience of synchrony rather reflects a non-verbal agreement between the two of maintaining contact.

The synchronisation of rhythms aimed for can also be seen in the physiological reactions of the partners. In an experimental trial set-up (McFarland, 2001), it was found that during conversation the breathing rhythms of friends tended to conform to each other. The listener's breathing rhythm conformed to the speaker's rhythm, and the more synchrony in breathing was complete, the closer to the switch of speaking turns they came. The similar breathing rhythm between participants in a conversation may also be seen when, for example, they burst out laughing at the same time. Everyone is surely familiar with such experiences from everyday life. We believe this information is useful for utilising breathing in therapy even if no actual breathing exercises are used. By breathing calmly yourself you can invite the patient's breathing to calm down. Many people do this naturally, by slowing down their speech rhythm, lowering their voice, and thus inviting the anxious or agitated person to calm down.

Steven Knoblauch (2000), a psychoanalyst and musician, describes the similarity of music and a therapeutic relationship when speaking about the synchronisation of interaction: good interaction is like improvisation by a skilled jazz band. Phenomena associated with correct timing and synchronisation can also be seen in nature, in the seasonal variation, waves in the ocean, heartbeat, cell function, and movement of atoms, molecules, and electrons. Poetry, dance, play, games, rhymes, and many other forms of expression are also based on rhythm. Rhythm and flow are central elements of breathing. The flowing, incessant breathing maintains the rhythm and, in a natural way, the experience of well-being.

In a genuine encounter between therapist and patient, the boundary between them yields but still remains. Healing and increasing well-being require an encounter and mindful presence; only in this way can people provide each other with true meaning. It is important for the helper to be able to be herself in her relationship with her patient, not just a person working in her professional role. The patient is able to exist only when the helper can genuinely identify with the patient's needs. It is also essential for recovery for the patient to realise that the helper is another person, not just "somebody". Patients often use impersonal language for a long time: "It is good to have someone listening." A genuine relationship is created when the patient confesses: "It is important for me to tell precisely you about this" (Buber, 1971).

Concepts related to psychophysical breathing therapy, and their association with breathing

Concept	Explanation	Association with breathing
Body memory	Implicit, preconscious conditioning of body reactions	Various breathing patterns also represent remembering
Implicit communication	Wordless communication through rythms, touch, looking, facial expression, posture and tone of voice	We also communicate through breathing rhythm and patterns
Body image	Image of one's own or someone else's body, bodily functions and breathing	The type of image affects breathing patterns
Object relations	Mental representation of relationship to another person	The mental representation and the type of relationship affect breathing patterns
Internal child	Image of oneself as a child or of the child in oneself now	The quality of the image affects breathing patterns
The soothing other	Image, memory or real person experienced as safe	A calm and neutral image of the other person calms down breathing
Potential space	Image of space in one's own mind and between oneself and the other	The image of breathing space and living space affects breathing
Good enough	Permissive image of oneself or of another one	Associated with calm, balanced breathing patterns
Self-compassion	Compassionate image of oneself and outlook on oneself	A compasssionate and calm attitude affects the breathing pattern
Transitional object	An item, issue or thought reminding of a soothing other	A breathing exercise may form a transitional object and thus calm and improve the patient-therapist relationship
True self	Experience of the true self (vs. false self)	Related to the ability to regulate breathing to become more balanced
Transference and countertransference	Redirection of experience from emotional interaction to another relationship, the other person's counteremotion to it	The patient's unconscious emotion/purpose may be visible/felt in the therapist's breathing

CHAPTER SIX

Mental breathing

Minna Martin, Maila Seppä, Matti Keinänen

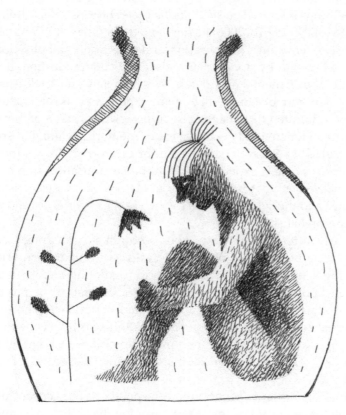

You?
I can taste the word in my mouth when saying it.
Smiles light up our faces.

Breathing reflects the state of the body, but also our inner mood and our current situation in life. Breathing puts us in touch with some aspects of our heritage and interactional history. Through physiological mechanisms, breathing patterns have a comprehensive effect on health. They also modify our posture, structure, and presence. Psychophysical breathing therapy can help to alleviate mental and physical problems caused by imbalanced breathing. In this chapter, we would like to consider further some of the ideas presented in this book in terms of the concept of mental breathing.

The ideas of psychiatrist and psychotherapy trainer Matti Keinänen have contributed to strengthening the theoretical basis of psychophysical breathing therapy. The *symbolisation-reflectiveness model* (Keinänen, 1997, 1999, 2000, 2001b, 2006) he developed is a unit combining physiology, early interaction, symbolisation, and reflection. Symbolisation, that is, self-expression by non-verbal and verbal communication, helps to *bind* and modify mental experience. When anxiety and restlessness are presented in symbolic form, they can be experienced as understandable and communicated to someone else, if necessary, instead of remaining as undifferentiated bodily experiences or memories waiting to erupt. If unstructured chaotic experiences recur or are overwhelming, they may later appear as panic experiences, fear of disorganisation, or emotional lability. *Reflection*, that is, the ability to observe and assess sensations, emotions, and thoughts, helps us to analyse the experiences and makes them comprehensible.

In early interaction that is good enough an integrated continuum gradually develops between physical and mental experiences. Breathing acts there as a mediating and regulating factor—a bridge between body and mind. *Mental mobility* consisting of the physiological state, undifferentiated emotional experiences, non-verbal and verbal experiencing, and perceptual ability is here called mental breathing (Keinänen, 2006). Such mental mobility or mental breathing can be considered a prerequisite for and expression of mental health.

Mental breathing as a concept corresponds to the concept of *mentalisation* (Bateman & Fonagy, 2006), meaning the ability to be aware of your own and other people's mental states, for example, desires, emotions, or thoughts. There are two types of mentalisation, implicit and explicit. Implicit mentalisation is basically unconscious, non-verbal, and not reflected upon. Mirroring of the other person's feelings in emotionally significant interaction and being in touch with the other person's emotions through one's physical reactions are examples of this. Explicit mentalisation, on the other hand, is conscious, verbal, and reflected upon. It can be used to interpret information obtained on the other person by implicit mentalisation. Observations about the other person's (and one's own) mind are thus basically physical. When parents mirror their children's emotions in their own bodies, they are simultaneously in contact with both themselves and their children. Implicit mentalisation in a child may therefore also involve a verbal, interpreting view. Mental breathing, that is, continuity between physical, implicit mentalisation and interpreting, explicit mentalisation, occurs in such interaction. In psychophysical breathing therapy, interaction between instructor and group (therapist and patient) follows the same principles. We believe that understanding one's own and other people's feelings is based on listening with a keen ear to physical reactions and, particularly, to breathing.

Levels of experience and expression formed through symbolisation-reflectiveness

1. Undifferentiated physiological and emotional experiences, non-verbal communication
2. Non-verbal mental experiencing, visual communication, in particular
3. Experience and communication based on conventional—for example, linguistic—symbols
4. Reflective ability, that is, observation, assessment, and expression of experiences
5. Mental breathing, that is, mental mobility between the above levels and in association with another person.

During development, each level builds on the previous ones, and none of the previous ones is lost. The mutual breathing between these levels creates the ability to soothe and express oneself both with and without words.

(Keinänen, 1997, 1999, 2000, 2001b, 2006; Keinänen & Martin, 2011)

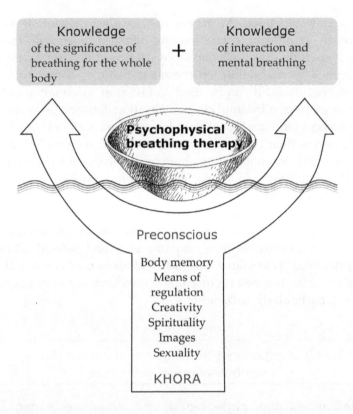

We will now look at each of the above levels considering the signifi-cance of breathing as a regulatory mechanism. At the end of the chapter there is a summarising table.

6.1. Undifferentiated bodily and emotional experiences and breathing

The earliest experiences of self and other are undifferentiated (Keinänen, 2006; Keinänen & Martin, 2011). This means that information on the internal and external worlds that is conveyed by the senses is experi-enced holistically instead of being able to examine specifically "what I see" or "what I smell". Babies receive information about themselves through the proprioceptive sensing of stimuli arising within the body, and about the external world through vision, hearing, touch, taste, and smell (Spitz, 1965). The joint (conesthetic) "sixth sense" integrates the sensations. When such sensing recurs, it creates the first permanent signs, or undifferentiated memories, of subjective experiences. To create good enough undifferentiated memories, the unconscious and conscious mind of an emotionally significant other (parent) is needed. The parent interprets and gives words to the child's early needs expressed non-verbally. By responding appropriately to such needs the parent creates the basic prerequisites for the child's *basic mental matrix* (Lehtonen et al., 2006), and thus for experiences of satisfaction and pleasure. Through early interaction and recurrent experiences of being nurtured, the baby gradually develops the ability to make more specific distinctions between emotional observations of himself and others. This is how he obtains information on the internal and external realities (Keinänen, 2001a, 2006).

It is typical for people suffering from imbalanced breathing that they have not been able to learn sufficiently well to differentiate between their sensations in interaction with others. Instead, they trust and cling to the other person, try to adapt to the expectations of others, and sense such expectations more readily than their own feelings. The apparent feeling of safety is bound to fulfilling the wishes of others. Their own wishes and boundaries cannot be clarified through such interaction, and being separate therefore becomes frightening. Fears begin to regulate their existence increasingly, and alertness, the fight or flight reaction being easily activated, becomes the prevailing physical state. They are thus exposed to stress, and in stressful situations they may, for example, breathe with their accessory respiratory muscles or use the diaphragm to breathe incessantly in and out and in and out. Simply being is not enough for them but they need to redeem the licence to exist by doing. Even relaxation becomes something that has to be "performed" if letting themselves be supported by another person or by gravity feels frightening or strange. Supporting oneself often manifests as inappropriate muscle tension and the use of accessory respiratory muscles.

In psychophysical breathing therapy, participants are told that they are allowed to be as they are. The therapist's calm breathing rhythm supports the permission to just be. Calm use of the voice and pauses in breathing also communicate this. In the beginning, the encouragement of an approving presence is more significant than teaching actual ways of breathing. Participants become able to relinquish the need to perform and find space for wondering at and listening to what is happening in their own body, for appreciating their own physical sensations.

Through the experience of existence and through breathing exercises it is possible to contact the basic mental matrix of the undifferentiated mind.

Tasks of the basic mental matrix
• To create unity with the world of experience • To create and maintain a sensation of being alive • To create a connection between various body parts and between mental and physical functions • To create a basis for the creation of images. (Lehtonen et al., 2006)

In addition, this develops the ability to experience satisfaction, calm down, become excited, maintain a day and night rhythm, and tune into moods and tones in interaction with others.

6.2. Non-verbal experience, expression, and breathing

In physical breathing, breath flows in and out. Similarly, in the mind a metaphoric "inhalation and exhalation" occurs between the self and others. In early interaction, the rhythmic compatibility between the child's needs and the parent's response, and the associated feelings of satisfaction and pleasure occupy a central position. Early undifferentiated experiences are stored as physical ways of reacting and experiencing but also as images. The mirror neuron system (Hari & Kujala, 2009) specialised in experiences of watching and hearing is at an early stage tuned in to receiving such experiences and creating equivalent images in the self. Some images can later be recognised and expressed in words, some are stored in the unconscious. Mental images thus form the first differentiated symbols (Keinänen, 1997, 1999, 2000, 2006). Early differentiated images of the self and the parent (object relation) are in essence sensation-based body images. At this developmental stage, children are not yet capable of assessing others' moods and they have no words for emotions even though they can receive information on others' moods through non-verbal communication.

In a breathing relationship, the child's images of himself and others can be differentiated. A child "inhales" images of how he feels his mother encounters him. If he feels that the mother understands him, totally good, loving images of the mother and the self are created. The child then metaphorically inhales from the atmosphere of the relationship the safety, approval, and tenderness of the mother. He utilises this for growth and reflects it back by his loving existence.

It is important for differentiation that alongside good experiences and images other types of experiences creating opposite, "bad" images can occur. As no mother is in reality perfectly good, disappointment and frustration create images of a "bad mother" and equivalent images of the child's self. Bad metaphoric images are created to guard the good image: images of witches, stepmothers, and dragons breathing fire give children permission to have negative emotions. It is more tolerable for children to place badness in the hands of a metaphoric figure than to experience the nurturer as bad. Reading fairy tales, stories, and poems thus enriches the world of images and helps to bind anxiety. This strengthens the child's ability to handle separation anxiety and other forms of anxiety. Later on, he develops the ability to integrate the images of good and bad. He becomes capable of accepting imperfection as a part of his own and other people's basic aspects.

At later stages in life, too, people often need help to accept "badness" as a part of themselves. Way into middle age, many people remain prisoners of their excessive kindness. They dare not disagree or make others feel bad. Encouraged by a therapist, they may be able to recognise sides in themselves such as opposition or a need to set boundaries. In a patient's words: "I now dare be a bitch every now and then."

Integration of good and bad

- The mother's/therapist's understanding attitude to the child's/patient's disappointment, anger, frustration
- Empathetic description, understanding, sharing
- Ability to bind bad and good mental images (icons) in an integrated experience
- "Bad" is thus transformed into an operating force, power, and energy
- Based on these, a reflective-integrative ability is established leading to the creation of stable ideas, regardless of mood, of oneself and others.

(Keinänen, 2006; Keinänen & Martin, 2011)

It is typical for our patients with imbalanced breathing to have developed strong denial mechanisms to prevent images and emotions from becoming conscious. On the other hand, no images or emotions may have been created in the first place. We have often heard participants say "How should it feel?", "What kind of an image would be correct?", or "I don't know what an image is". Repressing, forgetting, or denying dreams belongs to the same group of phenomena. As if dreams had nothing to do with the internal world or the person's own experiences. Non-judgmental contemplation of the rich imagery in dreams and images, and taking it into consideration, are ways that can be used by anyone to create symbolic tools, to reinforce such tools, and thus to understand and be healed. Instead of concerning themselves with rich imagery, people with breathing symptoms are more familiar with doing, keeping busy, and concrete activities, whether in the form of conscientious diligence at work or passionate physical exercising.

Mental images are among the most significant means of accomplishing change in psychophysical breathing therapy. If a patient has no images, it is particularly important to create, revive, and enrich them by diverse means. The patient may at first find this weird and strange. Instead of giving concrete advice or speaking about symptoms, we may ask them to draw images of themselves or their symptoms, use ready-made pictures or cards to express experiences, listen to fairy tales describing metaphorically common unconscious experiences, imagine, and play with breathing. In psychophysical breathing therapy, all being and doing is associated with the use of images and metaphors. They are used to enliven the experience of the patient's own body and to reinforce boundaries. The pause after exhaling clears the space for the chance to hear images arising in oneself. It often takes some time for patients to start realising that recognising and using images will help them to calm down and to understand themselves in a dynamic way. When a breathing exercise performed in therapeutic contact touches patients, it revives their feeling and experiencing minds holistically.

For her 1995 licentiate thesis entitled *Ahdistuksen psykosomatiikka* (Psychosomatic Aspects of Anxiety; only available in Finnish) Päivi Lehtinen studied the efficacy of breathing school. One of her results was that in a large proportion of patients, the world of images opened up in a new way. During participation in the group they had achieved significant contact with their repressed feelings and thoughts.

Utilising and reflecting on visual and physical images in therapy
• Attention is directed to physical experiences and the world inside the mind, and these experiences are reflected on • Music is used as a guide on this journey • Images such as body image, symptoms, or other images are drawn/painted • Participants convey information about themselves with the help of cards, items, stones, or other metaphoric symbols • A drawing that is made or a card that is chosen reflects the second position in a description of reciprocal object relation. We can discuss, draw, or choose a card to complete the reciprocal setting, the image of the other • Verbal metaphors, poems, and stories provide words for unconscious or preconscious emotions • The therapy room arouses images of safety, thus promoting the development and internalisation of a feeling of safety • Transitional objects during and at the end of therapy promote an increased feeling of safety.
Change begins with being able to imagine acting differently, but not yet trying to do so. Realisation occurs in the space created by images, not in rushing to do things.

6.3. Experience based on conventional symbols and breathing

The ability to verbalise emotions and share experiences verbally develops in good enough early interaction (Keinänen, 2006; Keinänen & Martin, 2011). Facial expressions, gestures, postures, other physical signs and expressions, as well as experiences during emotions create the basis for such symbolic experience and expression. This promotes the ability to understand one's own and other people's experiences and emotions through language. Enjoyment of arts is also often based on shared symbolic language. Breathing is provided with space to flow freely, and live breathing and its delicate regulation are able to function.

Undifferentiated affects may create a state of turmoil with adverse and often alarming physical sensations. To be able to understand our experiences, we need a form and a symbol for the experience and expression. If emotional energy is not tied to symbols (such as images or words) or if it is poorly developed, under- or over-regulation of emotions will occur. This will affect physiological regulation through muscle tension and breathing, for example. Breathing thus has a central regulatory task in the experience and expression of emotions. If mental breathing is disturbed, pauses in breathing and swallowing occur, and the respiratory capacity becomes superficial and restricted. As physical tension increases, mental anxiety is activated, further aggravating imbalanced breathing with its various symptoms.

In psychophysical breathing therapy space is created for experiences and emotions as they appear. They are given permission to be, named, and shared in interaction. In group therapy, identification with joint experiences and emotions is important for learning new things. The therapist describes to the group what she hears, sees, and understands. She also pays attention to what counter-emotions and thoughts the group arouses in her. She uses all this information to help her guide the group. Calmer and more realistic emotional experiences gradually arise in the group parallel to the original emotional experiences possibly feeding anxiety, shame, and unrealistic conclusions. Exposure exercises alone do not usually help if safety and help in regulation are not offered by the therapist.

6.4. Reflective ability and breathing

Reflective ability means the ability to examine what is happening in the mind and body and what we are experiencing (Keinänen, 2006; Keinänen & Martin, 2011). It is precisely reflective ability helping us to observe our own and other people's desires, wishes, feelings, and thoughts that is central for the ability to mentalise. Reflective ability thus means the ability to examine connections between various forms of experience and to compare our own experiences to another person's world of experiences. It creates a feeling of integrity, separateness, and being alive, as well as a trust in our own body and breathing and in the ability to cope with ourselves and others (Keinänen, 2003, 2015). When breathing becomes more difficult, it means that we may become conscious of what the anxiety may be associated with. "What is happening? What is happening in my body? What am I feeling? What comes to mind?" A reciprocal, soothing relationship with oneself (internal adult) is then applied as a means of self-regulation. This makes it possible to calm down one's breathing and mind and to know how to reinforce reality. "In spite of everything, I can still breathe" is an experience representing a functional self-reflective ability. Such a basic experience is associated with the ability to think insightfully, that is, to have *inspiration*, that appropriately describes the association between breathing and interaction. The Latin verb *inspirare* means to "breathe something into, arouse something in someone" (Keinänen, 2006; Keinänen & Engblom, 2007).

If such listening ability is lacking and we do not know what is happening in ourselves, experiences of anxiety and tension and associated experiences of pain will prevail. This is often associated with the experience that emotions have no essence bound to words or that they are experienced as frightening or anxiety provoking. If so, we are unable to wonder, soothe, understand, or apply the knowledge of what is happening in ourselves as anxiety increases. When the "inner child" panics, symptoms associated with imbalanced breathing are experienced as threatening and, at worst, fear of death may be activated.

The self-reflective ability may be revived and reinforced in a trustful relationship, such as in psychophysical breathing therapy. A sufficiently long therapeutic relationship is needed to gradually develop the client's/patient's reflective ability if it is very much deficient due to severely traumatic experiences in childhood, for example.

- Reflective ability acts as mental breathing integrating experiences from various levels
- This creates a bridge, an unbroken continuum from sensation to thought and vice versa
- Images, dreams, fairy tales, and creative activity, as well as a breathing relationship, act as a bridge from the unconscious to the conscious.

(Keinänen, 2015; Keinänen & Martin, 2011)

As the ability to reflect on ourselves and others develops, a separate consciousness, that is, sense of reality, is reinforced. Sensations are crucially important for the development of the sense of reality: I experience my body and recognise my breathing, therefore I exist. The development of a reflective ability joining and assessing images including various emotions signifies the gradual formation of stable attitudes lasting throughout life (Keinänen, 2003, 2015; Keinänen & Martin, 2011). The development of such an ability requires a breathing interactive relationship: providing space, being present, and listening to the other person activate the conscious mind, but also a comprehensive emotion arising from the basic mental matrix and helping to recognise the individual emotional tone of interaction. It is therefore characteristic of stable experiencing to have a permanent image of the self and others regardless of moods. If one cannot develop vital mental breathing in a relationship that is good enough, mental mobility will be repressed. Panic disorder with its physical expressions and emotional instability are examples of disorders of mental breathing.

6.5. Mental breathing table

We have compiled a table summarising thoughts on mental breathing and its application in psychophysical breathing therapy. The table is divided into four parts, each on a separate page, and each page can be examined from the bottom upwards or from the top downwards. This provides an understanding of the development of experiences and expressive ability and connections between various levels of experience. We suggest also examining the table "sideways", that is, comparing each level to equivalent levels on the other pages.

The first page summarises the thoughts on the symbolisation-reflectiveness model. The second page shows how imbalanced breathing may present as disorders on various levels of experience. The third page shows how problems on various levels and, thus, the development of self-reflection can be influenced by means of psychophysical breathing therapy. The fourth page summarises the thoughts on operationalisation of the concept of mental breathing. This page is useful for readers who wish to examine these phenomena more closely in their clinical work.

Mental breathing—mental mobility

4. Reflective-integrative experience / reciprocal communication
Ability to mentalise, meaning the ability of being aware of your own and other people's mental states, for example, desires, emotions or thoughts
Ability to understand one's own and another person's experiences
Ability to understand connections between one's own and another person's levels of experience
Ability to move flexibly between various levels of experience

3. Experience and communication based on conventional (e.g. linguistic) symbols
Learning words for emotions, and learning other concepts based on physical experiences
Learning in interaction to understand and use words expressing needs, desires, and wishes, and expressions related to boundaries, such as "yes" and "no"

2. Mental images, nonverbal communication
Early experiences are stored as images of oneself and the nurturing other obtained through the senses and bound to experiences of interaction.

Child	Nurturer
• Totally good/bad images are created. Some images are repressed to the unconscious.	• The nurturer empathically understands the child's development/state.
• Metaphoric images of the bad in fairy tales bind bad experiences of the nurturer/oneself. They thus develop to guard what is good.	• The good (parental affection) regulates bad experiences of them both (uncontrolled eruption of negative emotions).
	• The parent's own experiences of the bad help him to empathise with the child's experience.

1. Undifferentiated physiological sensations and experienced affects, conesthetic communication
Nonverbal interaction between parent and child creates the first physically experienced affects and the undifferentiated basis for the workings of the mind.

The child senses:	The child's experience becomes understandable if the nurturer observes and is capable of
• sees	
• hears	• seeing the child as he is
• feels	• intuitively hearing the nonverbal message
• tastes	• understanding through touch
• smells	• appreciating what the child prefers
• senses with his proprioceptive sense	• harmonising with the child through implicit communication
Experiences are joined by	• adapting and differentiating her rhythm intuitively to what is suitable for the child
• a conesthetic mutual sense	• encouraging the child to make contact

The ability to synchronise breathing rhythms is written in our heritage but we learn mental breathing in early interaction.

Imbalanced breathing

4. Reflective-integrative experience / reciprocal communication
Is not capable of breathing calmly or thinking clearly due to strong and
unclear emotions.
Has no self-reflective ability or ability to reflect on another person or is not
capable of applying the ability.
Is not used to sharing difficult or intimate issues or emotions.

**3. Experience and communication based on conventional (e.g. linguistic)
symbols**
Few or no words for emotions or images
Pauses in breathing, swallowing, rapid/narrow/superficial/pumping
breathing
Imbalanced use of respiratory muscles and muscle tension in various parts
of the body
Flexible dynamism of the spine disturbed, immobile pelvic area

2. Mental images, nonverbal communication
No images or repressed, weird or frightening images
"If I try to listen to my breathing, I get anxious."
"How should breathing feel?"
"What is an image?" / "I have no imagination."
"What do images have to do with my problem?"
"I need advice on how to get rid of my symptoms."
"When will we do actual breathing exercises?"
Wants to learn correct breathing.
Doing is familiar, just being is impossible.
Safety = conforming to others' needs and wishes.

**1. Undifferentiated physiological sensations and experienced affects,
conesthetic communication**
Complete adjustment or maladjustment to external or internal expectations
and requirements
Symptoms appearing as muscle tension or disturbed blood acid-base
balance
Regulation of difficult experiences by physical breathing
No reliance on one's own senses or clinging to guarding them
Just being is insufficient or impossible
Giving way to gravity (relaxation) impossible
Preparedness or fight or flight reaction easily activated
Impulses from one's own body frightening or unfamiliar
Fear and shame regulate existence
No boundaries or too strict boundaries
Panic symptoms
No ability to calm down; the soothing other is missing, or the person clings
to others.

"I am scared because I cannot get enough air."

Psychophysical breathing therapy

4. Reflective-integrative experience / reciprocal communication
Space is given and the patient is helped to develop his ability to mentalise and to associate words with experiences.
Metaphors are used.
An understanding is shared of the effect of one's own experiences on how the other person is experienced.

3. Experience and communication based on conventional (e.g. linguistic) symbols
The therapist describes what she hears, sees, and understands.
The therapist is active and curious about the other person's/group's internal world.
The therapist asks questions such as: "What do you feel in your body?", "How does breathing feel?", "What comes to your mind?", "What do you think about this?", "How are you really?", "How do you really feel?"

2. Mental images, nonverbal communication
Giving space for the other person's experience
Training together the visualisation of boundaries
Breathing with good and bad images
Using play as a tool
Using images and music to support breathing exercises
Using art pictures and pictures of nature to support exercises
Drawing one's own images of various experiences
Reading, writing, and processing of fairy tales, stories, and poems
Encouragement to enjoy nature and the arts
Working on dreams

1. Undifferentiated physiological sensations and experienced affects, conesthetic communication
Creating space for balanced development of physical and mental breathing
Learning to be present for oneself and others
Giving permission and space for being just as you are
Encouragement for approving presence
Helping to breathe soothingly
Guidance for listening to and appreciating one's own body
Teaching how to be with one's own emotions and sensations
Sensing: wondering, listening, watching, touching with appreciation
Being supported
Reinforcing body boundaries

"I breathe, therefore I live."

Systematic definition of psychosemiotic
ways of experiencing

4. Mental function reflecting on and integrating experiences (reflective-integrative ability)

Ability to mentalise, that is, examine and reflect on separate moods of oneself and another emotionally significant person in a time perspective
Includes:
Ability to integrate various experiences, such as the ability to compare one's own experiences to the experiences of another emotionally significant person
Does not include:
Behaviour, thought, and speech not reflecting affective moods or verbally expressed emotional images realised in interaction between oneself and another emotionally significant person

3. Experience based on conventional (e.g. linguistic) symbols

The mind creates agreed symbols for affects, emotions, and images.
Includes:
The person uses verbal symbols to bind and describe various affects, emotions, and images. Through verbal symbols, the person creates concepts for expressing his needs.
Does not include:
Behaviour, thought, and speech not associated with affective moods or verbally expressed appropriate emotional images in interaction between oneself and another emotionally significant person

2. Iconic or mental experience

Appropriate emotional, nonverbal images aroused by affects and related to another emotionally significant person
Includes:
Immediate appropriate moods related to oneself or to another emotionally significant person in, for instance, fantasies, dreams, dressing style or automatic symptomatic behaviours
Does not include:
Behaviour and speech not associated with affective moods or appropriate nonverbally expressed emotional images in interaction between oneself and another emotionally significant person

1. Indexical or undifferentiated emotional experience

Undifferentiated overall affective moods.
In emotionally significant interaction the person expresses with his look and manner how he is doing.
Includes:
Undifferentiated, generally or physically experienced affective moods.
This includes wellbeing brought on by satisfaction and/or a general feeling of dissatisfaction and discontent.
Does not include:
Behaviour and speech not associated with affective moods between oneself and another emotionally significant person.

There is no mind without corporality but there may be corporality without mind.

(Keinänen & Martin, 2011)

CHAPTER SEVEN

Applications of psychophysical breathing therapy

Minna Martin, Maila Seppä

I let breathing go around ...
Missing
Remembering
Silence.

B reathing school was originally developed as a short-term group therapy method for patients with physical symptoms of anxiety. Many health care and other professionals heard positive feedback on the effects of the group therapy and became interested in the method. Maila Seppä trained breathing school instructors from the beginning of the 1990s until quite recently. Today, Minna Martin provides training in psychophysical breathing therapy. People who have attended breathing school instructor training have also applied the method in working with other target groups. In many settings, forming a group is challenging and requires close cooperation with the referring party. Therefore, breathing school methods have been increasingly used for individual breathing therapy. The ways of thinking and working were thus combined with a great variety of methods. This is the reason why the term *psychophysical breathing therapy* began to be used alongside the term breathing school so as to broaden the conceived possibilities of using the method. The approach used in psychophysical breathing therapy has proved useful in practice even when the purpose is not to work directly with breathing. Psychophysical breathing therapy is also useful for supporting the capacity of therapists for self-regulation and coping.

We and the people we have trained have experience of treating the following states and disorders by using breathing as a tool, possibly combined with and/or supporting other forms of treatment

People suffering from overarousal
- Various kinds of anxiety
- Stress
- Functional physical symptoms, such as problems associated with breathing, the digestive tract, pelvic floor, or use of the voice
- Concentration and attention problems
- Difficult situations in life; for example, people attending bereavement groups

People suffering from underarousal
- Exhaustion, lack of resources, or fatigue
- Low mood or depression

People with fears
- Social anxiety
- Fear of childbirth
- Fear of dental or medical procedures

People with somatic diseases
- Respiratory diseases
- Allergies, atopic dermatitis, or urticaria (hives)
- Acute or chronic pain
- Surgical patients
- Sleep apnoea
- Cardiac diseases
- Diabetes

People with eating problems
- Weight management difficulties
- Binge eating
- Anorexia or bulimia

Support of self-regulation and interaction in relationships with patients and other people
- Support of early interaction, early childhood education, and other education
- Support of well-being in work communities
- Mental coaching of athletes
- Guidance of musicians and other performing artists.

(Martin & Seppä, 2014)

Most professionals seeking training have been physiotherapists or psychologists. Other groups of health care, interpersonal work and guidance, and teaching professionals have also been well represented. Training has been participated in by physicians from various fields, nurses, occupational therapists, social workers, pastoral care workers, clergy, teachers, kindergarten teachers, voice massage therapists, speech therapists, singing teachers and other music teachers, dance teachers, exercise and relaxation group instructors, and sports coaches.

Work with breathing has been combined with many methods and ways of working
• Various forms of psychotherapy, including trauma therapy • Physiotherapy and occupational therapy • Teaching and guidance • Dance therapy, art therapy, and other forms of creative therapy • Therapeutic methods based on learning theory (Alexander technique, Feldenkrais method, etc.) • Relaxation methods • Hypnosis • Mindfulness • Mind-body techniques: yoga, Pilates, Nia, etc. • Sports coaching and physical education • Instruction of dance and performing arts • Instruction of singing and other music.

7.1. Psychophysical breathing guidance in groups

We recommend breathing guidance in groups. Breathing problems occur in relation to other people and, therefore, they enter the scene and surface more easily in a group than in individual contact. Even though being in a group may activate fears, it also provides protection and eases the pressure to perform exercises "correctly" (Martin & Seppä, 2014). Individual work lacks identification with others and peer support. It relativises the significance of one's own problems to hear that other people have similar experiences (Martin, Heiska, Syvälahti, & Hoikkala, 2012). In addition, a group provides the opportunity to practise tolerating difference and separateness (Kajamaa, 2003). In a group, it is not important what we do but how we do it and that we verbalise experiences of doing and our own observations in interaction with a partner in the group and the whole group.

Breathing school as such is suitable for many target groups. In some groups, it is good to emphasise certain sections of the breathing school programme or certain exercises or to combine the method with other methods. We encourage such creativity. Breathing school is not, therefore, a fixed, prepared format but a basis for work. Next we give a few examples describing how breathing school concepts have been applied to various target groups.

7.1.1. Social anxiety groups

Social anxiety groups were originally set up in student health care (Martin, Heiska, Syvälahti, & Hoikkala, 2013) and have subsequently been used in school and occupational health care. Similar approaches have also proved useful in individual therapy and teaching. School and college or university are appropriate times for helping people with social anxiety symptoms because this is a time when they experience many situations giving rise to problems. People who do not seek help for social anxiety until adulthood often say that their problems started many years before. As in most cases problems first occur in adolescence if not before, they should be tackled as early and actively as possible, that is, ideally at kindergarten or preschool age, but no later than at school age. In this way, more severe symptoms could be prevented.

Even though various forms of anxiety may be difficult to separate, it is good to try to form groups of people with as similar problems as possible, so that the participants can feel that they are with a peer group. It is therefore advisable to form separate groups for those with social anxiety.

People with performance and social anxiety often have a tense and frightened manner, with restricted facial and bodily expression, superficial and broken breathing. They sustain the anxiety by demanding a lot from themselves but they may feel that their environment is demanding and cannot tolerate people with social anxiety. They fear that anxiety will be considered a sign of weakness (Rochat, 2009).

In a group, these people should be encouraged to be more compassionate and approving towards themselves. To change their attitudes, people with performance or social anxiety often need to understand sufficiently what lies behind their problem and to work emotionally on the significance of such background factors for their lives. Therefore, such groups should discuss the participants' histories, any conflicts in their self-images, their relationships, and any changes they have experienced during their lives that may have caused stress. In the course of the group work, a person with social anxiety may realise that moving to a new area and changing schools was the original source of their anxiety. As reactions are conditioned and become automatic, social anxiety can easily recur. The group should work on means of coping with social anxiety and on finding it more possible to deal with. Social anxiety cannot be totally eliminated because it is an inherent part of life. However, it is possible to learn to tolerate it with the help of soothing breathing. The soothing effect of breathing is highly significant for the success of exposure exercises. Participants help each other to gain courage and to be exposed in small steps; instead of avoiding they move towards relationships, instead of fleeing they enter social situations, instead of drawing back they assert themselves. Work with people suffering from social anxiety involves helping them to become visible, breathing together safely and calmly. Helped by the group it is possible for them to realise the positive aspects of social anxiety—it stimulates the mind and the body naturally, without trying. They can learn to trust eustress instead of being afraid and fighting against anxiety. Appropriate tension will help them as required in a particular situation. The titillating feeling of anticipation in a challenging situation may start to feel enjoyable.

Through breathing exercises, people suffering from social anxiety may learn to cope with their physical symptoms, which they often experience as unpleasant and uncontrolled and which attract their attention like magnets. They may learn to take good care of themselves by using breathing and self-compassion: "It's OK to be nervous or tense, I'm good enough. There's no need to worry, I'm allowed to be as I am. I'm allowed to be nervous or tense." With the help of the exercises, people with social anxiety learn to observe the difference between muscle tension and relaxation. In addition, they may observe that letting go and easing up on defences does not lead to chaos and insecurity but to improved well-being. In addition to calm breathing, the safe atmosphere in the group will help them to come out of hiding. Calm breathing may help people with performance anxiety in many ways; it may help the night before, and it can be used to calm down when waiting for their turn to perform. It is also possible to breathe calmly during their performance; it will help them to purposely slow down their speech rhythm and to make pauses. The pause after exhalation is an important bridge to taking a pause in speech. This gives the speaker the time to calmly observe any new thoughts arising in the situation, and enables him to tune in to genuine interaction with his audience. Calm breathing will also help the person to calm down after the performance.

7.1.2. Groups with physical symptoms

Participants in groups called "tough for the body, rough for the mind" suffer from various psychophysical symptoms, recurrent diseases, fears of disease, or problems based on stress or anxiety with physical symptoms. Such groups may include atopic patients, people exhausted by studies, and people with symptoms of panic disorder or with pains. Their common denominator is "something felt in the body" and at least a dawning idea that the symptoms may partly have to do with mental issues (Martin & Kunttu, 2012). The work is integrated with cognitive methods to understand the participants' attitudes to themselves and to bring phenomena up from beneath the surface for conscious discussion. The groups examine, as homework and by doing functional exercises, their relationships, emotions, self-image, body image, and stressful experiences from their histories, as well as means of coping. When simply observing and wondering about their background, people often find the explanation for the kind of emotions they have learned to associate with physical symptoms and falling ill and the kind of illness behaviour models they have learned in their close relationships. As in breathing school, participants here learn to just be, seeking a calm experience of living in their bodies instead of suffering, and, with the help of breathing, seeking space for examining their experiences. In addition, the groups work with boundaries, getting to know their own resources, body boundaries, territories, and spaces. Interaction with, support from, and the understanding of others are essential soothing factors.

Phenomena from early interaction are strongly present in these groups and often quite hard on the instructor. The process may start with the instructor's images and counter-emotions becoming stronger. These are vague at first, appearing as glimpses of something which vanish again, then returning with increasing intensity and atmospherically present in the group. Through this process, the group starts to speak "between the lines" of a common important issue, such as anger or disappointment or that nothing helps with their complaints. The instructor needs to verbalise the process and to help the group develop its self-reflective ability. Breathing has a central role in all this. It helps to calm down overarousal and, through an increased feeling of safety, creates space in the mind for participants to listen to their own needs and emotions. Discussion concerning the end of group work and being separated is an often moving part of the process. This builds a new way of letting go and moving forward in life.

These groups differ from the breathing school method we have described in that in breathing school there is less focus on participants' individual symptoms or mental problems, these rather being discussed at group level. In breathing school, some people speak about their problems and about the experiences and sensations aroused by the group; others do not speak much about these. Work in "tough for the body, rough for the mind" groups integrates various cognitive methods to encourage verbal sharing within the group. The age of the members affects the issues discussed in the group. In the original breathing school groups led by Maila Seppä, most participants were middle-aged or older adults while participants in student health care groups are mostly young adults.

7.1.3. Groups of people with fears

People with various fears often experience strong symptoms resulting from imbalanced breathing and symptoms mediated by the autonomic nervous system. They may realise, to some extent, that there is no reasonable cause for the fear but they often find it impossible to calm down sufficiently. The fears often concern the person's own body, of losing its integrity, or of its vulnerability. Such fears may include various fears of disease, fear of dental treatment, fear of injections, or fear of childbirth. As children, many people feared painful procedures or visits to the doctor but most people grow out of such fears with age. In some, however, early fears persist and may be reactivated in association with challenging situations in life. At various ages, we are exposed to ever more fears associated with our situation in life or developmental stage. There are therefore often unprocessed and unrecognised fears and relationship problems underlying the anxiety. In addition, many people suffering from fears have family members with various kinds of anxiety. Thus reaction models may be genetically or socially inherited.

Stairs of fear
Anxiety and fears over a person's life-span

Fears associated with old age: change of identity, being left alone at the end, helplessness, diminishing and loss of control of vital functions and senses, diseases, pain, and death. Forms of anxiety caused by unresolved fears: shame about being needy, bitterness and anger, anxiety about the unknown of death.

Fears associated with middle age: getting old and losing strength, getting sick, death of parents, disappointment; threats posed by lack of boundaries, fear of aggression and shame, empty nest grief, threats associated with the children's lives. Forms of anxiety caused by unresolved fears: generalised anxiety, fear of depression, and psychophysical disorders and symptoms.

Fears associated with early adulthood: demands of adult life, fear of loss of control. Forms of anxiety caused by unresolved fears: panic attacks, social anxiety, and generalised anxiety, the most severe form being personality disorder.

Fears in puberty: inadequacy of one's looks, personality or level of performance, not being accepted by others, pressures associated with sexuality or seeking one's own identity, fear of being revealed. Forms of anxiety caused by unresolved fears: anxiety associated with social situations, withdrawal from difficult relationships and situations, shame, worry, and pessimism.

Fears in latency period: diseases, traffic and other accidents, fires, being injured, death, being left out, isolation, and loneliness. Forms of anxiety caused by unresolved fears: avoidant and compulsive behaviour.

Fears in early childhood: fantasies, unreal things, nightmares, animals, bugs, dentists, doctors, certain foods, sleeping alone. Forms of anxiety caused by unresolved fears: separation anxiety and somatic symptoms.

People with similar fears may be brought together to form a fear group. However, the group should be kept small in order to avoid excess anxiety caused by the social situation, as many people with fears are ashamed about their problems. Work on breathing and self-knowledge is similar to that in breathing school in general and, in addition, target group relevant information and space for discussion should be provided. Additionally, stepwise fear exposure exercises may be used. For example, participants may be offered the chance to familiarise themselves with dental or medical instruments, premises, and personnel. In such situations breathing can be used as a method of calming down and self-regulation to control increasing anxiety. The significance of various transitional objects in calming down and increasing safety may be discussed. For some participants, the aim may be to conquer and face their fears, by having a dental check-up or treatment, for example.

In fear of childbirth groups led by midwives, the main aim is to help the pregnant mother to trust her own resources during delivery. Because many mothers-to-be have in the past often had to manage difficult situations on their own, it is important to also remind them that help is available if needed. Breathing will help the wandering mind to concentrate and prevent it from feeding images of fear so easily. The group is told that the pain associated with contractions is not dangerous but just means that delivery is progressing. Various positions to help in the first and second stages of labour are discussed. In addition, the group will discuss any fears. Fears of pain, of one's own or the baby's death, or of loss of control are quite common among women fearing childbirth.

The group concentrates on stopping, quieting down, and listening to their bodies. They practise breathing during contractions and during the pauses between contractions. They learn to receive pain during contractions by breathing in through the nose and slowly out through the mouth. The mother may hold her breath when in severe pain. The group is reminded of the importance of flowing breath also during contractions. A simple piece of advice may help here: during contractions, keep your face and jaw relaxed, teeth apart, and hands open. During exhalation, birth sounds are practised, singing at a low pitch sounds such as "aah, ooh, mmm". Use of the voice will balance breathing, relax muscles, and relieve pain. When singing, it is impossible to overbreathe or to hold the breath (Vuori & Laitinen, 2005). If the mother practises this during pregnancy, it will be easier for her to find a suitable way of breathing from her body memory during labour and to accept advice on breathing given by the midwife. Many exercises performed with pregnant women are also suitable for other patients suffering from pain or fear.

7.1.4. Pain management groups

Patients participating in pain management groups usually suffer from chronic pain, and many kinds of therapeutic interventions have already been tried to help them. Many additionally suffer from chronic sleeplessness and anxiety. Some are by now rather disappointed with health care and with the supporting effect of relationships in general. Therefore, it would be a good idea to offer pain management groups for patients at an earlier stage after the onset of pain symptoms. Adverse attitudes and behaviour increasing pain could thus be prevented.

Most people want to avoid pain and the associated fear. Protecting themselves from pain they may end up in a vicious circle. Protecting oneself from pain causes inappropriate muscle tension and laboured breathing, which leads to increased pain. Realising this increases the motivation to reduce overarousal and tension. It is unnecessary to address pain as such in the exercises; instead the patients should concentrate on the stress cycle caused by the pain.

In the group, patients suffering from pain will learn to observe their bodily sensations, including those not associated with pain. Observation of breathing is the first step, and the second step is associated with the observation of muscle tension. Listening to oneself is then extended to various parts of the body, learning to use different senses. Group members are encouraged to listen to their breathing in daily situations, too; they will thus start to notice how breathing and muscle tension vary in different situations. The primary goal is not relaxation and pain relief but developing the ability to sense subtle changes in the body through breathing. Patients suffering from pain will thus become more conscious of themselves, and their possibilities of affecting their state will improve.

Clients suffering from restlessness and pain are often incapable of sitting still but when we look at breathing together, simply observing it with a certain sense of wonderment, they quickly calm down and pain is alleviated. They often notice that they soon start breathing more calmly and feeling calmer, even though this is not a direct aim. One client reported that she was huffing and puffing about things, and that corresponding changes were easy to see in her body: her whole body was pumping breath like during sport.

Pain group instructors should understand the meaning of the gate control theory in pain management. According to this theory, pain is not a direct consequence of the activation of receptors in pain neurons. Observation of pain is regulated by interneuronal interaction. Weak stimuli, such as blowing, stroking, pushing, or the mere image of any of these, may relieve pain. Patients with pain often get concrete help from working with images: "Breathe into the pain or out of it." Images of compassionate and stroking breathing and opening up of the capillaries may help muscles to silently let go of the permanent tension in the painful area. Exercises involving boundaries and touching are also important for patients with pain. Many exercises done in pairs in breathing school are therefore suitable for patients with pain to do at home with their families. Use of a spike mat and heavy bean bags at home may also be helpful.

In pain management groups, shared experiences of pain add to mutual understanding. Many patients with pain feel that they are not heard. Outsiders may find it hard to observe other people's pain and to understand it. They cannot necessarily respond sensitively and patiently to people struggling with pain. In a peer group, experiences of being left outside and misunderstood can be shared. When emotions are given space and shared, the fear of being isolated decreases and breathing opens up, giving the body the chance to recover.

7.1.5. Groups with eating disorders

Weight management groups

Weight management problems are associated with many types of difficulties in self-regulation. Many overweight people find it hard to know when their physical sensations signify hunger, when anxiety or other arousal. Many say that they eat to deal with any state of affairs or emotion, whether joy, sorrow, disappointment, or being offended. Patients struggling with weight management find it hard to relax or to experience things calmly. They have weak self-knowledge and a distorted body image, just like those with anorexia, but the two groups sometimes have nearly opposite self-regulation problems. (Martin, Friman, Hannula, Lusenius, & Nieminen, 2016.)

Breathing as a tool for self-regulation,
self-expression and self-reflection in patients with
eating disorders

Anorexia	Binge eating
Excessive regulation	Insufficient regulation
Control	Immoderation
Constricted breathing	Accelerated breathing
Undernutrition	Overnutrition

Forbidden foods
Forbidden emotions and images
Difficulty identifying physical
sensations

Self-regulation is breathing between these

Self-control _____ Permissiveness in
in eating   relation to eating

      Regulation of eating by hunger and fullness
      Satisfying emotional needs primarily by other means than eating
      Expression of emotions as necessary

Weight management groups can be led by multiprofessional teams including, for example, a psychologist, nurse, and physiotherapist. In such groups, a psychological process offering the participants the opportunity to get to know themselves runs in parallel with instruction about a healthy and balanced diet and exercising. Participants get to know their history and any stressful experiences. They discuss contradictions they experience related to their personality and body image. They discuss difficult experiences in relationships, unconscious misbeliefs directing their actions, coping with challenging eating situations, and a negative relationship with exercising, and the opportunity for alternative means of coping is opened up. Work with images, observing to what extent their body image and mental images direct their actions and attitudes, is also essential. For example, to what extent have their attitudes to themselves as plump children affected their exercising and eating behaviours, gradually possibly making perfectly normal-weight children overweight adults? In addition, the groups discuss how fear of hunger and emptiness guides their eating behaviour. The leitmotif of the process, with exercises performed first individually and then in pairs, is breathing. Participants also listen to their breathing in eating meditation exercises.

Group members may at first find it confusing to see how breathing and weight management are interrelated. However, during the process many of them realise that calming down is the key to coping with urges to binge. Breathing also offers the key to improved self-knowledge. The body image becomes clearer, and they become increasingly capable of sufficiently accurate and subtle observation of their own state. This enables them to approve their experiences and respond to their needs. Breathing provides a time out: before eating, stop, think, feel what the situation is. One weight management group developed the tea cup meditation for this purpose. They learned to drink a cup of tea while looking at what their problem was. A hot drink cannot be gulped down impulsively but you have to slow down and sit still. While drinking, you can observe whether you are hungry or whether your sensations tell you something else. Do you feel restless or anxious, has something happened, are you angry, disappointed, or lonely? Instead of rushing to push problems and emotions away by eating, agree to stop and observe the situation while sipping your tea and breathing calmly. The calming breathing and warm drink release stress, which is quite common in people with weight problems. Severe stress is associated with glucose metabolism and sleep problems, both of which often aggravate weight problems.

In psychophysical weight management groups, the aim is not another diet or quick weight loss but improved self-knowledge and self-regulation ability, which in the long run may lead to weight loss. This way is naturally slower than people generally expect. However, in the group they can learn better ways of taking care of themselves than neglecting their needs by either binging or starving.

Anorexia-bulimia group

Eating management groups have three themes on which the breathing exercises are based. The first theme is calming down and getting the experience of just being. Through just being, participants learn to tolerate emptiness, as well as compassion for themselves and their needs. Once they have true contact with themselves, it is possible to feel the approval of others. The second theme is associated with visualising boundaries. The aim is to achieve separateness and to identify physical sensations, emotions, and attitudes. The internal experience is identified through exercises strengthening body boundaries. The third theme is activation of images and putting them into action. The aim is to reduce the mysticism associated with eating problems. Participants learn to identify, share, and modify images. Feelings of shame and inferiority are discussed, and sickness and symptoms are separated from the self-image. The aim is to accept frightening sides of themselves and to turn these into resources. Participants learn to set themselves and others boundaries and to say "no".

Through exercises, common themes arise to work on that reinforce the set targets. Insecurity, need of protection, excessive control, and fear of losing control are topics that may arise. Participants share the difficulty of tolerating contradictory needs and emotions in themselves and practise accepting these. Intolerable tension and stress symptoms are relieved and new ways found for calming down. Towards the end of one group a participant said: "Just imagine, this is a group of people with severe eating problems, and we have not once discussed eating but emotions and we have worked on real issues."

Guiding of patients with severe eating problems differs from that of other psychophysical short-term therapy groups in that the same aims and exercises create different group dynamics and a different relationship to the group. Guiding these groups may feel superficially easy and tempt the instructor to lecture on healthy habits. However, the most important tool is what happens in the instructor on the emotional and image levels. The instructor may have strong counter-emotions. Intolerable helplessness, stagnation, fear of losing face, strong feelings of badness, and shame may be activated in such a group. At the end of the group, the instructor may experience sadness and a feeling of being rejected. Through these emotions, the instructor will learn to understand undifferentiated emotions of group members. Through identification, the instructor can provide words for experiences and wonder aloud what responses the exercises activate in the group in each case. Group members appear to find groups conducted according to the principles presented above necessary because usually no one drops out prematurely. It is otherwise relatively common for patients with eating problems to break off the treatment process.

7.2. Individual breathing guidance

Group work is not suitable for everyone and suitable groups are not always available. In addition, many people may need first aid sooner than it is possible to join a group, and some will for other reasons benefit more from breathing guidance and attention to breathing in individual contact.

7.2.1. Breathing as an attitude creating space and as a tool

Therapists do not necessarily need to use actual breathing exercises with their patients. They can use breathing as a tool for self-calming and for creating potential space. In the company of anxious or otherwise agitated patients this may be sufficient. Therapists can pay attention to speaking in a peaceful rhythm, as if to say with the melody and tone of their voice, "Don't worry, everything is fine." By using calm breathing and speech, restless and anxious patients can be encouraged to calm down. This is useful information for anyone and for all daily interaction.

Patients can be asked to observe their breathing, how they experience it when speaking about something specific or pondering some mental image. The aim is to help them integrate verbal and physical experiences and to become conscious of small but significant changes constantly taking place in breathing that help to regulate experiences. Asking patients to observe their breathing does not mean that they should change it, but listening to breathing helps them to open up for non-verbal, unconscious, and preconscious knowledge.

Observations of her own and the patient's breathing, and conscious regulation of her breathing enable the therapist to tune in to and regulate the patient's experiences and physiological alertness. When therapists keep their breathing open towards their patients, they communicate the message that the current emotions are safe and acceptable. Observation of breathing helps the therapist to assess the correct working intensity, how the patients' autonomic nervous system reacts, and when patients should be helped to apply the brake or to lower their level of alertness. When the therapist notices that the patient starts holding his breath when speaking about difficult issues, she may pay attention to calming down her breathing and to creating space.

Breathing is a way to open up potential space where the experience of the self in relation to others can become conscious and reorganised. This way, it is possible to reach early non-verbal experiences and memories that are more difficult to reach through verbal work alone. Use of breathing as an information and communication channel means working at the interface between conscious control and unconscious reactions of the autonomic nervous system. By listening to her breathing the therapist learns to observe her physical sensations and reactions such as tension, irritation, or overarousal. At the same time she gets the chance to develop the ability to calm down, which is necessary because working with people presents challenges every day.

7.2.2. Calm breathing as first aid

Breathing guidance is appropriate first aid for patients with panic symptoms or in acute crisis. It is also suitable for various investigations and treatments causing anxiety or fear. In such situations, it is often hard to calm down, and in a state of alarm mental and physical symptoms increase.

In acute shortness of breath, the safe presence of a therapist speaking and breathing calmly helps to calm the patient. If it is appropriate for the therapeutic relationship, touching and manual assistance of breathing may also help in a difficult situation. The patient should be guided to extend his exhalation and to avoid gasping. Many patients hyperventilate without noticing it when they are agitated or crying, overwhelmed by strong emotions. Asking tenderly "I wonder if you could calm down your crying" may help them to gradually calm down. The patient should be assisted to find the lost pause after exhalation, during which the respiratory gas balance is restored. Inhalation automatically becomes gradually deeper when thinking "There is no hurry to inhale". It is good for many physiological processes to breathe through the nose. Nasal breathing prevents overbreathing.

The calm presence of the helper is of primary importance but many breathing exercises may also help in an acute situation or during a procedure. For example, the patient can place his hand on his stomach or use the image of holding the internal child in his arms to feel safer (p. 195). Grounding exercises and focusing on the soles (pp. 206–207) will help to get a hold of the present and to direct the attention away from symptoms. Releasing exhalation exercises (pp. 208–214) may help to break the vicious circle and to restore the sense of coping. Pursed lip breathing (p. 219) and sitting with your elbows resting on your thighs (p. 219) may also help to restore the balance in an acute situation. If all else fails, you can always breathe.

It is easier to calm down breathing if the patient has already received information on overbreathing: what happens there, what the reason is, what it leads to, what symptoms it causes, and if he has received advanced information on breathing, the mechanics of breathing, and the work of the respiratory muscles. It is generally advisable to remind patients about the significance of calm breathing. The aim is not so much to relax but to reduce overarousal. Guided breathing exercises are a better first-aid method than breathing into a paper bag because they support the development of the patient's self-regulation ability.

7.2.3. Breathing exercises in various individual patients

Guiding breathing exercises can readily be performed in a doctor's, physiotherapist's, psychologist's, or psychotherapist's office, in association with short- or long-term treatment or therapy, according to the patient's needs and interest. The visit can be started with breathing exercises before discussing other issues. Another alternative is to use guided breathing exercises when a suitable context presents itself in discussion. One-off guidance may be sufficient. That may be enough to help a patient to observe his breathing and to calm down his way of breathing. It should be emphasised that the aim of the guidance is not to influence breathing from outside or to teach techniques of breathing "correctly". It is sufficient for the patient to learn to observe his breathing in various daily situations. This may help him to recognise tension in both body and mind, but nothing needs to be done about such sensations or emotions. Better identification of sensations and emotions will improve the patient's self-reflective ability and help him to integrate the sensations and emotions as his own experiences. The process should preferably take place without forcing or trying.

Sufficient time should be reserved for breathing exercises and hurry and distractions should be avoided. In the first session, guidance may be provided sitting on a chair. If exercises are done for a longer time, both the patient and the instructor may close their eyes. When the instructor closes her eyes, the patient becomes free to concentrate on himself and will not need to fear being assessed. As the instructor will not be able to see the patient's reactions, it is good to ask the patient to report any unpleasant or frightening experiences, if these should occur during the exercise. Observation of breathing and image exercises are guided verbally. The patient can be given written instructions on the main exercises to take home so that he will not need to learn them during instruction. He can be asked to pick the exercises that he found easy or pleasant. At any further visits, changes in breathing and any other observations made by the patient should be discussed, as well as how the patient has used breathing exercises in his daily life. Recognition and approval of breathing will increase the patient's possibilities for self-regulation. Breathing exercises can be continued either sitting on a chair, standing up, or with the patient lying on a mattress or couch. Combination of movement and breathing can be practised or exercises performed with the instructor assisting breathing through touch.

All people with breathing problems, physical overarousal, restlessness, tension, stress, or anxiety may benefit from individual breathing guidance. Imbalanced breathing may aggravate many somatic diseases, and vice versa. Breathing therapy may be very beneficial as complementary therapy.

By relaxing breathing in small steps, physically anchored and automated experiences can be changed. Changed breathing will calm down the autonomic nervous system and muscle tone. This will help the patient to get in better contact with himself and to tune in to information, sensations, and urges arising from his body. This will create space for images associated with dawning emotions. Contact with emotions and the habits behind them will become deeper and richer. The aim is to increase the patient's choice of ways of expressing himself. Breathing exercises will thus provide a physical way to change.

7.3. Breathing guidance for families and couples

7.3.1. Breathing and early interaction

People with many kinds of problems benefit from breathing guidance; such groups have been widely described in this book. Problems with overarousal of the body and mind and activation of fears are quite common. Many of these phenomena are either directly or indirectly associated with disturbed natural flow of breath and inability to calm down. The problems are often rooted in the earliest stages of life, perhaps even as early as experiences in the womb and early interaction. Therefore, the mother should start practising calming down of her own and the child's breathing already during pregnancy by breathing calmly for the baby in the womb. In a tiny newborn baby's life, mental and physical experiences are present simultaneously in breathing, its problems and regulation. Breathing reflects the baby's overall state.

To be able to receive and interpret the baby's messages, the parent's mind and experience must include vacant potential space and the possibility of just being. Only through her own psychophysical experience and images can the parent understand what her baby is experiencing or needs. Such understanding is only possible if the parent herself feels sufficiently nurtured. It is therefore important for a small child's parents to be surrounded by a sufficient supportive network that can also give the parents the feeling of being nurtured and cared for. Such a supportive network often consists of grandparents, other relatives, and friends. Professional helpers may also have a significant role in supporting early interaction, as necessary. Support may be given by breathing calmly next to the anxious parent trying to calm down her baby. Recognition of her own physical experiences and needs will help the parent to nurture her child. In babies, all experiences and action can be seen as physical reactions, often first in changes in breathing.

Babies are usually capable of rhythmic breathing, breathing and sucking, right from birth. A calm baby is capable of breathing through his nose while holding the nipple in his mouth, whereas a restless baby will breathe through his mouth, which complicates both eating and breathing. In premature babies, who did not have the chance of growing sufficiently protected by the womb, respiratory organs are often under-developed. The first milestone in the development of small premature babies is coping with breathing independently; before this, they often need several weeks of mechanical ventilation. During this period, parents may mediate experiential continuity by voice and touch. When the parent keeps her hand on the baby's body, her breathing rhythm, heartbeat, and body temperature are mediated into the baby's experiences, calming him down. Preparedness to suck is supported during mechanical ventilation by encouraging the baby to suck on a dummy. This provides the premature baby with important experiences of pleasure. The sucking reflex is reinforced by letting the baby suck on a dummy while milk flows into his stomach through a nasogastric tube. In kangaroo care, the baby is placed on the parent's chest with as large an area of skin contact as possible for long periods of time. Both the baby and his parent rest and calm down, the parent's calm breathing stabilising the baby's condition. In studies, kangaroo care has been shown to promote small premature babies' growth and development. Only when babies are capable of breathing themselves can they learn to suck on the breast or a bottle. This requires the ability to alternate rhythmically between breathing and sucking. This is, after all, what the rest of our lives involves, adapting breathing to how we are acting.

7.3.2. Breathing as a tool in problems in a relationship

Ways of breathing develop in relation to other people and, consequently, breathing problems also appear in relationships. The relationship with the spouse is one of the most significant emotional relationships in our lives. In that relationship, early, conscious, explicit, and unconscious, implicit, memories and experiences of reciprocity are activated. We were created to seek corrective experiences throughout life. Partly for this reason we repeat what we are not conscious of. We have a deep wish for problems to be solved in a new way. At best, a relationship provides the possibility for reinforcing or correcting the experience of being safely supported and allowed just to be. This may reinforce the experience that we have strong boundaries and that we are separate. But a relationship may also repeat a tiresome, continuous fight at the boundary, and the pain of being unseparated. If so, the spouses are stuck and not able to continue their natural growth and development.

At best, being in a relationship may offer a safe haven of trustful closeness and distance, respect for one's own and the spouse's space, space for oneself and for the other person's otherness. On the other hand, the couple may lose the way and be driven into the frightening eye of the storm, and finally just try somehow to guarantee staying alive.

Well-being in a relationship essentially depends on how well its breathing, that is, dialogue, works. Couples with problems have breathing problems (Nissinen, 2013). When seeking help from a couples therapist they have often suffered from imbalanced breathing in their relationship for several years. The two "prairie dogs" have taken cover deeper and deeper in their burrows without really daring to come out into the common space of the relationship, the "prairie" of the safe emotional relationship, to feed on love, trust, affection, admiration, and turning to the other. Both as individuals and as a couple, they need the chance to feel sufficiently safe to gradually start coming out of hiding to examine and wonder about what is happening in themselves and in their interaction. They need safe others, a soothing environment, and a compassionate, supportive presence. They need space to start letting go and breathing.

It has been particularly significant to notice that the awareness of therapists, precisely, of the all-encompassing significance of breathing as a support for self-regulation and interaction can be truly helpful when examining the state of a relationship and helping a couple to find the way to continue either together or separately. In couples therapy, therapists should pay attention to both the state of the calming system and its activation and to finding the mutual breathing space, that is, the dialogue. This way, the distressed couple can be invited to start calming down and be convinced that there is no need to worry and that everything is fine. From the very first sessions, the couple can be helped to reflect on themselves, on how they and their relationship breathe. During sessions, it is essential to get an experience of safety provided by activating the calming system. This way, the session will provide a strong physical experience.

In these sessions, what happens here and now is significant. At best, the spouses may have an experience of being able to let go. A dialogue will start to come about, and the two can exhale, safely share various sensations, inhale, accept the other spouse's sensations and allow them to calmly influence each other and their relationship, descending to the pause in breathing. Such personal breathing moments shared as a couple are experientally psychophysical and help to restore missing needs for attachment, approval, to be loved, heard, and understood, needs that have perhaps for a long time been repressed in the mind and the body. Once a dialogue comes about and sufficiently balanced breathing is found, the therapist may often observe changes in the spouses' manner and body language and feel these sensations in her own body and breathing.

As breathing in the relationship is revived, the couple can be guided to strengthen the breathing in their relationship in therapy sessions and at home by doing various exercises together. Such exercises can be adapted for couples therapy sessions and relationship courses. On relationship courses, couples can experience peer support and, through joint experience, see that breathing problems in relationships are very common, human, and often treatable. Only the creativity of therapists and instructors limits the ways of adapting the exercises.

CHAPTER EIGHT

Breathing exercises

Maila Seppä, Minna Martin, Tiina Törö

*This breathing is movement that is pleasing to the ear,
chords being colours, silent observations.*

8.1. Assimilation and teaching of breathing exercises

Psychophysical breathing exercises seek to restore natural breathing appropriate to the physical needs of the body. The main aim of the exercises is to increase the awareness of how breathing reacts in interpersonal interaction. Mental and physical breathing occur in relation to others and to what is present in reality or in the mind, what is happening here and now or has happened in the past. The more people learn to register their mental processes and observe their physical sensations, the easier they find it to calm and restore their breathing rhythm, and the more naturally and easily they can influence their breathing. Breathing exercises can be used to practise the challenging skill of letting go. The exercises help a person to surrender to the pause after exhalation and, in doing so, to influence the regulation of breathing in general (Martin & Seppä, 2014).

> Accept what you cannot influence, and become aware of what you can regulate in yourself.

Each person must absorb the breathing exercises in her own individual way and adapt them as feels best for herself. Similarly, each person must, at her own pace, adopt a way of guiding other people's breathing that is appropriate for her. Each exercise is personal to the person practising it. The important thing is not learning the correct technique but rather learning a way of being. In a therapeutic relationship, this means being present for yourself and the other person, and this is reflected in communication and interaction and felt physically by both. Each section in this chapter is a tray full of options for you to sample. It can stimulate both people studying their own breathing and people teaching, guiding, or helping others.

You can perform or teach breathing exercises as you prefer, combining various exercises. It is good for people to start with ones they like because these will trigger and revive familiar and safe internal resources. However, bear in mind that exercises which initially provoke anxiety or unpleasant feelings may prove to be treasure troves of self-understanding. They may help the people doing the exercises to understand something they were not previously aware of in themselves or that they find worrying or hard to understand in their breathing. Through the breathing exercises, a safe atmosphere will develop in a group or in individual therapy. This allows the use of playfulness in dealing with frightening experiences. Exercises should proceed in small steps, remembering the significance of an accepting presence in everything we do and find in ourselves. These exercises are particularly recommended in the context of a stable therapeutic relationship where the person doing the exercises can obtain help with their integration.

Regardless of whether breathing guidance is being offered in a group or individually, the basic principle of "Do not guide another person's breathing" always holds. This means that we should not, for instance, dictate the rhythm for another person's breathing or specify how many times any exercise should be performed, how long an inhalation or exhalation should take, or what muscles should be used. It is good to keep in mind that in most cases guidance will not help to initiate introspection. We should therefore rather support the other person's ability to simply wonder about what is happening in himself. Nevertheless, the question "What is the correct way of breathing?" can provide a bridge for speaking about the use of accessory respiratory muscles and for examining breathing together. Even though the aim is to facilitate breathing, the focus should not be on training but on offering a chance to develop the ability to observe. This will support interaction with the soothing, compassionate, approving side of the self.

The exercises in this chapter are drawn from various sources, such as games and experiences from workout, dance, total expression, yoga, meditation, and therapy groups. Some have come about spontaneously in clinical therapy, some through creative cooperation in training groups. Some old, familiar exercises have been given new form and purpose. Many of them may be familiar to the reader. In psychophysical breathing therapy, however, they are recreated, offering an opportunity to absorb them individually. The exercises we use are designed in such a way that they make psychological and physiological sense in the respective contexts in which they are used. We have thus been able to integrate psychophysical breathing exercises with mental development and to increase our understanding of the origin of breathing symptoms. This knowledge has helped us to develop breathing exercises further.

We have tried to describe the breathing exercises in such a way that no precise instructions or illustrations are needed, and these are therefore not included in the book. This reflects our belief that breathing exercises should be performed by exploring inwardly, not by learning from an external model. It also reflects the main way of guiding breathing therapy.

> *I am not a health care professional and I have no experience of guiding other people. My son suffers from asthma and breathing problems, and I was given the breathing book as a present, with the advice to read the exercises aloud to him in a calm voice during his attacks. It is amazing how well we were able to work together! Reading aloud and concentrating on the exercises calmed us both.*

It is good to perceive the guidance of breathing exercises as implicit communication. Not only the words themselves, but how the instructor uses the language and her body and how she breathes are very important. When guiding exercises, the breathing therapist should achieve a feeling of safety and calmness within herself and convey this feeling to the other person by the calm rhythm of her breathing, her movements, touch and gaze, and the tone of her voice. This does not mean that the instructor cannot be nervous or afraid of feelings of helplessness, for example. Becoming aware of one's own emotions is part of the basic task. However, bearing responsibility for one's own feelings structures the relationship to the other person or the group, increases the feeling of safety, and relaxes the other party.

Interaction cannot be used to support breathing exercises if the exercises are just mechanically learned by heart. It is important to absorb being and doing oneself and express this through body language to the other person. The therapist's experience of self-regulation will facilitate a creative encounter, which often also means submitting to a flow where it is not necessary to know exactly what will come out of your mouth next. Therefore, training sessions should not be too accurately outlined in advance. They should be alive and therefore somewhat uncontrolled.

By your side

Now. You there, just breathing
at your own pace.
Telling a quiet story without words.
A story about how you are feeling now.
You there, just breathing
at your own pace.
Me by your side at my pace.
Can I hear your story, do I know how to listen?
Now, just here, now.
Myself, you.
Today you say to me:
"Be quiet but stay by my side.
Be quiet and hold my hand.
Be there but let me rest."
You there, me by your side.
We breathe,
quietly.
Now.

(Tuula Vesiluoma, during breathing school
instructor training in 2005)

8.2. Becoming familiar with being and breathing

We have grouped the exercises in this chapter so that their sequence supports the process of work with breathing. The sequence partly follows the programme of breathing school and our training groups (Martin & Seppä, 2014). However, some elements from each section are used in several sessions. This allows issues and ways of thinking to be repeated and processed in more depth from session to session. This kind of method is difficult to replicate in a book because each group is authentic and different, but the exercises in this chapter also follow and intensify the experience of mental breathing. You have to learn to walk before you can run, which means that the foundation must be laid first. As their work on breathing advances, people will grasp the idea that the concept of mental breathing can best be understood experientially within and during each exercise. The mind breathes through physical

experience, images, emotions, thoughts, memories, and associations, reflecting on experience and creating new connections and insights. We will repeat here in brief the idea of mental breathing associated with the breathing exercises.

All work and development starts from the *level of physical being*—the ability to just let oneself be. This sounds simple but for many people it already poses a problem. Lying down, alone, may be difficult for them. Closing their eyes may feel frightening, and an attempt to stay still may lead to fidgeting. In order to learn just to let themselves be, they often need another person to soothe and remind them that there is no need to worry, that everything is fine. Such calm being will later form the basis for all breathing exercises.

Images are powerful. Repressed and thus unconscious emotions and images live and materialise in our bodies in different forms, such as muscle tension or inhibited breathing. By connecting images to breathing exercises we build a bridge between physical and mental breathing.

Images supply the shield of *play*, meaning that breathing does not need to be performed or done correctly (See Booth, & Jernberg, 2009; Rosas & Rosas, 2004). Using images we invite the respiratory muscles to perform natural, appropriate work. Breathing is often guided by setting the pace for it and giving orders to the diaphragm and other respiratory muscles. But this can lead to "correct" breathing which is often in contradiction to the person's natural rhythm and need.

Recognising one's own emotions is an important goal for the work. Unbound emotional experiences have power over what happens in the body. It is hard to give expression to emotions that have not been perceived or named. We cannot regulate unnamed emotions, and they may be activated in situations experienced as overwhelming and then remain contained within the body, causing symptoms of tension and anxiety. Anxiety is central to the development of many breathing symptoms. People are afraid of anxiety and use drugs to suppress it instead of wondering what it might represent. To ward off threatening mental content, the unconscious may develop symptoms related to breathing, that is, hyperventilation.

We also train the conscious mind to understand the *power of thoughts and words*. This refers to our internal dialogue—what we say to ourselves or require from ourselves and how we calm down. Automatic thoughts activate feelings provoking anxiety, leading to the activation of tension. Watchfulness fed by muscle tension affects breathing, leaving it less space. The experience of tension often additionally triggers feelings of shame and inferiority that influence the expression of emotions. By adopting a new kind of terminology and a new way of thinking, it is possible to calm breathing and clear the ground for self-understanding and self-compassion.

Mental breathing is mobility through all these levels. When we become conscious of how we feel and how breathing feels, of what kind of images and emotions arise, of the kind of effect that talking to ourselves has, and of how all this affects introspection and self-understanding, we use our *reflective* ability. Either the mind—mental breathing—moves and exerts its influence on us or we prevent it from moving by holding our breath, hence preventing ourselves from being moved. Change always begins with movement, whether in the form of letting go helped by an image or physical movement, or of calming down, or of a forceful burst of exhalation. We may then be able to connect the experience here and now to past memories, situations, or experiences of relationships or to how we are feeling. Through breathing, it is possible to find a new, creative view on things.

Stop and listen to how the mind inspires the body and how breath brings mobility to the mind.

Just let yourself be

This is a merciful expression. It entails deep-down approval of what is. We have received plenty of feedback on how significant this permission is. It reaches deep into our basic experience of ourselves, alleviating unconscious shame. It provides space for our own rhythm and way of breathing. It gives us time to watch and listen to what is happening in ourselves (Winnicott, 1987). In a state of just being, we can learn to observe our sensations and physical experiences without judging or criticising. This in turn reinforces our self-reflective ability (Kabat-Zinn, 1994, 2013). Even though such calm existence is easiest to find in positive idleness, it is not the same as passivity but can be applied at the foundation and in the background of any activity. At first, just being is easiest to practise by concentrating on breathing only, without doing anything else. Soon, however, it can be practised whilst in the middle of daily chores.

Just letting yourself be

- You can just let yourself be, rest, and let everything be as it is
- Let your breathing be as it is. Become aware of the sacred rhythm of breathing
- Simply wonder about what is. This will give you an astonishing freedom; all observations are fine
- Let your mind float free and your head become empty of thoughts. They will come and go, do not cling to them
- Feel your body from the inside, a part of your consciousness following the emptiness, filling, pulsing, and flowing in your body
- Become aware of the effect of gravity on breathing
- Become aware of the effect of letting go in your body
- Learn to wait calmly in a state of alertness and silence.

Accepting presence

Training an *accepting presence* supports observation of reality and increases permissiveness towards oneself. It helps us to stop at the current experience, whatever it is: discomfort, tension, pain, blockage, or the experience of internal flow or well-being. Instead of accepting, we are used to judging ourselves and comparing what is to what and how we think things should be. Experiencing permissiveness towards yourself—built on the permission to just let yourself be—is the basis for a change in breathing. A helper can rarely be completely capable of understanding how another person's breathing feels or how that person should breathe. Each of us must develop an accepting attitude towards our self, with the resulting calming breathing (Kabat-Zinn, 1994, 2013). However, this requires tools and a supportive relationship with another person. First we need help to stop for a moment so that we can encounter and appreciate our feelings. It will then gradually become possible to influence breathing even while feeling anxious. Influencing the breathing is like grasping a handle which enables us to consciously guide what is happening inside us. When panicked or under stress, people experience severe helplessness or fear of helplessness. Through breathing and with the support of another person it is possible to find soothing words and images that help.

How to practise just being

- Observe breathing
- Find soothing words
- Achieve accepting presence
- Give space for a compassionate wave of breathing
- Become aware of images, emotions, and thoughts
- Concentrate and become aware of yourself
- Breathe down to the bottom of your pelvis.

The quality of doing is affected by

- Basic experiences of doing
- Ways of learning
- Resistance to change
- How others perceive my performance or doing
- Whether I am allowed to do as I wish
- The significance of gaze and quality of touch as regulating factors.

The quality of doing, and integration of being and doing
in breathing

In being and doing, everything happens in relation to others. The joy or
requirement of doing, and being the target of doing, are learned early.
In breathing exercises, it is important to consider the effects of these.
Through doing something together we strive to revive the feeling of
being understood and the unity of being and doing. At best, the exercises
revive presence, knowledge of your own body, vivacity, and joy. The
most significant aim is to practise consciousness of the act and quality of
doing (Jalarmo, Klemola, Mikkonen, & Mähönen, 2007; Wildman, 2006).
We also learn to recognise the significance of different forms of the use of
power. We explore directions of movements and their effects on breathing. In breathing exercises, movements as such are not essential but the
way of performing them is. Doing together, playing, and using images
override all requirements to do things right and facilitate the revival of
natural breathing. Movements can be performed with eyes closed, listening to the instructor, and it is not essential for all group members to
do them in exactly the same way. What is most important is to establish
contact with one's own breathing through movement.

The combination of being and doing can be practised in many daily
chores, too. Awareness of breathing can be practised while listening to a
lecture or reading a book, for example. It is possible to clean or wash the
dishes listening to the breathing. We soon notice that learning, curiosity,
and surprising insight thrive in this state. With time, the state of being
may become natural. As with any new habit, it is eventually assimilated
through countless repetitions.

Breathing and change

- Breathing starts deep inside and should be allowed to occur
  naturally
- Doing is movement with a target that always occurs in relation
  to an object, such as another person
- Observation of doing represents consciousness of what is
  happening in your body
- Observation of doing also represents consciousness of what
  is moving in your mind, in other words, awareness of your
  thoughts, images, and emotions

- People often find a change when they become aware of something in a new way
- On the other hand, changes and reorganisation also happen in us without our being conscious of them. We learn without trying or noticing
- In breathing school, changing and learning represent alternating developments occurring in the conscious and unconscious, and a dialogue between them.

Factors promoting or hindering the change

- To be at ease is a virtue
- Both excessive use of force and fear of our own power increase control and upset our natural balance
- Fear of our own power is associated with a fear of emotions
- A counterforce is needed to enable us to get to know our own power and to use it—this can most practically be found in relation to another person
- When we do not interfere with the course of events, with what is going on inside us, we can feel the flexibility and pliability of the spine when breathing
- The position in which we are may become our personal way of being
- Movement may become personal and feel like implementing our own existence and being quite natural
- All this will enable us to find out things about ourselves at our own pace.

Support and change—flow and connection with the ground

Dynamism, pauses, and flow are basic words for describing breathing. A back-and-forth wave-like motion is an essential part of all movement, and it is important to experience it in breathing. The physical experience of flow represents an all-encompassing feeling of being alive and becoming free. It is intertwined with the experience of basic trust created in early interaction, depending on how we have been supported and whether we have been able to trust an adult. In this connection, we learn what it means to be alive, the experience of emotions, and trust in the usefulness of the body. Our relationship to the ground and gravity is built through flow. These experiences affect breathing. Whenever we lose contact with the supporting surface, with the ground beneath us, this affects the quality of breathing (Farhi, 1996).

Giving support can be practised in pairs. One of the two lies on her back. The helper takes hold of each limb in turn, with a firm but soft grip. He raises and holds it, making sure that he gives sufficient support to the limb so that the person listening to her breathing will not need to do any muscle work. Holding and supporting represents soothing of each limb, with a touch saying, "There is no need to worry, everything is fine." After being held, the limb is gently returned to the ground. Finally, the helper lifts and holds the breather's head, placing his hands beneath the head and trying a tiny movement of the cervical spine. He then lowers his hands until the backs are resting on the floor, while continuing to hold the breather's head for a little while longer. At the end of the exercise the two discuss any observations made during it.

The experience of being supported can also be practised alone. Lie on your back and, one limb or muscle group at a time, tense your muscles hard so that it feels as if you are nearly lifting from the floor. On exhalation, slowly start letting the tension go. Gradually relax and feel how the ground supports you completely.

Experience of tension and anxiety symptoms and excessive holding onto oneself are reflected in symptoms

- Sleep problems, difficulty falling asleep
- Tension and anxiety symptoms
- Imbalanced breathing
- Feeling dizzy—the "top" feels dizzy if the roots are not firmly in the ground.

Symptoms are alleviated by

- Consciousness of bodily experiences, what is happening in oneself
- Awareness of the effect of gravity: making contact with the ground when sitting, standing, or walking

- Slow movements in low starting positions
- Becoming sensitive to the experience of flow.

Before exercises that require touching, the instructor should demonstrate what will happen, explaining the purpose of the exercise. In this way, she will show respect for the autonomy of the other person. She will then need to observe how the exercise is performed and what happens in the group. This will increase trust and safety within the group.

> In one group, fear of touching was roused in connection with the exercises. In many professions, touching may really be a big taboo. This was discussed but recurred every time a new exercise was introduced. The group only calmed down when the instructor said, "There is no need to worry, everything is fine. I will be by your side watching all the time."

The presence of a regulating and soothing other creates a feeling of safety. On the other hand, it is important to have respect for and be conscious of boundaries in all interaction. For this reason, inexperienced groups should not be left to do the exercises entirely alone. Respect for boundaries is especially important when working with individual patients.

8.3. Observation and examination of breathing

Observation of one's own breathing

When attention is turned to breathing, at first the flow of air in and out can be observed, paying heed to how it feels. Listening to breathing may also trigger unpleasant images and emotions. Breathing may appear frightened, like a small, shy child who is being watched. We gradually get used to listening to our breathing. Simply contemplating and wondering about breathing represents working towards accepting ourselves with all our emotions, images, and thoughts. For us to tolerate working on this, help is often needed from someone else. Soothing images, and the safe company and comforting breathing of another person will help. These resources strengthen our self-reflective ability, restore our sense of reality, and help us to become aware of and approve our emotions and sensations. We experience that "There is no need to worry, everything is fine". Merely learning to observe breathing often takes time. Breathing can be influenced only later. It is therefore good to start by playing with breathing and observing the movement caused by breathing in ourselves.

> Imagine that your breath flows to beneath your navel, to your lower abdomen and pelvic floor, the home of breathing. Move your ribs or breathe into your back.

Awareness of breathing can be practised with the following concentration exercise. This exercise is suitable for people with no previous contact with breathing or with working with their bodies. After this exercise, it may be easier to move on to image exercises.

> Take a comfortable sitting position with your feet firmly on the ground, back supported, shoulders down and hands resting on your lap. Close your eyes. You can start getting to know your breathing by asking yourself how you actually know that you breathe. You will get information about this by listening to your sensations. Be sure not to judge yourself or try to change your breathing in any way. Let it be as it is today, right now.
>
> Move your attention to your face and the top of your head. Allow the muscles in this area to relax. In daily contact with other people, our facial muscles do a lot of work without our noticing it. If there are conflicts in relationships, muscles become increasingly tense. Pay attention to the area around your eyes and any sensations behind them, and allow your muscles to soften. Let your teeth come apart but allow your lips to be softly closed. This will relax the jaw area, as well.
>
> Direct your attention to your nose. You can listen to the air flowing in and out through the nose. If you pay really careful attention, you might feel the air flowing and perhaps even the temperature of the air in your nose. You have probably experienced that in very cold weather, below zero Celsius for example, the sensation is particularly strong, but at room temperature the sensation can be quite subtle. If you observe really closely, you may feel the tiny muscles in your nose working to assist the flow of air.
>
> Next, follow the flow of air into your pharynx and throat; you may feel the flow and the temperature even here. Let your attention move down to your shoulders, collarbones, breastbone, and ribs in your upper chest. Let your chest drop into a resting position and relax after the constant watchfulness for inhalation. Feel the yielding and flexible movement of your chest when you breathe. You may notice a hint of a yielding movement as

far as in your upper arms. Notice how breath flows all the way down to
your fingers.

Continue listening to your breathing with your body. Become aware of the
movement of your abdomen, like the ebb and flow of waves on the beach. You
can listen to waves coming and going by placing your hand on your abdomen.
Your own hand is present for your breathing, intensifying your observations,
kindly and keenly receiving your breathing. Sense the wave of breathing all
the way to your lower abdomen and pelvic floor. You can feel breath flowing
down to your buttocks, thighs, legs, and all the way to your toes.

Practise getting to know your breathing and concentrating on it as
described above. Alternatively, concentrate for a moment on just a part
of the exercise, such as sensations in your nose or your hand resting on
your abdomen. Your hand may represent the memory of a "safe other".
There is nothing to worry about, everything is fine, if you can use your
own hand to calm your breathing.

Sacred breathing rhythm

To influence breathing, first observe and concentrate on your breathing
movement and rhythm. The rhythm and way of breathing represent
your state of being more genuinely than what is consciously going on
in your mind. The rhythm is private and personal, completely internal and untouchable. By this we mean that from the outside we cannot
know much about how anyone else should breathe or be. It is sometimes hard even to let ourselves be as we are.

Pause to listen to your sacred breathing rhythm. Sit or lie down, and place
your hand on your abdomen to listen. This is where getting to know your-
self and wondering begin.

Helping another person

The therapist should start by working on her own breathing. It is good
to remember that our way of breathing affects others. Even later on,
the use of breathing for therapy does not always mean influencing
the other person's breathing directly but rather working on one's own
breathing. Knowledge of breathing and interaction is useful for everyone in daily life.

Breathing as a tool
• Breathing is the therapist's or helper's tool for calming herself and her breathing • Breathing creates potential space in both one's own mind and the other person's mind • Potential space is created between the person being guided and the guide • The melody and tone of the voice convey the message "There is no need to worry, everything is fine" • Calm breathing and speech encourage anyone who is restless or anxious to become calmer.

Before examining or helping anyone else, we must work on our own breathing. It is also good to practise being present and listening. The following exercise, which can be done at home or with a colleague, for example, is suitable for this purpose.

Listening task

Choose a partner for the task. Sit close to the other person and decide who will speak first and who will listen. Both partners should keep their eyes closed for the duration of the exercise.

The speaker will first speak uninterrupted for five minutes about "when I woke up this morning". He can describe what the morning was like, what he did in the morning, who was there, what feelings arose, etc. The listener will concentrate on listening to his speech, its rhythm and melody, how it feels in her body, what sensations she observes, what happens to her breathing, what urges to react arise, what she would like to say, and how it feels just to listen.

After five minutes, switch roles. Each person then gives feedback on what they felt and observed in themselves. The purpose is not to comment on the other person's story but to talk about how you found the experience of listening.

This exercise is used to prepare for the following one.

Examining another person's breathing

The person being examined lies down on her back and the examiner takes a comfortable seated position next to her. The examiner should be open to his own breathing rhythm and to how he is feeling, simply wondering about any tension. He listens with his hands and identifies with the other person's breathing rhythm in trying to understand her.

The person being examined is asked to close her eyes and listen to what is happening inside her and how breathing feels. She is asked to speak about this. The examiner can say: "Place your hand on where you feel you're breathing best and listen there for a while." He can then say: "May I place my hand on yours?" If this is OK, they listen together to the breather's rhythm. The breather is then asked to show with her hand a place where she cannot feel her breathing well enough and where she would like some help. This time the examiner can ask if he can place his hand on the immobile spot. The breather can place her hand on his and show how intensively she wishes to be helped. This way they will both help each other. The examiner can place his hand under the breather's lower back. He will help inhalation and the natural breathing wave in the pelvic spine by gently lifting the breather at her lower back or at the attachment point of the diaphragm. He allows his hand to descend softly during exhalation and perceives through his hand whether a natural pause occurs in breathing. The examiner must not regulate the breathing rhythm but follow it and, through touching, give the breather space and an opportunity to express herself. Preparedness is expressed largely as in a discussion—by taking listening pauses every now and then. Going with the movement, giving space and attention provide the breather with an experience of being understood. The moment of encounter thus becomes satisfying for both.

They can explore ways of facilitating breathing by gently pulling on the breather's ankles in the rhythm of her inhalation. This helps the diaphragm to work in the right direction and reveals any tension in the pelvic area. Softly drawing on the neck in the rhythm of the breather's inhalation and pressing on her chest during exhalation may also release breathing.

Observation of breathing in daily life

We urge people to transfer the observation task to their daily lives. They can thus learn to listen to themselves in order to deepen and expand their consciousness of their breathing and of themselves as a whole.

> I was taking a walk with my dogs, and we were walking at a brisk pace. Suddenly something cracked in the forest. The dogs and I stopped, clearly alert. I noticed how the dogs' chests turned immobile and I felt like bursting. As we heard nothing more from the forest, the dogs exhaled in a long sigh and continued their walk happily. What did I do when exhalation stopped? I inhaled again, increasing the tension in my chest. I started following this phenomenon, and it confirmed what I had learned in breathing school about the effects of automatic fear reaction on muscles.

We keep repeating to our patients: "Remember, you can always breathe." This is a helpful thought in situations provoking anxiety. Only once you have realised this can you make changes by doing actual breathing exercises.

But what if you cannot breathe or breathing is difficult and feeble, after surgery for example? Many people are familiar with the sensation of not being able to get enough air, no matter how hard they gasp. Or you may have in your head a compulsive idea that you should know how to breathe right. How can you breathe if fear of death is choking your throat, you don't have the strength, or you feel like running away in panic?

It is possible for people to breathe unconsciously and consciously at the same time. This makes it possible to influence breathing even when it is difficult. Exhaling consciously through pursed lips and inhaling through your nose down to your pelvic floor encourage the calm course of breathing. The presence of a soothing other will facilitate and support this. Just practising conscious breathing techniques by yourself when facing panic symptoms may for some time provide you with a feeling of having your breathing under control. On the other hand, such techniques may strengthen obstacles based on muscle tension, making breathing harder and adding to the symptoms. Breathing is regulated by the breathing centre in the brain stem, ensuring it continues automatically. You can use this information to calm and support yourself or others. It is wiser to learn to listen to your breathing than to try to control it. This is the beginning of a long path towards becoming conscious of yourself.

How can natural breathing be learned? First you should learn to stop and tell yourself that there is nothing to worry about, that everything is fine. This is the sentence mothers have used since time immemorial to calm their children, and children use it to calm their toys or pets. Little Helena held a struggling kitten in her arms, stroking it and saying "There is no need to worry, everything is fine ..."

> When calming down, the breathing rhythm slows and breathing movement becomes smaller.

Concentrating and becoming conscious of oneself with the help of a partner

> The helper places her hands at the area of the body where change or treatment is needed. This may be a sore spot, tense muscle, cold feet, or, perhaps, an empty-feeling place in the chest. The person being helped does the actual work by exhaling into the cup of the helper's hands. An image of the partner's hand receiving whatever it is the breather wishes to get rid of may help. The person being helped may also imagine spraying cleansing breath into the sore spot.

Circulation is activated in the capillaries, with a simultaneous change occurring in the mind. As a positive body memory arises, the effect of the exercise becomes deeper; that is, the self-regulating, soothing other is activated. Calm touch causes the secretion of oxytocin, a stress antagonist, activating a natural desire to open up and lean on the other person. The usefulness of this exercise has been confirmed, for example, in adjustment training courses for cancer patients and their spouses or other near ones. Alleviation of pain during the exercise was experienced as almost miraculous. In a training group, someone said: "I no longer ask my partner for massage but for him to keep his hand on the spot into which I wish to breathe change."

> I was in hospital to try out treatment with new medication, and I thought the medication was causing intolerable side-effects. When I could not bear them any longer, I rang the bell. The nurse who came in saw that I was hyperventilating heavily and believed that was the reason I was feeling so bad. She said she would bring me a sedative. When I understood the reason, I told her I would not need it. I told the nurse that I had learned a way of calming my breathing, and I asked her to place her hand on my chest. I closed my eyes and breathed. My breathing gradually calmed and the unpleasant symptoms were alleviated.

8.4. Body image and other images

Images reinforcing the connection to our bodily experience and to experiences of interaction are used to support breathing exercises. Images arise based on experiences of being, and on awareness of breathing and of the body being alive. We learn to direct our attention to images arising in the body and to reflect on them.

The significance and use of images are individual and personal. Images suggested for exercises can always be replaced by others that are more useful and applicable to the person doing the exercises. In addition to conscious use of images, strong memories or symbolic images may arise spontaneously during breathing exercises. They are like dreams that do not appear to be associated with anything. Such images and dreams can provide a basis during daytime consciousness for simply wondering about the state of the mind and body and about issues causing restlessness, but also about wishes and possibilities of becoming free.

> Breathe with your hands resting on your abdomen. Feel the waves rising and falling. The image of ocean waves will relax and calm you.

Lie on your back with your knees bent. Use the image of a broad rubber band inside you. One end of the rubber band is attached to your pubic bone, the other end to your pharynx, underneath the tongue. Inhalation will stretch the band and exhalation relax it again. You can play with the rubber band like a child might, first stretching it as much as you can and the next time as little as possible. Examine what type of extension feels good right now. The movement should be produced by breathing, not done consciously with your muscles. The exercise will enable you to feel your large muscles loosening, to feel the flexibility and suppleness of body tissues, and how relaxing it is to let go.

You can try doing the same exercise the other way round: let the rubber band relax when inhaling and stretch when exhaling. Examine how your spine becomes longer during exhalation. In this version the point of origin of the movement may shift to the middle of the spine, from where the band stretches simultaneously upward and downward.

Many image exercises are particularly easy for children. One mother reported that after breathing school she had always played breathing games with her children who were under school age. She was astonished to discover that a couple of years later one of her children, who was then at school, was capable of applying what he had learned. He had felt nauseous when travelling on the school bus. After returning home he said, "I breathed like in the rubber band exercise and the nausea went away."

Imagine breathing in a colour. Let your exhalation spread it through your legs and all the way down to your toes. Feed your toes with the colour. You can choose a different colour for each breath, if you like, and give each toe what it appears to need. Your toes are like children in a large family, they rarely get individual attention. For them, "we" almost always comes before "me". By breathing separately for each toe, you can provide each with individual attention. At the same time, take in the feelings arising in you towards your feet or toes or other parts of your body. Breathe for the parts needing your attention, for tight and tense or painful spots and, particularly, for places that you have a problem with or find it difficult to accept in yourself. Breathe compassion and acceptance into these parts of your body. Cherish the thought "I could actually have more compassion for myself".

To practise breathing with images, first lie on your back, with your eyes closed. You can either listen to calm music or be in silence. Do the exercises a few times and see how they feel. Then let the image go as if blown away on the wind, and let your breathing go on as it wishes. Later it is important to breathe in various positions and various places to become familiar with breathing and the use of images and to have them available, when necessary. Listen to how it feels to work with your eyes closed and later with your eyes open. Concentrate on your breathing or do the image exercises particularly if you are stressed, anxious, tense, or restless. You can breathe consciously where and whenever you like, at traffic lights, in the theatre, on a bus, when queueing in a shop ... You can treat yourself by calm and conscious breathing.

Exercises to strengthen body boundaries

A developmental process continuing throughout life—the *separation-individuation* process—occurs in relationships. This idea, originally expressed by the child psychologist Margaret Mahler (Mahler & Bergman, 1975), was later complemented by the idea of *attachment-individuation*, emphasising that we become individual and separate precisely through a safe relationship and successful symbiosis, not so much through emphasis on being separate. During the development process, consciousness of our own boundaries and separateness, as well as of our own desires and will, gradually arises and becomes stronger at our own, natural pace. What is important is the integrity of the boundaries and the internal permission to be separate and as we are. The body of an individual with his own emotions and thoughts is autonomous. At the same time, we must remember that support from another person may also be needed for breathing exercises.

The occurrence of breathing symptoms always depends on the degree of individual differentiation. People with breathing symptoms often have significant difficulty in experiencing separateness and their boundaries. For this reason, exercises strengthening body boundaries are done before actual breathing exercises. By visualising boundaries we develop the ability to observe what is happening in ourselves, to sense experiences of inner space and associated rhythms, to notice experiences of flow and changes in them, to become aware of experiences of controlling orifices of the body and images associated with bodily excretions or products. Drawing is an excellent task for making the body image real. Through drawing, a person can describe how he experiences himself and how he feels he has been encountered.

In a group of middle-aged people, a grandmother drew a plump, sweet
image of herself that looked like her. At the end of group work, the body
image was drawn again. The image she then drew represented a bird fly-
ing free. On seeing the first drawing again at the last group meeting, the
grandmother said that when drawing it she would have liked to add a tail
and hooves because she felt like the devil. But she was too shy to do it then,
being hardly able to tolerate that image of herself. We spoke about how
even the slightest need to define our boundaries first feels difficult. During
the group work, the grandmother had learned to say "no" to her children
and grandchildren. At first, the image of herself as bad in this way had
been frightening. Through working with images and breathing, the setting
of boundaries started to feel permissible and even liberating.

It is not always easy to separate between images and deeds, between
what is experienced in our imagination and what is real. Through body
image drawings, we can safely permit what becomes conscious. This
opens up and adds to experiences of the self. Accepting forbidden sides
becomes easier. Drawings done early in the course of group work often
include black and locked inner spaces, cages and constricted spaces.
During the work, changes take place. Drawings become brighter and
open up, cages and obstacles disappear. Spaces become larger and there
are wings to carry people.

We sometimes observe directly that chronic muscle tension serves the
function of maintaining boundaries: "I demand perfection of myself,
I am always criticising and keeping a watch on myself. I am anxious,
therefore I exist." When our boundaries become clearer through exercises we can gradually let go of tension.

Strong, conscious muscle tension strengthens the experience of body
boundaries. Try closing your eyes and tensing your muscles as much
as possible. Clench your fists, frown, bite your teeth together, be tense
and sense your boundaries, your existence. Gather up all your ten-
sion and all the watchfulness and energy generated by your anxiety.
Maintain the tension for some time and then relax with a sigh of relief
at letting go.

In the "defending my borders" exercise, lie on your back, tense one
side of your body, including the outer sides of your leg and arm and the
outer parts of your neck and head on the same side. Conjure up an image
of a country preparing to defend its territory, assembling its troops and

securing its borders. Strengthen the image with the thought that no enemy will be able to cross these borders. Slowly let go of all tension. You will then feel peaceful. Afterwards, become aware of the experience of a new kind of boundary. Repeat this on the other side. Finally concentrate on becoming aware of the intact, whole shape of your body.

You can also visualise your body boundary in your mind. In your imagination, draw or paint a continuous boundary around yourself. You can use any colours and as heavy a line as you like. Some prefer a thin, sharp pencil line on the floor, while others prefer to paint their sides using a wide brush. Start from the top of your head and work down, continuing all the way around yourself until you have drawn an unbroken line around your whole body. Should any part of you require more reinforcement, you can revisit those parts. You can also paint the upper surface of your body with a soft brush, following the recesses and hills on your body. This is a useful concentration exercise to calm and relax muscles. Many people have started doing this exercise every day at home.

Boundaries can be reinforced in pairs, with one person tracing the other person's boundaries from the top of the head down to the soles of the feet, first on the left, then on the right side. Boundaries should preferably be traced using the neutral back of the hand, not the intimate palm. The person doing the drawing draws the boundaries carefully on the floor with her fingertips. The grounding sensation of the fingers touching the floor feels quite different to the recipient from drawing with the fingertips in the air (we recommend trying the difference!). Please note that boundaries should never be drawn between the lower limbs or between the fingers. In this way, we respect the other person's intimate areas. In the group, the instructor first explains what will happen, then demonstrates the exercise describing its purpose, emphasising respect for the other person's bounda-ries. This exercise can also be done in groups of three. If two people act as assistants, first one draws the left side, then the other draws the right side. Then both the assistants draw a confirming line at the same time. Many experience this moment as very harmonising. After the exercise, it is good for the person being treated to turn onto her left side for a while to allow her to assimilate the experience. The assistants cover her with a blanket and tuck her in carefully.

Boundaries can also be drawn in pencil on a large piece of paper. One person lies down on a large piece of paper, and the other draws around her, following the body boundaries as closely as possible, again from the head down to the soles of the feet. If she wishes, the person being drawn may fill in the boundaries on the insides of the legs herself, once she has got up. A life-sized drawing like this can later be strengthened and coloured. It can be used for many kinds of image and drawing tasks.

An adult older brother played with his youngest brother, drawing his boundaries on brown wrapping paper. He then drew a Superman outfit on the little brother's picture. The parents mounted the drawing on cardboard, and it was hung on the wall in the little brother's room, where it reminded him for many years about the time spent playing with his big brother whom he admired, increasing his courage and giving him extra strength.

A ball can also be used to visualise boundaries; balls are particularly suitable for visualising the back of the body. The ball can be big or small or spiked. Big or small gym balls, tennis balls, golf balls, and massage balls are suitable. One person lies down on her stomach, and her partner rolls the ball in calm, circular movements on her back. This way, the partner can also visualise the backs of her legs and the soles of her feet. This exercise is often quite relaxing. Some groups find it easier to accept the exercise if it is offered as ball massage and a means of relaxing tense muscles.

Visualisation can also be done in pairs by kneading gently with the hands. It is done on the back of the body, with the partner lying on her stomach on a mattress. Slowly kneading with your hands visualise various parts of your partner's body—her head, back, arms, and legs. The image of a mother bear nurturing her cub can also be added playfully to the exercise.

Weights can also be used for visualisation. With your partner lying face down, place bean bags measuring 25 x 25 cm and weighing 2–3 kg on her back and legs. Alternatively, a heavy blanket can be used. One can comfortably lie under a weight for a long time.

Patients love to have bean bags placed on their chest at the beginning of group sessions. Many have said that they made bean bags for use at home and use them to relax after work, for example. The experience reminded many people of a similar experience of safety and reinforcing their boundaries when they slept under old, heavy covers in a summer cottage or at their grandmother's home, for example.

One mother reported that when she was making a bean bag to use in breathing school, her son came to her and enquired what she was doing. The mother explained how the bag was used, and when the bag was ready it immediately disappeared into the son's room. The bag became so dear to the son that every night he fell asleep holding it. He took the bag with him when he slept over at his grandmother's or anywhere else and he also took it to camp, even though his parents tried to stop him because it made his backpack so heavy.

> *The experience of boundaries can also be reinforced by using a spike mat. You can lie on your back on the mat or stand or sit on it. The experience will relax your muscles and activate the superficial circulation. You will feel your body boundaries clearly for a long time. If you wish to have a particularly strong experience, lie on your back on the spike mat with heavy bean bags on your chest.*

Being grounded

Patients with hyperventilation symptoms often also suffer from dizziness and difficulty walking straight. The physical and mental sides of hyperventilation are mutually intensifying. Many people describe a feeling of "being drawn to one side" all the time. In a supine position, difficulty trusting one's own body and its supportive surface, and fear of submitting to gravity manifest themselves as excessive tenseness and a state of constant preparedness. Whenever you lose contact with gravity, that is, when you cease to be grounded, the natural flow of breath is prevented. The activation of fears and experiences of insecurity arising from interaction cause tension in the body. All exercises associated with awareness of the body and gravity reinforce ego identity and balance the body.

People guiding breathing exercises and people doing the exercises alone should pay attention to and be aware of gravity. This means using a large supportive surface in the initial position, whether sitting, standing or lying down.

> *Feet often need to feel the contact to earth confirmed. Whenever you start feeling anxious or worried, remember to put your feet firmly on*

the ground. Ground your soles to the floor if you are sitting or standing. Breathe through your soles into the floor. Let tiny roots grow into the ground.

Stand with your feet slightly apart, knees and hips soft and supple. The exercise is best performed barefoot. Tilt your pelvis forward a little. Take a straight but relaxed position, with your arms hanging loosely at your sides. Your partner will root your feet to the ground as if you were a tree being planted. The image of roots pushing deep into the ground may intensify the experience. In this context, the roots of your family, where you come from, may be activated from your history. Your partner helps you by stroking your legs, ankles, and feet calmly towards the floor. In this way he roots your legs. He will test the results of his work, like the wind, by shaking you gently at the knees, hips, shoulders. Listen to your breathing. Feel how firm your steps are when you start moving after this exercise.

A kindergarten teacher who had attended breathing school said good-bye to a group of children in the spring using this exercise. Children continuing in the kindergarten were trees, those leaving were winds shaking and hugging them.

If your partner is lying on his back, you can ground his upper limbs by kneading them firmly from the fingers up to the shoulders and then taking hold of the shoulder and sliding your hand all the way down to his fingers again. This may give your partner a feeling of empowerment, of "being able and capable"; arms are important in this respect.

Use of music to support exercises

Gentle, melodic music will help the breather to concentrate and communicate that there is no need to worry, that everything is fine. Music offers safe arms that allow him to submit to just letting himself be. The use of silence requires skill. Submitting to silence may feel odd, strange or anxiety-provoking if frightening thoughts or images rush into the mind. When there is a pause, the breather's stern super-ego may be activated to watch what he is doing and demand that he performs the exercise correctly or tries harder. Flowing music will encourage the breather to let go as he breathes. Rhythmic music, on the other hand, will strengthen his boundaries and sense of reality.

Use of music with exercises often creates positive imagery for the exercise and for making associations

- Music opens the way for images
- It strengthens the experience of being supported
- It comforts and calms
- It creates potential space in the mind and in interaction
- It revives and feeds the basic mental matrix
- It arouses emotions, memories, and associations
- It creates boundaries for the exercise, protecting the group from external stimuli
- It supports the exercise
- It provides rhythm and energy and wakefulness
- It may sometimes annoy you and make you restless. Even this provides the opportunity for thinking "I wonder what this is all about?"
- Conscious use of silence also provides space for images.

8.5. Exhalation

Change begins with exhalation

Exhalation occurs in two simultaneous directions. Most of us are familiar with exhalation as directed out of the body, towards the external world and people. In contrast, the idea that the releasing exhalation movement is at the same time directed inward, facilitating venous flow and the work of the heart, and relaxing muscles, may be new to us. Accepting this idea makes it possible to stop holding on and to use muscles appropriately. Relaxing the diaphragm helps breathing to achieve a resting pause and the breathing rhythm to become calmer. Calm exhalation involves surrendering and submitting to your own body. The exercise gives concrete expression to the experience of forgiveness, forgiving oneself and others.

Breathing symptoms begin with unconscious muscle tension preventing natural exhalation. Understanding this has helped us to develop new kinds of psychophysical breathing exercises.

Exhalation
The key to change

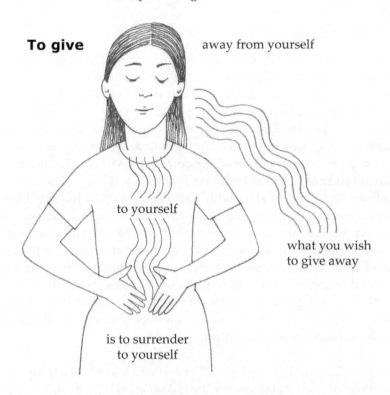

To give   away from yourself

to yourself

what you wish
to give away

is to surrender
to yourself

Otto Fenichel (1931) has said that all breathing disorders are
disorders in object relations, the conflict between individual and object
being reflected in a conflict between the individual and her lungs. It
was this thought that originally led Maila Seppä to pause and examine the significance of interaction when she encountered patients with
symptoms. In early childhood interaction the child develops a belief
of what she is allowed to express and how she is allowed to be. The
body learns to regulate its reactions, breathing, and muscle tension very
early. This occurs by holding back, controlling or swallowing expressions, needs, and emotions. In early interaction, feelings of shame may
occur that will exert an unconscious influence throughout life. Shame
may arouse a fear of being evil inside. Shame may also be preserved
in the body as a package of tension: "Now that I am aware of my
anguished shame and can breathe calmly with it, understanding and

cherishing self-compassion, I no longer feel the familiar muscle tension in my body," said one breathing school participant.

Letting go and listening to exhalation

When exhaling, we let go of the active work of the diaphragm and other inhalation muscles. Exhalation is a releasing, down- and sideward movement. It can be felt as a tender, releasing flow from the face, over the chest and abdomen towards the pelvic floor and groin. This kind of exhalation is like stroking oneself. Descending towards the pause is an essential part of free exhalation. A natural pause can only occur if the diaphragm is relaxed and breathing corresponds to physical needs.

To get to know or to change one's own or another person's way of breathing, it is best to start with passive exhalation. Just let it occur without making an effort, as if opening the string tying a balloon. This allows us to experience the air "escaping". At the same time, it gives us a good opportunity to simply wonder about what happens in the body when letting go. We can take note of the tension and withholding in the chest and respiratory muscles or the boundaries of the chest.

Letting go is a good intensifier for exhalation. Under stress, the respiratory muscles are overaroused. In states of fear, they are often completely under unconscious control.

> *When exhaling, give a sigh of relief, let go of muscle tension in your face, shoulders, chest, and abdomen, all the way to the groin.*
>
> *You can practise letting go by using the image of how nice it feels to ride down a long, gentle slope on a bike. You do not need to pedal or apply the brake, just let go … If you like skiing, you can use the image of shining snow and skiing down a gentle slope.*
>
> *Lie on your back. On inhalation, bend one of your knees gently; on exhalation let your leg straighten again through external rotation of your hip.*
>
> *Lying on your back, breathe in through your bones and let exhalation flow into your muscles.*

Using words for exercises will help to make a permanent change. It is important to listen to the words we say to ourselves when doing an exercise. The effect of words reaches deep into the unconscious, and internal speech is significant for how we live in and use our bodies

(Saaristo, 2000). At school, pupils may be asked to write "I will not talk in class" a hundred times—but repeating "Am I breathing right, do I know how to breathe?" over and over again will not help here. We recommend using experiential words during exhalation and in association with the experience of breathing. Such words provide nourishment for mental breathing.

Phrases reinforcing exhalation
• I will ease off • I will let go • It is flowing through me • Breath is flowing • I will let it occur by itself • I will not interfere with the course of breathing • I will set it free • I will give it away.

> *The calm image of soft mist floating out from between the lips in a lingering sigh calms and deepens exhalation.*
>
> *Imagine a slide in a playground. Slide down it during exhalation and climb back up the ladder during inhalation.*

Exhalation opens up a flow, an experience of giving to oneself. In natural exhalation, the respiratory muscles relax and return to a good state of preparedness for working again. Pressure in the abdomen is released, helping the veins do their work. Letting go opens up the opportunity to become aware of the experience of internal flow following the relaxation of muscles. The significance of following the flow of air in breathing is also emphasised in yoga and meditation. We believe that the experience of flow elsewhere in the body represents a continuation of this flow.

The experience of flow has been described by, for example, Hägglund and Piha (1980). The flow of breath continues to extreme limits, and for some people experiencing this internal flow may be frightening. It may be difficult to describe such a personal experience to someone else, particularly to a person to whom the experience of flow is completely foreign. However, if the experience of flow is familiar, it is natural to say in training sessions that people breathe with their whole bodies.

Anyone watching the breathing of a newborn baby can see this. In a little baby, breathing flows and pulsates. It is visible all the way down to his toes. We do not breathe with our lungs alone but with our whole bodies down to the cellular level. Physiologically the experience of flow is based on the effect of breathing on heart rhythm and on the circulation of body fluids (blood, lymph, and cerebrospinal fluid). The concept of cellular breathing can be reinforced by examining the experience of flow.

We have written that breathing forms a bridge between the mind and body. We use the metaphor of a breathing bowl, an inner space consisting of a vessel with an opening through which the mind breathes from the body. The mind breathes life into the body. This image will reduce the habit of performing and doing. The respiratory muscles will then be able to work in a relaxed way.

> *Let your breath flow into the space, cup, or bowl in your lower abdomen or pelvic floor. Let your exhalation flow out from there. Refill the bowl with another inhalation; half a cup will often suffice. This exercise allows you to bypass control by the diaphragm and make room for natural breathing.*

Many people believe firmly that breathing is done by the lungs alone—in and out. This kind of splitting also happens when people view different organs as if they were parts of a machine that various specialists treat in turn. We believe that breathing symptoms are connected with the whole personal history, that is, whether the person has learned to value what is happening inside him and whether he has permission to express it. The experience of internal flow is a tool for taking control of your own body.

The following exercise is useful for calming yourself if you find it difficult to quieten your mind. An image and exhalation are used for this three-part exercise. It is an appropriate exercise to do at night before going to bed.

> 1. *Breathe calmly, lying on your back, and imagine that you are breathing out through the top of your head. You can intensify the image by thinking that the top of your head is porous, full of tiny holes, or that you have a dolphin's blowhole there. Or you can imagine that you are spring-cleaning your brain. Continue doing this for a while.*

2. *Exhale calmly through your genitals, that is, through the vagina or through the penis. The use of images will stop you from thinking about whether you are doing this correctly. This phase of the exercise will relax your lower abdomen and pelvic floor and make room for the diaphragm to move.*

3. *Exhale through your feet and soles. This will extend and deepen the relaxing effect.*

The above exercise using images will improve circulation in the lower limbs, and relaxed exhalation will facilitate venous circulation. Many people suffering from hyperventilation symptoms say they have cold feet and fingers and poor circulation. The cold feeling has a clearly physiological background: hyperventilation reduces superficial circulation, and the feeling of cold, in turn, increases the tendency to hyperventilate. The symptoms of people suffering from poor circulation may therefore be alleviated when their breathing changes. Images can also be used to direct exhalation consciously into certain places in the body, such as sore or tense spots, cold fingers, or a place where there is an empty feeling inside. People with harmless resting tremor can also find relief in the calming effect of releasing exhalation. Similar image and breathing exercises are used for the mental coaching of competition athletes. Studies have shown the usefulness of such exercises: capillary circulation increases, improving metabolism (Douillard, 1995). We have also successfully taught patients with pain or poor peripheral circulation to use exercises with images for relieving their symptoms.

> *Direct your exhalation into the pain or coldness that you are feeling or breathe through it. Let the pain or coldness be as it is. If possible, let go of observing the pain or coldness, of trying to control it, or tensing your muscles against it. Your experience should not be judged but allowed to be as it is. Submit to the pain or coldness. The pain or coldness will die away or become tolerable when you breathe into it.*

In many people, symptoms arise, or are at least intensified, because their abdominal muscles are chronically tense for some reason. Back pain, gynaecological complaints, post-surgical conditions, traumatic sexual experiences, and taboos associated with sexuality may cause chronic tension in the abdominal area. Tense or overtrained abdominal muscles do not give the diaphragm room to move, and breathing therefore occurs in the upper body using accessory respiratory muscles. This may result in hyperventilation. Physiotherapists may be able to help to relax lower abdominal and pelvic floor muscles and to use exercises with gentle stretching and relaxation of thigh adductor muscles to release unconscious tension.

Pause after exhalation

Respiratory training has traditionally been considered to consist primarily of training respiratory muscles or expanding and deepening inhalation. It was thought that a large inspiratory capacity would guarantee correct and good breathing. Exercises consisted of drawing the air in forcefully, puffing the chest. This has been shown to lead to a feeling of being overwhelmed, and to exhalation becoming a short groan. In people suffering from panic anxiety, placing the emphasis on deep inhalation often increases symptoms. On the other hand, during a panic attack people may be afraid of letting go of air in exhalation for fear of suffocating. But being open to the experience of breathing will not cause us to lose any of our experience of the self. When breathing flows rhythmically back and forth in the body, with pauses in between, it flushes the body and revives it.

Breathing is often associated with images that are physiologically incorrect. One persistent health myth is that we need more oxygen to improve cellular metabolism and that carbon dioxide is a waste gas that we must get rid of (McKeown, 2004; Rakhimov, 2014). In our images, oxygen signifies a perfect, good mother you can never get enough of who will eliminate all anxiety. Carbon dioxide, on the other hand, is like a threatening, bad mother. It is also considered a waste that must be disposed of by expelling the breath fiercely. Hyperventilation is thus used to prevent shameful, forbidden, and feared emotions from entering consciousness. It is understandable that the feeling of not getting enough oxygen arising during hyperventilation activates a fear of death—making the person gasp for more oxygen. In reality, we need an appropriate ratio of oxygen and carbon dioxide to feel well. People often do not realise that, through physiological mechanisms, a lack of carbon dioxide reduces the amount of oxygen reaching the cells.

Tasks of carbon dioxide
<ul><li>To regulate breathing</li><li>To hold a key position in the process of normal cellular intake of oxygen</li><li>To relax smooth muscle surrounding the airways, arteries, and capillaries</li><li>To reduce neural activity.</li></ul>

In our images carbon dioxide should therefore be seen as being on a par with oxygen. Physical exercise often helps by producing carbon dioxide. In addition, we suggest breathing less, breathing naturally and as needed. Let us wonder at, observe, and practise keeping a pause after exhalation to increase and level out carbon dioxide levels. Inhalation as needed makes it possible to keep a pause after exhalation.

The experience of a resting pause after exhalation and the discovery of natural breathing are among our main goals. The pleasantness of such a pause is new for many. The pause provides breathing with rhythm; it expresses the rhythm of life, including the basic dynamics of combining being and doing. When people get used to the pause, they learn to recognise and tolerate emptiness in themselves. Images and emotions arising during the pause, "on the screen of silence", are highly valuable. It is possible to achieve a space and an experience of your own mode and rhythm of breathing there and to practise accepting your own individual pattern. The rhythm, depth, and volume of breathing are highly appropriate unless they are meddled with or unless emotions send out warnings of danger. The pause can be compared to a wave dying away on the beach. If you are not experienced in having pauses, they may at first be impossible to notice or may be very short. Gradually the body and the whole self will dare to submit to the pause and wait calmly for the following impulse to inhale. The pause is not a passive state; when practising, consciousness is present there.

In stressed breathing, the diaphragm pumps in and out and in and out without pause. Such breathing stresses the heart muscle and transmits to the central nervous system a message signifying danger. The body is in a state of alarm, and this reinforces a rapid breathing rhythm. Observing the place of the pause, gradually prolonging it, and yielding to it can be used as first-aid measures for calming down. To learn the pause we use "the mother of all breathing exercises", the body twist familiar from yoga, which makes it possible for even novices to find the pause.

> *Lie on your back with your knees bent and wide apart. Exhale, and during inhalation allow your knees to tilt slowly to the right, towards the ground. Exhaling gently, turn your head to the left. Breathe a few times while still in the twisted position and consciously enjoy the stretching of your upper body and neck. You can also bring your awareness to inhaling along your spine. During an inhalation, slowly return to the initial position. During exhalation, let go and feel your exhalation fade out to a pause. Wait to feel the impulse to inhale arise in your body. Do the exercise again, this time letting your knees fall to the left.*

This exercise produces the physical equivalent to the words we use in breathing school, "There is no need to worry, everything is fine" or to the familiar expression "a sigh of relief".

Assisted exhalation

Another person may *assist exhalation* with her hands. The person being assisted can lie on his back, on his side or face down. The person assisting should ensure that her partner is in a good position and that her touch feels firm and comfortable. She should press on her partner in the partner's rhythm and with suitable strength. She can use her hands or a ball for this. If she is pressing on the side of the body she can use her knuckles or arm. It is good to pause now and again during assisted exhalation, and the exercise should proceed at a calm pace. It is important not to push through any body armour or muscle tension. Before mental strengths develop, it is necessary to protect oneself by breathing and tension. The voice can often be used as a natural part of the exercise.

> *The breather lies on his back, the assistant sitting behind his head and placing one or both of her hands on his sternum or below his collarbones. As he exhales, the assistant pushes obliquely down towards the tail bone, thus helping the breather to empty his lungs. She can let one of her hands slide from the breastbone down towards the navel, or use a large, soft ball and let it roll from the breather's chest towards the navel during exhalation. The assistant may also assist exhalation by pushing on the breather's*

shoulders, on the ridges of his shoulder blades or on his sides. She can draw his arm obliquely downwards during exhalation, while using her other hand to help the shoulder blade to move.

The assistant can place the breather's soles against her stomach. She can help him to empty his lungs by rounding his lower back and pushing his knees onto his stomach during exhalation.

If the breather is lying on his side, exhalation can be assisted with the help of chest movement. On inhalation, the person assisting can help the breather's chest to open up by drawing his shoulder back, and on exhalation push the shoulder forward. Upper limb movement can be included in this wave-like motion. The assistant can also move the breather's shoulder and hip in opposite directions or draw them further apart and closer together as if playing the accordion.

If the breather's shoulders are chronically raised, the assistant can press them softly down along with exhalation. This can be done using both hands at the same time or assisting the right and left shoulders alternately.

Active exhalation

Exhalation involves fantasies of what is inside your body or what may be whirling in your mind. Fantasies of spirits or a soul hiding there may manifest themselves as a fear of their being released or escaping with the breath. Unpleasant symptoms such as a lump in the throat or difficulty swallowing represent a condensed form of this problem. Breathing difficulties will affect speech, as will needless swallowing throughout the day. When we do this, we press the back of the tongue against the palate, tightening the pharynx. Pain and spasmodic feelings associated with anxiety often concentrate in this area. Sometimes, conflicts may appear as constant smiling. It confuses other people when someone has a smile on his face even when speaking about an unpleasant topic. A person smiling compulsively or presenting herself as an overly nice diplomat may clench her jaw or grind her teeth at night. The larynx and the diaphragm are used for regulating emotions and consciousness of them. Anxiety and unconscious feelings of anger increase permanent tension in the jaws and the pharynx, which is reflected in the regulation of voice and affects the work of the diaphragm. Asking "I wonder what you are swallowing?" or "What is it that would be hard for you to express?" may help such issues to become conscious. We can focus on relaxing the masticatory and laryngeal muscles whenever we remember.

Let your jaw relax, teeth come apart, and your tongue rest in your mouth.
At the same time, let your face and the muscles maintaining facial expres-
sions relax. Now concentrate for a while on a breathing exercise that you
like. If you are alone, you can let your voice sound during exhalation.

We emphasise releasing exhalation and freedom of expression. In the teaching of classical singing, too, pressure-free, gentle exhalation is emphasised. The idea is that exhaling with pressure will make the diaphragm tense, causing compression of the trunk muscles and the lungs. After inhalation, when exhalation starts, the inhalation muscles are not relaxed but continue working. This is how we regulate the volume and the flow rate of exhalation. The moment of relaxation is perceived as an opening and preparatory (not loose or phlegmatic) phase of breathing. A singer may be afraid of letting go or finding herself short of air. The risk of revealing something uncontrolled or not daring to express forbidden sides of oneself may also cause anxiety. Fears relating to the use of space, that is, the feeling of not having enough space or not daring to fill it with one's voice are also significant. The fear of breathing all the way down may also prevent proper use of the voice.

It may be difficult to let the voice sound out on exhalation. Letting out the uncontrolled sound of one's voice in the presence of other people may invoke early experiences of shame. Exhaling audibly using the voice requires all one's courage and strengthens the ego identity.

Exhalation can be practised by consciously increasing the strength of movement or voice, shouting, and huffing or blowing to empty the lungs. Uttering a shout and exhaling when performing a strike, as is done in many types of martial arts, will strengthen the voice. It is good to be playful when trying to accomplish change through exercises as this will keep things relaxed, and shared laughter will lift inhibitions.

Breathe out everything that you wish to get rid of, and let in what you
wish to have in its stead. For example, use an image to exhale tightness
and tension, and inhale calmness and restfulness.

The exercise can also be done in pairs. Stand close to and facing each
other. Keep your knees supple and your posture in every way relaxed but
straight. During a long exhalation, sing a vowel, such as "Aah" (as in
"car"). Using your voice together with someone else requires courage, but
it can be a great experience. The voice will resonate in your body and you
will feel as though you are both jointly enveloped in a sound of well-being.

In your imagination, blow at a candle to make the flame flicker or die.

Let the exhalation out of your mouth in a burst, not caring about how it sounds.

Imagine that you are a dragon breathing out fire and smoke. It is good to have a partner in this exercise. This will prove that we cannot cause any real harm by breathing.

Hiss like a cat to exhale through your teeth. Intensify the exercise by pretending to use your sharp nails to scratch. This exercise is particularly suitable for people with asthma.

Shadow-boxing in a relaxed, rhythmic way, with each blow exhale and say "Huh—huh—H U H—huh—huh—HUH!"

Standing firmly with your legs apart, punch the air yelling "Yes!" Feel the joy and sense of power increase. In your mind, you can thank and praise yourself for your success.

If you notice that you are out of breath, blow out a few times through pursed lips.

Imagine a plunger inside you that rises up from the pelvic floor during inhalation and moves down, pushing the air out from down there, during exhalation.

Sitting with your elbows resting on your thighs, press your palms together and make a long "s" sound. Be aware of the pressing hands as you hiss. Feel the power in your muscles, exhalation, and voice. This is a good exercise for grasping power.

Lie down on your back with your knees bent. While inhaling calmly, raise your arms up and back towards the floor behind your head. During exhalation, return them to your sides. Do this first calmly for a few times to learn the movement of your arms. Then gradually let your arms fall to the ground during exhalation, feeling the power of the movement and the speed of your arms. Intensify the movement further by using your voice. You can sigh, moan, shout, or say "Out!" or "Go!" while your arms fall forcefully to the ground during exhalation. Think about things that you are ready to let go of: emotions, events, situations in life, memories, or difficult relationships, everything that you would like to get rid of. Imagine that you are throwing away everything that is burdening you. This exercise is like real spring-cleaning in the attic. Enjoy your voice, your power, and the thought of being able to decide for yourself.

In one social anxiety group, we threw away issues using arm movements. Playing and having permission to throw things out inspired the group to discuss power. In the discussion, many different experiences of being humiliated and mistreated were touched on. Such exercises may help to bring up experiences that can then be discussed. Playing together increases safety and a trust that you are allowed to say things aloud and that those things will be accepted. When you get permission to use force instead of being hushed, you get close to experiences of, perhaps, having been insulted, betrayed, humiliated, or felt helpless or frustrated. Being allowed to feel as you do is an integrating experience.

> *A similar exercise can be done using the legs. Lying on your back, bend one knee to your stomach in preparation. Kick your leg straight, sliding your heel along the ground and shouting "Out!" Try the words "Go!" and "Enough!", too. Repeat the exercise with your other leg. As above, you can use your voice, and words and thoughts of throwing away and letting go in association with this exercise.*

8.6. Breathing and the experience of space

Inner space and images

Inhalation is associated with observing and experiencing inner spaces; that is, recognising one's boundaries from the inside. The experience arises from the movement of the abdomen, from the chest rising and expanding. The experience of space leads us to the concept of emptying and being filled. A fear of emptiness is a very basic fear that activates breathing symptoms. Any empty space must be rapidly filled, lest an outsider find a way to invade it. People who talk incessantly fill the emptiness with speech. In this way, they ensure that others cannot argue with their thoughts. Other people fill the empty space with activity, eating, or watching TV. They must never feel empty or bored.

About space exercises
• All breathing exercises are space exercises, particularly when being done in relation to another person or a group   • Images are used to clear inner space, space for your own internal reality, for example, in "visualising the inner space", or "the mind breathing in yourself"

> • This is an experience of becoming empty, the letting go associated with exhaling, and at the same time of the expansion of your own inner space.

Finding and tolerating the empty space during the pause after exhaling reinforces the experience of your own internal reality and clears the way to a potential space in your mind. There you can simultaneously interact with the external world or with objects. When you learn to become calm, you do not need to fill the empty space immediately. You do not need to fear that the bad in someone else's or your own mind will invade the space and fill it.

> *Lie on your back with your knees bent. Breathe into the space down on your pelvic floor. With exhalation, let go of everything you have been holding onto. As you stop holding on, you may notice a tiny, inconspicuous opening at the spot where inhalation begins. Stay for a while in the space at the opening. Let inhalation flow naturally without paying attention to it, allowing your mind to rest.*
>
> *Open the mental door into your inner space. Breathe there or into it.*

Inhalation is associated with feelings of pleasure and experiences of receiving and of personal power. In inhalation, the experience of accepting unconditionally is activated. With this image, you can reinforce and reach the flowing movement inside you and relax your muscles.

> *Lie on your back with your knees bent. Concentrate first on the pelvic floor. Use the image of an elevator moving inside you. Inhalation will raise the elevator, exhalation lower it slowly to rest in the lower abdomen and on the pelvic floor.*
>
> *Lie on your back with your knees bent. Breathe into the soft empty space on your pelvic floor. Allow the space to expand sideways all the way to your ovaries. Men can use the image of expanding breathing to beneath their iliac bones. In the images, the space will expand to the form of an ellipse.*
>
> *Breathe in and out through your porous breastbone or through a hole in your navel. The image of opening a window or an outlet in your breastbone will help. Alternatively, you can imagine that your breastbone is made of a porous material that lets air through easily and is easy to breathe through.*

Space exercises assisted by a group

We have often heard people say "There is not even space to breathe in that group" or "That person takes up all the space". The regulation of breathing, like everything we think or do, always occurs in relation to other people. Space and breathing exercises done in a group are therefore useful. In such exercises, one person (the instructor or the partner) gives the breather verbal permission for his own breathing rhythm or concretely helps him to expand or empty his breathing space. The mere soothing presence of the other person intensifies the experience of space.

> *The person examining himself lies on his back. The person assisting sits at his feet and places her hands calmly on his ankles. She first concentrates on observing his breathing, relating for a while to his breathing rhythm, and only then starts assisting him. She takes a hold of his ankles to pull on them during inhalation to change the position of his pelvis and provide his diaphragm with more space. During exhalation, the assistant lets go. It is important to imagine the pulling first, allowing it to be felt only in the assistant's own body. Actual pulling will deepen and facilitate inhalation. The assisting movement should be soft and round, with at first gentle and then gradually increasing use of force. The use of force can be increased substantially, particularly in men with well-trained muscles. The assistant should follow her partner's breathing rhythm and not attempt to change it. In fact, the assistant's movements should preferably lag slightly behind those of the breather, following his movement. If this "breathing together" succeeds and feels good, it can be continued for some time.*
>
> *The exercise works equally well if the assistant pulls on the breather's ankles during exhalation. In our experience, some people prefer it this way. Others prefer their ankles to be pulled continuously. This requires slightly more strength from the assistant but may really arouse a feeling of letting go and creating space.*
>
> *This exercise can be performed with the assistant sitting behind the breather's head, lightly holding his neck and gently pulling on it. Or the exercise can be performed with the assistant supporting exhalation. In this case, she places one of her hands on the breather's chest, at the breastbone, and pushes it obliquely downward during exhalation.*
>
> *These exercises can be further intensified by pulling at both ends, that is, with the breather lying on his back, one assistant at his feet and*

another at his head. They pull along with inhalation and let go during exhalation. Again, pulling should be started slowly and calmly, listening to the breather and respecting his rhythm. The breathing space and rhythm should be controlled by the breather.

Expansion of the experience of space can be assisted if the breather lies with his knees bent and arms extended horizontally to both sides. The assistants take hold of his wrists, pulling them slowly sideways during inhalation and letting go during exhalation. The pulling can also be done during exhalation, to explore which version feels more pleasant.

The exercise based on the image of a starfish can be done alone or in a group of six. On inhalation, the centre rises, on exhalation, air flows into all five arms, that is, the limbs and the head, at the same time. In a group, one assistant is assigned to each arm of the starfish. The assistants gently pull on the arms along with breathing, thus creating space.

For a special treat, after the exercise the assistants can hold the breather's little fingers, stretching them gently and softly during inhalation or exhalation. This can also be done with the little toes. Moreover, this can be done either pulling simultaneously in all four directions or alternating between pulling on the little toes and the little fingers. In this exercise, the breather in the middle may experience his boundaries becoming stronger.

This exercise activates the pause after exhalation, which may be long. Assistants should be sure not to activate inhalation but to wait calmly. We encourage the breather to have the courage to give feedback and tell the assistants what feels good and what doesn't. In breathing school, this exercise has been found very useful and pleasant. Through understanding and assisting, it emphasises cooperation and empathy.

The following space exercise is not suitable for everyone, as it may arouse various associations provoking anxiety, and demands a certain mobility of the shoulder joints. Nevertheless, in the best case it can provide a rewarding excursion into the experience of space.

The breather lies on his back, with his hands clasped behind his neck. The assistant sits behind his head and takes a firm hold underneath his elbows. A second assistant can be used for this exercise, as necessary, just to hold the breather's ankles firmly, ensuring that his lower limbs are grounded. The first assistant lifts the breather's elbows very slowly from the ground, the breather breathing calmly at his own pace and examining any changes in how he is feeling. The breather can focus on how it feels to surrender to being supported, what kind of images arise at various stages of his elbows being lifted, whether he notices any muscle tension or release of tension, etc. The assistant continues lifting the elbows until they touch each other. She then presses the breather's lower arms briefly and lightly against his temples. The breather becomes aware of his head in the narrow space between his arms. The assistant then lowers the breather's arms to the initial position, again moving slowly. When the arms touch the ground, the assistant pushes them open, stretching the breather's chest muscles. The assistant lifts the breather's clasped hands to behind her own neck and, by lifting her upper body, stretches the area between the breather's shoulder blades. Finally, she opens the breather's arms placing them obliquely upwards on the floor and strokes them from the breastbone out towards the fingers. At the end of the exercise she helps the breather to turn onto his left side. This will allow the experience to be integrated.

Opening up of breathing space

These exercises are suitable for more advanced learners who have worked with their breathing for a slightly longer time (Klemola, 2013).

Opening up of lower breathing space: Sitting in the squatting position breathe towards your tail bone, lower back, and pelvic floor. Allow breathing to stretch your tissues softly and to expand the space in the pelvic area. At the same time, allow your back muscles to stretch, with your back rounded from the neck all the way down to the "tail".

Opening up of central and upper breathing spaces: Sit on a chair or stand in a firm position on the floor. Intertwine your arms to form a "garland", round your upper back and breathe into the space between your shoulder blades, opening it up.

Opening up of upper breathing space in the sitting or standing position: Breathe space into your upper neck.

Breathe out pronouncing vowels (aah, eeh, eee, ooh, ooo) in your mind, recognising in which direction the vowels create space in you.

Combine voice with exhalation, using, for example, vowels, sighs, or other speech sounds.

In the sitting position, focus on breathing into a "balloon" in your abdomen. The balloon will expand with each inhalation. Continue this until the balloon has expanded to the size of the whole universe, to infinity. The balloon will then gradually start to shrink, its centre point being in your abdomen.

Stand with your knees relaxed. In your imagination, take hold of a
balloon and imagine it expanding and emptying slightly as you breathe.
Then imagine that you are a pear-shaped balloon yourself, filling up and
being emptied in the same way.

8.7. Inhalation

Inhalation is receiving

Inhalation lays down the conditions for receiving, determining whether
inhaled air can flow in effortlessly.

Life begins with the first breath and breathing continues cyclically
until the end. We need oxygen to enable the body to use food as fuel
for energy. Breathing is normally unconscious, automatic, and in balance, but if we wish to, we can become aware of it and influence it
consciously. Automatic regulation processes can be bypassed to a certain extent. We spontaneously breathe more deeply when we smell, see,
or experience something pleasant, such as the scent of a rose, the sea,
a forest, or a spring morning.

Even very small children store sensations comprehensively through
their senses, and the respiratory tract acts as another assimilation route.
The most significant example of positive assimilation is breathing in,
sucking on, and ingesting the bringer of all good—the mother. This
experience is often reciprocal, with parents feeling the desire to smell
the baby's head or using images such as "You are so sweet I could eat
you". If the environment is sufficiently safe, approving, and receptive,
a safe and permissible way of regulating breathing is created.

Inhalation can be practised in pairs, looking at each other's faces. Inhale
extending your arms towards your partner; on exhalation, bring your
hands back to your chest and experience giving to yourself. This experience
may revive the feeling of receiving without doing or making an effort. You
can just let yourself be; opening up to receive everything that is flowing in.
There is enough air and you can have all you need, unconditionally.

In breathing school, we also discuss greed in connection with breathing
exercises. Even adults sometimes need permission and support for taking in rather greedily.

If the body and its automatic regulation mechanisms are governed
by fears and conditions and have learned that the body should be used

cautiously, breathing will be weak and superficial. Breathing muscles, particularly the diaphragm, then work under tension, with the brakes on. Chronic anxiety may develop in the body, intensifying the fear of not getting enough air. The person will start gulping in air, which will aggravate the situation. Breathing according to one's needs will become impossible. Many people (or their bodies) are afraid of delicate, calm, barely perceptible breathing. A fear of death is activated: "What if I stop breathing altogether?" We therefore think it is important, in addition to teaching breathing and movement exercises, to teach people to listen to themselves and become aware of their own emotions, sensations, and images.

> Breathe into the home of breathing, the soft spot in your abdomen beneath the navel, and into the chest.
>   Lying on your back, breathe calmly into the space, bowl, or cup we visualise on the pelvic floor. When inhaling, think about the word "yes" or "OK". Receive and give to yourself.

Inhalation can be intensified by reminiscing about a flower with a lovely scent and inhaling the scent. At the same time, you can move your head back and forth a little to deepen your breathing. Reminiscing about a pleasant memory or any other pleasant thing will deepen breathing. When entering a forest or walking by the sea, we often do this instinctively, breathing in the fresh air. We have used pictures of nature scenes for this purpose. Like good experiences in nature itself, looking at such pictures has been found to lower the blood pressure and stabilise the pulse rate.

Nasal breathing

Nasal breathing will prevent overbreathing and regulate the breathing volume. The nose is an effective filter that also warms up and moistens the air. Inhalation slows down, the diaphragm is activated, and consciousness of breathing and of oneself are improved. Many breathing school participants have said that they have narrow nasal passages, a deviated septum or chronic rhinitis complicating nasal breathing, which may have contributed to hyperventilation symptoms. Others may suffer from the opposite phenomenon; lack of use of the nose may have led to its obstruction. Nasal irrigation with saline solution or alternate nostril breathing from yoga may help if the nose is stuffy. The image of breathing into the two cerebral hemispheres or between them may also open up the airways (McKeown, 2004; Rakhimov, 2014).

> *Imagine that you are drawing in air through your nose into a bag in your stomach or into a balloon, relax and let exhalation occur spontaneously, emptying the bag or the balloon.*

Breath-holding after inhalation

Many breathing guides suggest pausing and holding your breath after inhalation (Klemola, 2013). In the therapy we provide, we do not empha-sise this. In our experience, people unconsciously hold their breath quite enough. The primary goal of the exercise is to experience a natural flow of breathing and find the natural pause after exhalation. Patients with panic anxiety often have overwhelming tension of the accessory respiratory muscles, and holding their breath will add to this and to the anxiety, increasing the symptoms. Only when people become familiar with their breathing and the function of their bodies can a pause after inhalation be added to the exercises. This experience can help them find their own boundaries from the inside through the resulting pressure.

> *Breathe against your inner boundary by drawing your lungs as full of air as you can. On exhalation, slowly let the air flow out.*

8.8. Breathing and movement

Combining movement and breathing

When combining breathing and movement, you have to learn to walk before you can run. Start with a tiny, familiar movement, such as extend-ing your thumb on inhalation and bending it on exhalation. When com-bining breathing and movement, even a more advanced learner may feel breathing involves more than the two tasks, in and out … A child needs to learn from the very beginning to combine breathing with doing: "I breathe and suck." Even as adults, many people find it dif-ficult to do two things at a time: "I peel a potato, stop, breathe, and con-tinue peeling." This is easier to become aware of once you have learned to observe what is happening in your body in daily life.

Movements of the arms, legs, and back are usually not thought to be accompanied by breathing. Therefore, concentration on simple movements of these parts should be used for the exercises. This will stop the mind obsessing about controlling breathing as such or about correct performance. Movements help breath to flow rhythmically and a conscious wave of breath, again, helps natural movement (Jalarmo, Klemola, Mikkonen, Mähönen, 2007; Rosas & Rosas, 2004; Wildman, 2006). All exercises involving movement can be done changing the direction of breathing every once in a while and examining which way feels most pleasant. It is also good to concentrate on letting breathing start and movement follow in the rhythm of breathing. Your own interest in the experience imbues the exercise with feelings of presence and being in a relationship (Blitz, 1985).

> Sit or lie down with your palms open. Imagine that your hands are flowers and your fingers the petals. The flower opens up and closes again in the rhythm of breathing. Change the direction of breathing and examine which way feels more pleasant. You can also allow your hands to conduct a dialogue: one closes while the other one opens up.
>
> Lie on your back with your legs extended. Inhalation will bend your ankles and exhalation relax your feet. Change the direction of movement as in the preceding exercise and try conducting a dialogue between your feet.
>
> Lie on your back. On inhalation, raise your arms up towards the ceiling, then relax and exhale letting them return to your sides. Do the same exercise consciously guided by your breathing: start the movement with a delay after inhalation has begun, as if inhalation is lifting your arms up; exhalation will lower them again. Movement and breathing merge. Examine the difference between the two versions of the exercise.
>
> Lying on your back extend your arms sideways with your palms up, and consciously breathe in a feeling of space. On inhalation, take your arms to the floor behind your head. On exhalation, let go and yield to the soft stretching of your whole body. Then allow inhalation to lift your arms up towards the ceiling; during exhalation, stretch them towards the ceiling. Inhalation opens your arms to your sides, expanding the space within your chest.

Breathing down to the pelvic floor

All breathing exercises are based on pelvic floor exercises. Constant tension of abdominal muscles prevents the natural downward movement of the diaphragm. Flaccid abdominal muscles or excessively tense pelvic floor muscles do not support the abdominal organs or assist natural exhalation, either. This may be associated with functional disturbances of the pelvic floor described in Chapter Four.

Self-reflection

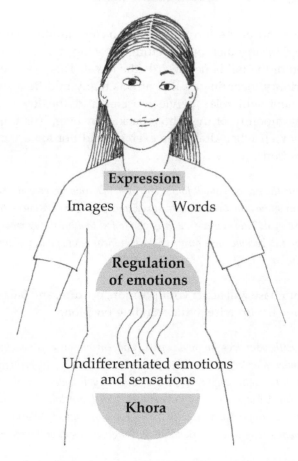

Expression

Images   Words

Regulation
of emotions

Undifferentiated emotions
and sensations

Khora

To practise breathing down to the pelvic floor, start by lying on your back. The image of a bowl with a flexible bottom into which you breathe is useful. Flexible movement of the pelvic floor will make room for the diaphragm to work. During inhalation, when the diaphragm contracts, the pelvic floor will relax, and vice versa.

Lie with your knees bent and feet on the floor. During the whole exercise, remain conscious of the pelvic area and spinal movements. Breathe into the bottom of your inner space. On inhalation, your navel area rises, the lower back comes off the floor, and the pelvic floor relaxes. During exhalation, the pelvic floor is contracted. Your tail bone and navel approach each other, your back is rounded and lower back pressed against the floor. The flowing, enjoyable wave-like motion of your spine continues all the way up to your neck.

This exercise can be performed using varying amounts of force and emphasising, for instance, either letting go or emptying through intensive traction of the tail bone towards the navel. This exercise will help with the urinary incontinence that afflicts many middle-aged women. The movement will relax pelvic muscles and the lower back and improve the mobility of the whole back. However, it is important to listen to yourself when doing the exercise and not force yourself into extreme positions.

Continue the exercise on all fours. During inhalation lower your back so that your spine forms a downward curve, and during exhalation arch your back like a cat. This exercise will help you to feel that breathing movement flows and to become more aware of the significance of spinal mobility for breathing.

Training your base will affect your position, posture, and balance; therefore, continue the exercise in the standing position.

Stand with your legs hip-wide apart. Concentrate on experiencing the floor under your feet, submit to it while simultaneously supporting yourself on it. Let your weight rest on the whole of your soles. Become aware of gravity. Become aware of the support from the pelvic floor muscles. Become aware of the midline with the help of your spine. Let the breathing movement strengthen the extending, flowing movement of the spine.

Willpower starts from your legs and lower back below the waist and bounces to your upper body like from a trampoline, utilising the bones to create a counter-stretch up to the base of the skull. Placing your legs too wide apart will stiffen the pelvic area, while overextended, locked, knees will stiffen your lower back and prevent the natural work of the diaphragm.

Alive, breathing spine

When we speak about breathing exercises we often use images emphasising the importance of muscles on the front of the body and of training this area in breathing. But tense muscles on the back of the body and an imbalance between various muscle groups also often disturb breathing. Tension and imbalance cause locking, stiffness, and pain in the back and thereby result in impeded breathing. In natural, unimpeded breathing, we can perceive the flexible movements of the vertebrae. Experiencing the breathing wave in the spine reinforces awareness of the midline of the body and improves coordination between upper body and pelvis. Use of images releases and sensitises the use of intervertebral muscles (Franklin, 1996).

> *Sit on a chair or a large ball. Use your buttocks to perform a circular movement around your seat or move the ball similarly; shift your weight using your pelvic muscles. Relax your muscles while doing this. Stop the movement and become aware of your midline and spine. Use the image of your consciousness, your "experience of yourself" rising up your back. Breathe calmly. Repeat the movement from the beginning.*
>
> *Sit on a chair with your knees apart, feet firmly on the floor. First concentrate on your tail bone. Utilising the above image, draw the inhalation up along your spine. Exhale letting the breath flow down the front of your body to the starting point. Let go, relax. Let your spine come alive with your breathing.*

The spine represents strength, responsibility, and adulthood. For example, we often speak of "putting our back into something"—or, on the contrary, describe a person as being "spineless".

> *Elliptic breathing utilising an image and visualisation: Lie on your back, knees bent, feet firmly on the floor. Inhalation starts from the tip of the tail bone and continues along the spine up to the head. Concentrate on the midline and on becoming aware of the spine. Your sensitivity to the role of your spine in breathing will gradually increase, and your trust in your body will also start to grow. Exhalation curves from the top of your head down along the front of your body. This way, you can visualise the elliptic form of breathing, and your breathing can flow in an even, calm wave. This is a good exercise for doing in bed in the evening, for example.*

In any breathing exercise, sexual sensations may arise spontaneously; this may happen during this exercise, for example. If so, notice your sensations gently and enjoy them without a target or any need to put them into practice. This represents your creative power. Whether inhalation rises to the level of the chest, the mouth, or the top of the head varies naturally from individual to individual. This exercise can be done equally well sitting on a chair. We have received plenty of positive feedback for both versions. One patient said: "The bus is the worst place for my panic disorder but I have to take the bus to work every morning. But now my commute has become considerably easier. I sit there with my breath moving elliptically ..."

Rest your back by drawing your knees up to your stomach, with your arms clasped around them. Rotate your knees slowly, using your lower back to draw a small circle on the ground. Allow your breath to flow and enjoy the stretching of your lower back.

Continue in the same position. Imagine that you are a wide bowl full of precious liquid. Tilt yourself slowly from one side to the other, taking care not to splash any liquid over the rim. Feel the shift of weight on your cheek, your flank, and your pelvis. Breathe slowly in step with tilting.

Lie on your back with your knees bent. Focus on the tip of your nose as a tool, and use it to draw an ellipse in the air. Change the direction. Breathe evenly, as if power is flowing from your breath to move your head. Become aware of what happens in your neck and shoulders. Rest and listen to the relaxing effect of the movement.

Stand with your back straight, knees supple, and feet firmly grounded. Become aware of your uppermost cervical vertebra. Start by tilting your head slightly forward while exhaling. Continue the movement one vertebra at a time towards the ground, stopping the movement each time you inhale. Each exhalation will release and relax your muscles further. Continue bending forward as far as feels good. Beware of pushing yourself or using excessive force. Stay in the extreme position to breathe for a while and to listen to yourself. Continue by gradually straightening up again. This time, each inhalation will extend your spine, one vertebra at a time. Stop the movement during each exhalation. This will give you time to send relaxing thoughts to your back muscles and to become aware of the space between the vertebrae.

8.9. Breathing and interaction

Breathing exercises in interaction

In the following exercises, the partner and the group are used to expand the significance of the exercise in the area of self-knowledge. We have explained repeatedly how important it is to understand breathing, and changes taking place in it, in relation to interaction. This knowledge has helped us to develop breathing exercises and to evolve them further, as well as to understand the origin of breathing symptoms. The unconscious body memory guides what happens in us. Understanding this points us to how breathing and well-being can be influenced. Appropriate exercises improve the ability for self-reflection, that is, they bring consciousness to the interaction between the experiencing self and the observing self.

Simple exercises done in pairs, with the emphasis on inhalation and looking at the partner's face, continue the experience of *inhaling what is good*. For homework, we have suggested going to the market. When talking to friendly vendors there, we can observe our breathing and what we notice in interaction. We can learn to become aware of the movements in our mind and our automatic thoughts. Physical freezing and clinging to thought patterns causing fear is typical for states of anxiety. In addition, it has been found that anxious people do not use their senses to test reality but to observe their symptoms, thus increasing their sensations. Turning the head slightly and looking with curiosity at what is going on around them may help to take their thoughts away from unpleasant sensations.

The following exercise was developed in breathing school when a young woman sighed, "If only someone would breathe for me even for a moment."

> One person sits with his back against the wall and legs apart. He holds large cushions for his partner to lean on. The person sitting in front of him leans on the cushions and on his chest. The person behind can, if he so wishes, place his hands on his partner's shoulders and breathe evenly and calmly "on her behalf". The person he is holding can let go of her worry about breathing and just let herself be. Submitting to being supported by the breathing rhythm of the person sitting behind you resembles the bodily experience of letting your mother take total responsibility for your self-regulation. In this exercise, the importance of the person in the adult role calming down his own breathing can be emphasised. He should keep his eyes open during the exercise to keep consciously responsible.

Some group participants find this a corrective experience. It may represent a return to a shared rhythm, to being nurtured and supported. Switching the roles arouses interesting discussions. What does it mean to be supported, what does it mean to support or to breathe in the role of an adult? We have recommended doing the exercise at home when watching TV, for example. You can support the other person's breathing by breathing calmly and thus revive someone who is exhausted. When a hyperventilation attack is beginning, you can go close to your spouse, for instance, to listen to his or her calm and deep breathing. A participant in breathing school instructor training reported:

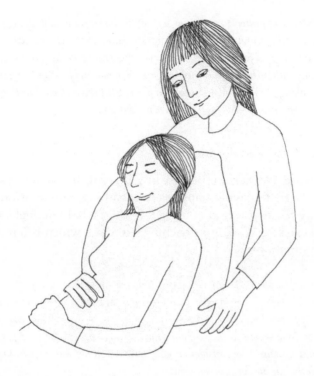

The partner exercise was really rewarding. I could not have guessed how deeply such a simple exercise could affect me. It was blissful to submit to being the recipient. I felt the other person as being present, safe, and calm. It was easy to relax, and I felt happy. On the following day, I realised that as a baby I had missed precisely that, the experience of a parent calmly present, in no hurry to go anywhere and with time to spend with me. I believe my mother must even then have been quite efficient and busy, taking care of my basic bodily needs in an exemplary way but not knowing how to stop, to just be and wonder. At least this is how she was later on when I was big enough to remember. The exercise reminded me strongly of the importance of giving my time to my children, of just being close to them. I have sometimes hastily urged my daughter to give me a hug in the evening without really stopping to pause and experience the moment. I have now been able to do that and received a positive response from my children.

The role of the giver was more difficult for me. As I had just been in a blissfully relaxed state, I noticed that I worried whether I could offer my partner a good enough experience of being held. I observed my breathing and felt nervous vibration. I felt that I had to really work to be able to be in an adult's responsible position without becoming nervous. The effect of the exercise appeared to continue even after the training day. Being close had touched me, and emotions with no name and no target emerged. There was anxiety and fear with no target. The bus trip home felt exceptionally difficult with no one to share my feelings. At home, my husband supported me, making me feel safe and mirroring me. Still the awkward feeling did not pass quickly. I felt heavy for three or four days.

Space, nearness, and distance

These exercises can help familiarise us with typical psychophysical reaction models, that is, what happens in breathing, how tension changes in the body, what you find you are thinking, what you feel like doing. The basic exercise is an "approaching exercise" which is familiar from everyday situations:

The exercise should be done in pairs. One person stands still, sensitive to observing herself, her images, emotions, and, in particular, changes in her breathing rhythm, while her partner approaches her walking slowly. This can be done several times, varying the walking speed. When the partner reaches a distance he considers appropriate, he stops, and the two look at each other in the eye for a moment.

The person standing still can also be allowed to make a small corrective movement, approaching the walker or moving further away from him. This way, both can influence the situation and express their needs for being close or more distant.

In the third phase, the person standing still extends her arms at shoulder width towards the person approaching. She should listen to her real need and either allow her arms to open for the person approaching or protect her own space with her hands, turning her fingers towards each other to form a gate.

Roles are switched, and afterwards the thoughts and emotions aroused by the different approaches can be discussed. Many people have said at the beginning of the exercise, "Yes, of course you can come close to me, go ahead." It may then be surprising to see how they actually feel during the exercise. They may react with their breathing, and familiar situations may come to mind. It is therefore good to encourage the group to practise expressing their own space. Support is also often needed for maintaining appropriate separateness. The instructor can mention that it is important to see the other person as a whole. If you stand with your nose right against the other person's nose, it is hard to see him.

We have encouraged people to utilise this experience in daily interaction. Reactions aroused by the family and changes in tension between colleagues have been the most interesting. Where people have previously blamed the circumstances and other people for their social anxiety symptoms, they are now more interested in examining what is happening within themselves. After the exercise they may have a more compassionate attitude towards their ways of protecting themselves, becoming more aware of their mixed messages in situations where their bodies are communicating something different from what they are saying. With time, they may become able to take responsibility for a change towards becoming more genuine.

> The following exercise is performed in pairs with a chair between the two partners. Standing facing each other, look into each other's eyes and maintain eye contact throughout the exercise. Looking into each other's eyes and breathing, allow tension to arise between you. Examine how the tension changes when one of you climbs up onto the chair. The situation can be intensified by the person standing on the floor kneeling down. Both should observe what is happening in them. Look at each other's faces. Observe changes in your breathing, tension, thoughts, and emotions. Then switch roles and repeat the exercise.

In many instances, the person looking up has said that it was confusing to notice how one of his life's authorities immediately came to mind. People have found it equally surprising to experience how small they felt. There is no space even to breathe, they dare not decide for themselves. On the other hand, the person down in a "child's" position may develop a deep feeling of trust; the other person being responsible, he is allowed to be helpless and small. The person up on the chair may feel guilty and uncomfortable in her body. It is, after all, inappropriate to feel pleasure at placing oneself above another person, not to mention intensified feelings of having power. A wish to help the person below may be activated. The person up on the chair may be annoyed and wish to come down at once. Breathing evenly will clarify the emotions in this exercise, and positive consciousness of oneself may develop.

The height difference achieved by using the chair is utilised to activate internal events—body memories. The goal of the exercise is to understand this. We often talk about equality but also realise how difficult it is to put into practice. Under what circumstances can a parent and a child be equal? The experience of an encounter can only happen in an equal relationship. In groups of professionals, this exercise has aroused significant discussion and understanding for how easily our bodies react to interaction.

We recommend this exercise for doing at home between parent and child. It is an empowering experience for a child to become big by stepping on a chair and to breathe there watching his parent lower down. However, we do not recommend that the parent step on the chair to become even bigger; it is sufficient for the parent to stand on the floor and breathe love towards the standing child.

Territory exercises

As a child becomes more differentiated, he learns to control himself, his body, and the surrounding space in relation to others. There are many words and expressions reflecting this taking control of space: "mine", "my own chair", "my mother". Today, many children have their own rooms, and they naturally learn to control their own space. They hang signs on their doors: "STOP—knock before you enter" or "Girls not admitted". Various symbols can be used to mark a person's own territory. People passionately defend their fishing waters, chanterelle sources, or, in coffee rooms at workplaces, their own chairs. By doing so, they strive to increase the feeling of safety: within their own territories they are allowed to have their privacy. In any case, the aim is to have the possibility for creating potential space. They can then learn to compromise between their own wishes and the needs of their environment and yield or reassert themselves, as necessary.

Sentences such as "I haven't even got space to breathe" or "Don't worry about me, I'll be fine" reflect lack of space. When you ask your guest whether he would like to have some coffee, he might say "Don't bother just for me" instead of saying simply "Yes, please". A person neglecting his own needs and wishes places someone else's needs ahead of his own, trying to please and be polite. He has not become autonomous or developed a fully reasonable feeling of being allowed to own his body and influence the use of space. Difficulty saying "no" is an example of the same phenomenon.

This exercise is performed similarly to the approaching exercise. Stand still and be prepared to listen to what is happening inside you as your partner approaches. Use conscious breathing. Recognise the point where your partner enters your territory. React by saying "stop" and reinforcing the word by raising your hand in front of your chest, palm towards your partner, who is approaching. Your partner, who was approaching slowly, stops at the point where you react.

Many versions of the stopping exercise can be produced. The difficulty of recognising any particular boundary around oneself is quite common. In therapy groups, this exercise has been used to study mixed messages, and it has increased the understanding of why a person's words are not taken seriously and why people do not believe him. The exercise is associated with everyday life. Many mix-ups are due to a lack of boundaries and not being able to open your mouth to express your thoughts and wishes. The difficulty of saying "no" has been discussed in nearly every group. Group members are confused about the conflict between their own wishes and other people's expectations. Participants often fantasise about renaming the breathing school as "No school", "Power school", or "Anger school".

The exercise is performed with the two partners facing each other. They take hold of each other with an arm-wrestling grip and look each other in the eyes throughout the exercise. The partners gradually increase the force, continuing to breathe all the time.

Another alternative is for the partners to stand facing each other in a walking position, with their palms against each other. In this power exercise, the image of moving heaven and earth to achieve something is activated.

The aim of these exercises is not to compete but to get to know your own power in relation to the other person. In addition, they provide the opportunity for becoming aware of any images and thoughts that arise and of one's fears associated with the use of one's own power.

Stick fight in pairs: Each partner holds a stick, grasping it firmly in both hands, the hands slightly further apart than shoulder width. On exhalation, they hit the midsections of their sticks diagonally at each other. After each swift blow, the partners change the direction of their sticks, so that first one hand, then the other is in the upper position. The blows should be kept playful and follow the same rhythm. The partners look each other

in the face. The sticks must be strong because there is plenty of power in
swift blows!

In this exercise, it is possible to observe any hindrance to breathing and
fear of extending the abductor muscles all the way. "I might hurt myself
or my partner." Blows may turn into just a vague swinging if you are
afraid to use your strength assertively and seriously, if playfully.

Children fight with each other about every possible thing, clothes
and other possessions. Sometimes they fight over who is allowed to
own their mother or father.

> *Gym balls of various sizes are useful for play between adults. In this exer-*
> *cise, two partners fight over a ball while continuing to breathe. One part-*
> *ner says: "Mine! My own!" The other may use various means of obtaining*
> *the ball, cajoling his partner or trying to take it by means used by children.*
> *This exercise offers the protection of being a game; the fight can dissolve*
> *into laughter, relaxing both parties.*

Big balls are very useful for active, joyful finding of your own power in
breathing exercises.

> *One person holds a therapy ball firmly in place, while her partner keeps*
> *kicking it (or hitting it with his fists) joyfully. The kicks or blows can be*
> *accompanied by images of targets. Such images can be used to reinforce*
> *the movement and to release inhibitions. In play, no one will be really*
> *hurt. The person holding the ball should make sure that the kicker's power*
> *is directed out towards the ball and the other person and that he uses his*
> *abductor muscles in a relaxed way.*

If a therapy ball of 120 cm in diameter is available, there can be two
kickers at a time in the group. Two assistants hold the ball in place. In
addition, each kicker has a personal assistant either holding his shoulders to keep him in place or, if the exercise is done with the kicker lying
on the floor, standing at the kicker's shoulders so that the kicker can
hold on to her ankles.

The kicking exercise should be continued until the kicker feels tired,
and even then he should listen to whether he would like to do it again.
The first experience of fatigue is most often due to automatic changes
in breathing. A change may occur if a person becomes angry. If he

does not approve of the feeling, it will frighten him. Even feelings of anger activated in play may at first feel forbidden. This exercise has often proved particularly important in groups of young people with eating disorders. Many adults have also been brought up to believe that it is not appropriate to express anger. This exercise may provide participants with an experience of taking control of power while using it safely in relation to others.

We have often marvelled at the unintegrated power flourishing in inefficiency and muscle tension symptoms. Assertiveness often becomes one of the most significant words and goals in therapy. Constructive self-defence without surrendering or aggressively violating the other person's boundaries is important for mental balance. Assertiveness can be practised in the imagination by using the wall plaque exercise.

Practising assertiveness and self-respect

Make yourself a wall plaque including the following thoughts. Place the wall plaque in a place where you can encounter the thoughts every day.

I have the right
- *to my emotions*
- *to my thoughts*
- *to my sensations*
- *to my breathing rhythm*
- *to being separate and to my body boundaries.*

I honour and respect
- *my emotions*
- *my thoughts*
- *my sensations*
- *my breathing rhythm*
- *my separateness and my body boundaries.*

Notice then how these thoughts affect
- your breathing
- your other bodily experiences
- your attitude towards yourself
- your relation to your family members, colleagues, friends.

A participant in breathing school instructor training described her experiences with this exercise as follows:

> *Luckily, these things are in order in my life—that was my spontaneous reaction on being given this task for homework. I know and feel that I have the right to my own emotions, thoughts, sensations, and breathing rhythm. I was glad that, in addition to myself, my relatives also honour and value my emotions, thoughts, and sensations, and even my breathing rhythm. The very next day, I painted the sentences on beautiful paper and attached it to the door of my closet.*
>
> *A few days later, I was disappointed and angry at myself for not keeping calm in a difficult situation with my children. I had felt strong anger that I tried to dispel, and later it burst out even more forcibly. Yet a few days later, I was tearfully angry about being anxious about a coming situation at work and about not having stayed calm in another situation at work.*
>
> *This woke me up. Was this me respecting and valuing my emotions? I had never understood how much I fought against my emotions. Was it any wonder then that I became exhausted? I now understand this, and I am bewildered. Since this insight I have wondered how I know when having my emotions under control means that I do not respect them. What would happen if I did not try to control them at all? When it comes to joy, that wouldn't be a challenge, but what about fury? Crying is a piece of cake but what about wanting to shout 'Shut up, everyone'?*
>
> *At home, they have begun to wonder why mother is angry so much more often than before. But, sure enough, she does not blow her top any more.*

This example sums up the essentials of what we wish to convey in this book. We have heard many similar stories from our patients and training groups. A change in the way of breathing does not only represent a change in the tidal volume or the use of appropriate muscles. The change affects the whole person and her relationships, from increasing the ability to calm down to the ability to value her emotions and the courage to express them.

REFERENCES

Aalto, A. -L., & Parviainen, K. (1985). *Auta ääntäsi* [Help your voice]. Helsinki, Finland: Otava.

Aron, E. (2003). *The Highly Sensitive Person: How to Thrive When the World Overwhelms You*. London: Element.

Bartley, J., & Clifton-Smith, T. (2006). *Breathing Matters. A New Zealand Guide*. Auckland, New Zealand: Random House.

Bateman, A., & Fonagy, P. (2006). *Mentalization-based Treatment for Borderline Personality Disorder: A Practical Guide*. Oxford: Oxford University Press.

Baumbacher, G. (1989). Signal anxiety and panic attacks. *Psychotherapy*, 26(1): 75–80.

Beebe, B., Knoblauch, S., Rustin, J., & Sorter, D. (2005). *Forms of Intersubjectivity in Infant Research and Adult Treatment*. New York: Other Press.

Berceli, D. (2008). *The Revolutionary Trauma Release Process: Transcend Your Toughest Times*. Vancouver, Canada: Namaste.

Blitz, G. (1985). *Yoga. La règle du jeu* [A yoga guide]. Paris: Union Européenne de Yoga.

Boadella, D. (1994). Styles of breathing in Reichian therapy. In: B. H. Timmons, & R. Ley (Eds.), *Behavioral and Psychological Processes to Breathing Disorders* (pp. 233–242). New York: Plenum Press.

Booth, P. B., & Jernberg, A. M. (2009). *Theraplay: Helping Parents and Children Build Better Relationships through Attachment-based Play.* San Francisco, CA: Wiley & Sons.

Borysenko, J. (1988). *Minding the Body, Mending the Mind.* Toronto, Canada: Bantam.

Bourne, E. (2015). *The Anxiety & Phobia Workbook (6th edition).* Oakland, CA: New Harbinger.

Broom, B. (2007). *Meaning-Full Disease: How Personal Experience and Meanings Cause and Maintain Physical Illness.* London: Karnac.

Brownridge, P. (1995). The nature and consequences of childbirth pain. *European Journal of Obstetrics & Gynecology and Reproductive Biology, 59*: S9–S15.

Buber, M. (1971). *I and Thou.* New York: Touchstone.

Caldwella, C., & Himmat K. V. (2011). Breathwork in body psychotherapy: Towards more unified theory and practice. *Body, Movement and Dance in Psychotherapy, 6*(2): 89–101.

Chaitow, L. (2002). Biomechanical influences on breathing. In: L. Chaitow, D. Bradley, & C. Gilbert (Eds.), *Multidisciplinary Approaches to Breathing Pattern Disorders* (pp. 83–109). Edinburgh: Churchill Livingstone.

Chaitow, L., Bradley, D., & Gilbert, C. (Eds.) (2002). *Multidisciplinary Approaches to Breathing Pattern Disorders.* Edinburgh: Churchill Livingstone.

Chaitow, L., Bradley, D., & Gilbert, C. (Eds.) (2014). *Recognizing and Treating Breathing Disorders (2nd edition).* Edinburgh: Churchill Livingstone.

Coffee, J. C. (2006). Is chronic hyperventilation syndrome a risk factor for sleep apnea? Part 1. *Journal of Bodywork and Movement Therapies, 10*: 134–146.

Damas-Mora, J., Davies, L., Taylor, W., & Jenner, F. A. (1980). Menstrual respiratory changes and symptoms. *British Journal of Psychiatry, 136*: 492–497.

Dębiec, J., & LeDoux, J. (2009). The amygdala and the neural pathways of fear. In: P. Shiromani, T. Keane, & J. LeDoux (Eds.), *The Post-Traumatic Stress Disorder: Basic Science and Clinical Practice* (pp. 23–38). New York: Humana Press.

Dewan, M. J., Steenberger, B. N., Greenberg, R. P. (Eds.) (2012). *Art and Science of Brief Psychotherapies: An Illustrated Guide (2nd edition).* Arlington, VA: American Psychiatric Publishing.

Diamond, D. B. (1987). Psychotherapeutic approaches to the treatment of panic attacks, hypochondriasis and agoraphobia. *British Journal of Medical Psychology, 60*: 79–84.

Douillard, J. (1995). *Body, Mind and Sport.* New York: Three Rivers Press.

Durand, E., Dauger, S., Vardon, G., Gressens, C., Gaultier, C., de Schonen, S., & Gallego, J. (2003). Classical conditioning of breathing patterns after two acquisition trials in 2-day-old mice. *Journal of Applied Physiology, 94*: 812–818.

Eisenberger, N. I. (2012). Broken hearts and broken bones: A neural perspective on the similarities between social and physical pain. *Current Directions in Psychological Science, 21*: 42–47.

Engel, G. L., Ferris, E. B., & Logan, M. (1947). Hyperventilation: analysis of clinical symptomology. *Annals of Internal Medicine, 27*: 683–704.

Epstein, M. (2005). *Open to Desire: Embracing a Lust for Life. Insights from Buddhism and Psychotherapy*. New York: Gotham.

Farhi, D. (1996). *The Breathing Book: Good Health and Vitality through Essential Breath Work*. New York: Holt Paperbacks.

Faulkner, W. B. (1941). The effect of the emotions upon diaphragmatic function. *Psychosomatic Medicine, 3*(2): 187–188.

Fenichel, O. (1931). Respiratory introjection. In: *Collected Papers of Otto Fenichel* (1953) (1: pp. 221–240). New York: W. W. Norton.

Franklin, E. (1996). *Dynamic Alignment through Imagery*. Champaign, IL: Human Kinetics.

Friedman, M. (1945). Studies concerning the etiology and pathogenesis of neurocirculatory asthenia: IV. *American Heart Journal, 30*: 557–566.

Gerhardt, S. (2004). *Why Love Matters: How Affection Shapes a Baby's Brain*. New York: Brunner-Routledge.

Gibbs, D. M. (1992). Hyperventilation-induced cerebral ischemia in panic disorder and effects of nimodipine. *American Journal of Psychiatry, 141*(7): 1589–1591.

Gilbert, C. (2002a). Biochemical aspects of breathing. In: L. Chaitow, D. Bradley, & C. Gilbert (Eds.), *Multidisciplinary Approaches to Breathing Pattern Disorders* (pp. 61–81). Edinburgh: Churchill Livingstone.

Gilbert, C. (2002b). Interaction of psychological and emotional effects with breathing dysfunction. In: L. Chaitow, D. Bradley, & C. Gilbert (Eds.), *Multidisciplinary Approaches to Breathing Pattern Disorders* (pp. 111–129). Edinburgh: Churchill Livingstone.

Goleman, D. (2006). *Social Intelligence: The New Science of Human Relationships*. New York: Bantam Dell.

Graveling, R. A., Pilkington, A., George, J. P., Butler, M. P., & Tannahill, S. N. (1999). A review of multiple chemical sensitivity. *Occupational & Environmental Medicine, 56*: 73–85.

Hägglund, T.-B., & Piha, H. (1980). The inner space of the body image. *Psychoanalytic Quarterly, 49*: 256–283.

Hari, R., & Kujala, M. V. (2009). Brain basis of human social interaction. From concepts to brain imaging. *Physiological Reviews, 89*: 453–479.

Harris, T. (1969). *I'm OK, You're OK*. New York: Galahad.

Heller, M. C. (2012). *Body Psychotherapy: History, Concepts, and Methods*. New York: W. W. Norton.

Hough, A. (1992). Physiotherapy for survivors of torture. *Physiotherapy*, 78(5): 323–328.

Hruska, R. J. (1997). Influences of dysfunctional respiratory mechanics on orofacial pain. *Dental Clinics of North America*, 41(2): 211–227.

Ikonen, P., & Rechardt, E. (1993). The origin of shame and its vicissitudes. *Scandinavian Psychoanalytic Review*, 16: 100–124.

Jalarmo, I., Klemola, T., Mikkonen, K., & Mähönen, Y. (2007). *Asahi*. Helsinki, Finland: Edita.

Jennett, S. (1994). Control of breathing and its disorders. In: B. Timmons & R. Ley (Eds.), *Behavioral and Psychological Approaches to Breathing Disorders* (pp. 67–80). New York: Plenum Press.

Kabat-Zinn, J. (1994). *Wherever You Go, There You Are: Mindfulness Meditation in Everyday Life*. New York: Hyperion.

Kabat-Zinn, J. (2013). *Full Catastrophe Living: Using the Wisdom of Your Body and Mind to Face Stress, Pain and Illness (2nd edition, revised and updated)*. New York: Bantam.

Kajamaa, R. (2003). Lyhytkestoiset psykoterapiaryhmät [Short-term psychotherapy groups]. In: R. Pöllänen & T. Sitolahti (Eds.), *Ryhmä hoitaa, teoriaa ja käytäntöä* [The group itself treats; theory and practice] (pp. 356–364). Helsinki, Finland: Yliopistopaino.

Keinänen, M. (1997). The meaning of the symbolic function in psychoanalytic psychotherapy. Clinical theory and psychotherapeutic applications. *British Journal of Medical Psychology*, 70: 325–338.

Keinänen, M. (1999). The evolution of the internal dialogue during the psychoanalytic psychotherapy process. *American Journal of Psychotherapy*, 53: 529–543.

Keinänen, M. (2000). Internalization and symbolization in the process of psychoanalytic psychotherapy: a case study. *Nordic Journal of Psychiatry*, 54: 347–354.

Keinänen, M. (2001a). The evolution of the psychosemiosis in the psychic development of the child. *Semiotica*, 135: 25–39.

Keinänen, M. (2001b). On symbolic function and its role in psychoanalytic psychotherapy. *Psychoanalytic Psychotherapy*, 15: 243–264.

Keinänen, M. (2003). The transformation of the internal dead mother into the internal living mother in the psychoanalytic psychotherapy of anorexia nervosa. *Israel Journal of Psychiatry*, 40: 220–231.

Keinänen, M. (2006). *Psychosemiosis as a Key to Body-Mind Continuum: The Reinforcement of Symbolization-Reflectiveness in Psychotherapy*. New York: Nova Science.

Keinänen, M. (2015). The psychosemiotic model for understanding the body-mind continuum: Implications for psychotherapeutic applications. In: P. Rosenbaum (Ed.), *Making our Ideas Clear: Pragmatism in Psychoanalysis* (pp. 215–241). Charlotte, NC: Information Age.

Keinänen, M., & Engblom, P. (2007). *Nuoren aikuisen psykodynaaminen psykoterapia* [The psychodynamic psychotherapy of young adults]. Helsinki, Finland: Duodecim.

Keinänen, M., & Martin, M. (2011). Mielen hengitys paniikkihäiriön psykodynamiikassa ja psykoterapiassa. [Mental breathing in the psychodynamics and psychotherapy of panic disorder]. *Psykoanalyyttinen psykoterapia, 7*: 68–83.

Kerr, W. J., Gliebe, P. A., & Dalton, J. W. (1938). Physical phenomena associated with anxiety states: the hyperventilation syndrome. *California and Western Medicine, 48*(1): 12–15.

Klemola, T. (2013). *Mindfulness.* Jyväskylä, Finland: Docendo.

Knoblauch, S. (2000). *The Musical Edge of Therapeutic Dialogue.* Hillsdale, NJ: The Analytic Press.

Korkeila, J. (2007). Astman ja ahdistuneisuushäiriöiden välillä merkittäviä yhteyksiä [Asthma and anxiety disorders]. *Suomen Lääkärilehti, 38*: 3409–3415.

Korkeila, K. (2006). Mikä suojaa stressiltä ja stressihaitoilta? [What protects us from stress and its detrimental effects?]. *Suomen Lääkärilehti, 40*: 4085–4090.

Korpela, T. (2012). Hengittääkö puhallinmusiikki raskaasti? [Does wind instrument music breathe heavily?]. *Musiikin suunta, 3–4*: 75–90.

Kristeva, J. (1984). *Revolution of Poetic Language.* New York: Columbia University Press.

Kunttu, K., Martin, M., & Almonkari, M. (2006). Nykyopiskelijakin jännittää esiintymistä, mikä avuksi? [Even today students have performance anxiety, what could be done about it?]. *Suomen Lääkärilehti, 44*: 4585–4588.

Kvåle, A., Johnsen, T. B., & Ljungren, E. (2002). Examination of respiration in patients with long-lasting musculoskeletal pain: reliability and validity. *Advances in Physiotherapy, 4*: 169–181.

Laine, A. (2012). Hengitys itsesäätelyn ja vuorovaikutuksen tukena [Breathing as a support of self-regulation and interaction]. *Scandinavian Psychoanalytic Review, 35*: 71–74.

LeDoux, J. (1996). *The Emotional Brain.* New York: Simon and Schuster.

Lehtinen, P. (1995). *Ahdistuksen psykosomatiikka* [Psychosomatic aspects of anxiety]. [Licentiate thesis in psychology.] Turku, Finland: University of Turku, Department of Psychology.

Lehtinen, P., & Laine, T. (1988). Hyperventilaatiosyndrooma psykologiselta ja psykiatriselta kannalta [Psychological and psychiatric aspects of the hyperventilation syndrome]. In: B. Falck, P. Lehtinen, & M. Tuhkanen (Eds.), *Hyperventilaatiosyndrooma* [Hyperventilation syndrome] (pp. 63–80). Turku, Finland: Kiasma.

Lehtinen, P., Tammivaara, R., Seppä, M., Luutonen, S., & Äärelä, E. (2000). Hyperventilaatio ja sen hoitomahdollisuudet [Hyperventilation and its treatment modalities]. *Duodecim, 116*: 1969–1975.

Lehtonen, J., Partanen, J., Purhonen, M., Valkonen-Korhonen, M., Kononen, M., Saarikoski, S., & Launila, K. (2006). Nascent body ego. Metapsychological and neurophysiological aspects. *International Journal of Psychoanalysis, 87*: 1335–1353.

Lin, J. M., & Peper, E. (2009). Psychophysiological patterns during cell phone text messaging: a preliminary study. *Applied Psychophysiological Biofeedback, 34*(1): 53–57.

Lowen, A. (1967). *Betrayal of the Body*. New York: Collier, Macmillan.

Lyons-Ruth, K. (1998). Implicit, relational knowing: Its role in development and psychoanalytic treatment. *Infant Mental Health Journal, 19*(3): 282–289.

Mahler, M. S., & Bergman, A. (1975). *The Psychological Birth of the Human Infant*. New York: Basic Books.

Martin, M., Friman, A., Hannula, R.-L., Lusenius, M., & Nieminen, M. (2016). *Painavaa asiaa kevyemmästä elämästä—Hyvinvointiopas painonhallintaryhmille* [Weighty comments on a lighter life—a wellbeing guide for weight management groups]. Helsinki, Finland: Ylioppilaiden terveydenhoitosäätiö.

Martin, M., Heiska, H., Syvälahti, A., & Hoikkala, M. (2012). *Satoa ryhmästä—opas hyvinvointiryhmän ohjaajalle* [Yields from group work—a guide for group instructors]. Helsinki, Finland: Ylioppilaiden terveydenhoitosäätiö.

Martin, M., Heiska, H., Syvälahti, A., & Hoikkala, M. (2013). *Jännittäminen osana elämää—opiskelijaopas* [Social anxiety as part of life—a guide for students]. Helsinki, Finland: Ylioppilaiden terveydenhoitosäätiö.

Martin, M., & Kunttu, K. (2012). *Psykosomaattinen oireilu—potilasopas* [Psychosomatic symptoms—a patient guide]. Helsinki, Finland: Ylioppilaiden terveydenhoitosäätiö.

Martin, M., &, Seppä, M. (2014). *Hengitysterapeutin työkirja* [A breathing therapist's workbook]. Tampere, Finland: Mediapinta.

McDougall, J. (1989). *Theatres of the Body: A Psychoanalytic Approach to Psychosomatic Illness*. London: Free Association.

McEwen, B. S. (1998). Protective and damaging effects of stress mediators. *New England Journal of Medicine, 338*: 171–179.

McFarland, D. (2001). Respiratory markers of interaction. *Journal of Speech, Language, and Hearing Research, 44*: 128–145.

McKeown, P. (2004). *Close Your Mouth: Buteyko Clinic Handbook for Perfect Health*. Dublin, Ireland: Asthma Care.

Mehling, W.-E. (2001). The experience of breath as a therapeutic intervention—psychosomatic forms of breath therapy. [A descriptive study about actual situation of breath therapy in Germany, its relation to medicine, and its application in patients with back pain.] *Forschende Komplementärmedizin und Klassische Naturheilkunde, 8*: 359–367.

Monsen, K. (1989). *Psykodynamisk kroppsterapi* [Psychodynamic body therapy]. Oslo, Norway: TANO.

Muurimaa, M. (1997). *Kuunteleva kosketus* [Perceiving touch]. Helsinki, Finland: Kehitysvammaliitto.

Nissinen, R. (2013). Integratiivisen paripsykoterapian pitkä tutkimusjakso [The assessment process of integrative couples therapy]. In: V. Malinen (Ed.), *Integratiivinen paripsykoterapia* (pp. 74–112). Helsinki, Finland: Psykologien kustannus.

Ogden, T. (1994). *The Subjects of Analysis*. Northvale, NJ: Jason Aronson.

Porges, S. (2011). *The Polyvagal Theory: Neurophysiological Foundations of Emotions, Attachment, Communication and Self-Regulation*. New York: W. W. Norton.

Rakhimov, A. (2014). *Normal Breathing: The Key to Vital Health*. Las Vegas, NV: CreateSpace Independent Publishing Platform.

Richter, P., & Hebgen, E. (2008). *Trigger Points and Muscle Chains in Osteopathy*. New York: Thieme.

Rinpoche, S. (1992). *The Tibetan Book of Living and Dying*. New York: HarperCollins.

Rochat, P. (2009). *Others in Mind: Social Origins of Self Consciousness*. New York: Cambridge University Press.

Rosas, D., & Rosas, C. (2004). *The Nia Technique: The High-powered Energizing Workout that Gives You a New Body and New Life*. New York: Broadway.

Rothschild, B. (2000). *The Body Remembers: The Psychophysiology of Trauma and Trauma Treatment*. New York: W. W. Norton.

Saaristo, T. (2000). *Taikasanat: Eli miksi antaisin anteeksi* [The magic words: Why would I forgive]. Helsinki, Finland: Dialogia.

Salzman, H. A., Heyman A., & Sieker, H. O. (1963). Correlation of clinical and physiologic manifestations of sustained hyperventilation. *New England Journal of Medicine, 268*: 1431–1436.

Schore, A. (1994). *Affect Regulation and the Origin of the Self*. Hillsdale, NJ: Erlbaum.

Seligman, M. E. P. (1991). *Learned Optimism*. New York: Pocket.

Selye, H. (1974). *Stress without Stress*. Philadelphia, MD: Lippincott.

Shear, M. K., Cooper A. M., Klerman, G. L., Bush, F. N., & Shapiro, T. A. (1993). Psychodynamic model of panic disorder. *American Journal of Psychiatry, 150*: 859–866.

Siltala, P. (1993). *Haen sanojani kaukaa: naiskirjailijan luovuus* [I seek my words from afar; on the creativity of female authors]. Helsinki, Finland: Yliopistopaino.

Siltala, P. (2002). Tunteet, mitä ne ovat, mistä ne tulevat, mitä ne merkitsevät ihmisen mielenterveydelle ja sairaudelle [Feelings: what are they, where do they come from, what is their significance for mental health and disorders?]. *Suomen Lääkärilehti, 57*: 3369–3373.

Spitz, R. (1965). *The First Year of Life*. Madison, CT: International Universities Press.

Stäubli, M., Vogel, F., Bärtsch, P., Flückiger, G., & Ziegler, W. H. (1994). Hyperventilation-induced changes of blood cell counts depend on hypocapnia. *European Journal of Physiology and Occupational Physiology, 69*(5): 402-407.

Stern, D. (1985). *The Interpersonal World of the Infant*. New York: Basic Books.

Stern, D. (1998). The process of therapeutic change involving implicit knowledge: Some implications of developmental observations for adult psychotherapy. *Infant Mental Health Journal, 19*(3): 300–308.

Stern, D. (2004). *The Present Moment: In Psychotherapy and Everyday Life*. New York: W. W. Norton.

Stinissen, W. (1988). *Deep Calls to Deep: A Study in Christian Depth-meditation*. Basingstoke, UK: Marshall Pickering.

Stone, A. M. (1992). The role of shame in post-traumatic stress disorder. *American Journal of Orthopsychiatry, 62*(1): 131–136.

Tähkä, V. (1993). *Mind & Its Treatment: A Psychoanalytic Approach*. Madison, CT: International Universities Press.

Thomas, M., & Bruton, A. (2014). Breathing exercises for asthma. *Breathe, 10*(4): 313–322.

Timmons, B., & Ley, R. (Eds.) (1994). *Behavioral and Psychological Approaches to Breathing Disorders*. New York: Plenum Press.

Tuomola, M. (2012). Hengitys kehon ja mielen siltana [Breathing as a bridge between body and mind]. In: L. Matikka, & M. Roos-Salmi (Eds.), *Urheilupsykologian perusteet* [The basics of sport psychology] (pp. 170–180). Tampere, Finland: Liikuntalääketieteellinen seura.

Uvnäs-Moberg, K. (2003). *The Oxytocin Factor: Tapping the Hormone of Calm, Love, and Healing*. London: Pinter & Martin.

van den Bergh, O., Stegen, K., & van de Woestijne, K. P. (1997). Learning to have psychosomatic complaints: conditioning of respiratory behavior and somatic complaints in psychosomatic patients. *Psychosomatic Medicine, 59*: 13–23.

van Diest, I., Stegen, K., van den Woestijne, K. P., Schippers, N., & van den Bergh, O. (2000). Hyperventilation and attention: Effects of hypocapnia on performance in a Stroop task. *Biological Psychology, 53*: 233–252.

van Dixhoorn, J. (1997). Functional breathing is "Whole body breathing". *Biological Psychology, 46*: 89–90.

van Dixhoorn, J. (2007). Whole-body breathing: A systems perspective on respiratory retraining. In: P. Lehrer, W.Woolfolk, & W. Sime (Eds.), *Principles and Practice of Stress Management (3rd edition)* (pp. 291–332). New York: Guilford Press.

van Dixhoorn, J. (2009). Whole-body breathing III: Clinical application/ implementation. *Biofeedback, 37*(1): 36–40.

van Dixhoorn, J., & Duivenvoorden, H. J. (1985). Efficacy of Nijmegen questionnaire in recognition of the hyperventilation syndrome. *Journal of Psychosomatic Research, 29*(2): 199–206.

van Dixhoorn, J., & Duivenvoorden, H. J. (1999). Effect of relaxation therapy on cardiac events after myocardial infarction: A 5-year follow-up study. *Journal of Cardiopulmonary Rehabilitation, 19*: 178–185.

van Lieshout, R. J., & Macqueen, G. M. (2012). Relations between asthma and psychological distress: an old idea revisited. *Chemical Immunology and Allergy, 98*: 1–13.

Voice Massage. www.voicemassage.fi/en.

Vuori, H. -L., & Laitinen, M. (2005) *Synnytyslaulu* [Birth sounds]. Helsinki, Finland: Edita.

Wildman, F. (2006). *Feldenkrais: The Busy Person's Guide to Easier Movement.* Berkeley, CA: The Intelligent Body Press.

Wilhelm, F. H., Gerlach, A. L., & Walton, T. R. (2001). Slow recovery from voluntary hyperventilation in panic disorder. *Psychosomatic Medicine, 63*: 638–649.

Wilhelm, F. H., Gevirtz, R., & Roth, W. T. (2001). Respiratory dysregulation in anxiety, functional cardiac, and pain disorders. *Behavior Modification, 25*(4): 513–545.

Williams, M., Teasdale, J., Segal, Z., & Kabat-Zinn, J. (2007). *The Mindful Way through Depression: Freeing Yourself from Chronic Unhappiness.* New York: Guilford Press.

Winnicott, D. W. (1951). *Playing and Reality.* London: Penguin.

Winnicott, D. W. (1987). *Babies and Their Mothers.* Boston, MA: Da Capo Press, 1992.

INDEX